God Bless,

[handwritten signature]

W9-BZF-571

Into
the
Mouth
of
the
Cat

By Malcolm McConnell

Fiction

Matata

Clinton Is Assigned

Just Causes

Nonfiction

First Crossing (with Carol McConnell)

Stepping Over

Into the Mouth of the Cat

Middle Sea Autumn (with Carol
McConnell)

Into the Mouth of the Cat

The Story of Lance Sijan, Hero of Vietnam

★

Malcolm McConnell

W. W. Norton & Company

New York

London

Copyright © 1985 by Malcolm McConnell
and Carol McConnell

All rights reserved.

Published simultaneously in Canada by Stoddart,
a subsidiary of General Publishing Co. Ltd,
Don Mills, Ontario.

Printed in the United States of America.

The text of this book is composed in Baskerville,
with display type set in Cheltenham Condensed.
Composition by The Haddon Craftsmen
Manufacturing by (to come)
Book design by Elissa Ichiyasu

First Edition

Library of Congress Cataloging in Publication Data
McConnell, Malcolm.
Into the mouth of the cat.
1. Sijan, Lance P., d. 1968.
2. United States. Air Force—Officers—Biography.
3. Vietnamese Conflict, 1961–1975—Prisoners and prisons,
Vietnamese.   4. Prisoners of war—United States—Biography.
I. Title. U53.S55M33 1985   959.704'348 [B]   84-14901

ISBN 978-0-393-01899-8

W. W. Norton & Company, Inc.,
500 Fifth Avenue, New York, N. Y. 10110
W. W. Norton & Company Ltd.,
37 Great Russell Street, London WC1B 3NU
1 2 3 4 5 6 7 8 9 0

To the

Memory

of

Captain

Lance Peter Sijan,

United States

Air Force

Medal of Honor

and for

the Sijan family

and the

American

prisoners

of war

Contents

Code of Conduct
for Members of
the Armed Forces
of the
United States

I

I am an American fighting man. I serve in the Forces which guard my Country and our way of life. I am prepared to give my life in their defense.

II

I will never surrender of my own free will. If in command I will never surrender my men while they still have the means to resist.

III

If I am captured I will continue to resist by all means available. I will make every effort to escape and aid others to escape. I will accept neither parole nor special favors from the enemy.

IV

If I become a prisoner of war, I will keep faith with my fellow prisoners. I will give no information or take part in any action which might be harmful to my comrades. If I am senior, I will take command. If not I will obey the lawful orders of those appointed over me and will back them up in every way.

V

When questioned, should I become a prisoner of war, I am bound to give name, rank, service number, and date of birth. I will evade answering further questions to the utmost of my ability. I will make no oral or written statements disloyal to my country and its allies or harmful to their cause.

VI

I will never forget that I am an American fighting man, responsible for my actions, and dedicated to the principles which made my Country free. I will trust in my God and in the United States of America.

"Let every nation know, whether it wishes us well or ill, that we shall pay any price, bear any burden, meet any hardship, support any friend, oppose any foe, in order to secure the survival and the success of liberty. "This much we pledge and more. . . ."

Inaugural Address,
John Fitzgerald Kennedy

A
Personal
Note
from
the
Author

While writing the story of
Lance Sijan's heroism in Indochina, I was constantly faced with the
challenge of maintaining verisimilitude within a compelling dramatic narrative without sacrificing historical accuracy. This problem
became acute when I began to re-create Sijan's lonely struggle in
the mountains of Laos during the seven weeks separating the unsuccessful search and rescue effort and his arrival at the Bamboo Prison
in Vinh. To compound the difficulty, I realized that the accuracy of
my manuscript would be rigorously scrutinized by the Research
Department of the *Reader's Digest*, the publication that had commissioned the book, and which has a reputation of demanding absolute
authenticity from its writers.

I was extremely fortunate, however, in being able to call on Guy Gruters, the only surviving prisoner of war with whom Sijan shared the details of his incredible evasion. Gruters is an exceptional person; at the Air Force Academy he was known for his intelligence, his energy, and, above all, for his uncanny memory. In Vietnam as a forward air controller flying missions in the misty gorges of the central highlands, Gruters sharpened his unusual powers of concentration and observation. When he and Bob Craner's Misty Super FAC jet was shot down over the Rao Nay Valley of North Vietnam and they were taken prisoner, Guy Gruters made especially good use of his mental acuity to resist interrogation in the Bamboo Prison near Vinh.

But it was when Craner and Gruters were brought together with Lance Sijan in Vinh that Gruters began to rely most heavily on his ability to memorize large volumes of complex information. Once Guy Gruters realized that Lance Sijan, his former Academy squadronmate, had, despite near-mortal wounds, evaded capture in the wilderness of the Laotian mountains for an astonishing period of forty-six days, Gruters knew that he had an obligation to memorize as many details of this historically important story as Sijan himself could recall. For the next two weeks in Vinh, on the battering truck ride north to Hanoi, and in their three-man cell in the Little Vegas section of Hoa Lo Prison, Gruters encouraged Sijan to talk about his lonely ordeal. He learned that Sijan's indomitable spirit of resistance was linked to his will to survive and that this emotional struggle was somehow maintaining life in Lance's ruined body.

After Sijan died, both Craner and Gruters vowed that if they survived captivity, they would do their best to preserve and disseminate the story of Lance Sijan's heroic struggle. During the brutal, desolate years of captivity and solitary confinement, Guy Gruters honed his powers of concentration through a disciplined memorization effort during which he preserved every detail that Lance had told them.

Fourteen years later, Guy Gruters was still able to recall Lance Sijan's exact words. In three long anguished interviews, he gave me detailed accounts of the events that took place between the night of November 9, 1967—when Sijan ejected from his crippled Phantom above the Ban Loboy Ford—and January 21, 1968, when the North Vietnamese removed Sijan from the cell in Hoa Lo Prison.

In effect, Guy Gruters had become the surviving memory of Lance Sijan. It was Gruters who brought me the vivid pictures of Sijan hanging injured in his parachute harness, still shocked by the violent explosion of the Phantom's bombs, staring down through the chalky glare of the flares at the naked laterite roadway of the Ho Chi Minh Trail north of the target. Through Gruters's memory of Sijan's words, I learned the heartbreaking story of the unsuccessful search and rescue effort—as seen by Lance on the ground. Gruters provided dramatic details of Lance's horrible ordeal among the thorn vines, razor-edged limestone, and hidden sinkholes of the rugged karst over which he dragged his wounded body.

During the course of these emotionally wrenching discussions with Guy Gruters, I was slowly able to fit together the important events of Sijan's struggle. From the tapes and transcripts of the interviews, I built the narrative scenes that recreate Sijan's astonishing endurance and valor. Later, I supplemented this rich source with assistance from military intelligence officers who had experience on the ground along the Ho Chi Minh Trail and who also had access to graphic reconnaissance material that rendered the terrain, the weather, and the enemy order of battle in great detail. I am confident my dramatization of Sijan's astonishing performance is as accurate a record as it is now possible to write.

The events and people portrayed in the book are real; I have created neither characters nor dramatic scenes from my imagination but have, instead, re-created in dramatic narrative actual events. To supplement Gruters's incredible memory, I drew on the memories and war diaries of Sijan's other colleagues as well as on official combat histories for details.

Among the many people and organizations that have further assisted me in this project, I am especially grateful to the following:

The Office of Air Force History, Mr. William Heimdahl; Air Force Office of Public Affairs, Lt. Col. Eric M. Solander and Lt. Col. Donald Gilleland; United States Air Force Academy, Office of Public Affairs, Mr. Willis Ketterson and Maj. Chuck Wood; *Airman* magazine, Lt. Col. Fred A. Meurer, USAF (Ret.). Fred Meurer is a talented journalist and dedicated officer. It was he who first broke the ground in telling Sijan's story.

Major Hobie Hobart of the 113th Tactical Fighter Wing gave one a real sense of what flying the F-4 Phantom was like during my orientation flight on that aircraft.

A number of former prisoners of war have been particularly helpful, including:

Lt. Col. Lee Ellis, Lt. Col. Tom Moe, Lt. Col. John H. Alpers, Jr., Col. William J. Baugh, and Rear Adm. James Stockdale.

Col. Robert Craner, who did so much to disseminate Lance Sijan's story among his fellow prisoners of war, died of a sudden heart attack before this book was begun. His invaluable contribution to the story came through the tape-recorded interviews and detailed notes made by Col. Fred Meurer when he was editor of *Airman*. Congressman John McCain, Air Force Col. Ronald Webb, and Col. George (Bud) Day, USAF (Ret.) Medal of Honor, who knew Bob Craner well in North Vietnamese prison camps, also contributed invaluable assistance by providing details of Bob Craner's memorable performance as a POW. Colonel Craner's untimely death was a loss for his family, for the Air Force that he served with such brilliant dedication and, years later, to me as an author. From all who knew Bob, I have learned what an exceptional person he was. In combat, he was a brave and tenacious pilot, a leader of the Misty FAC's Forward Air Controller squadron that did more than its share to blunt the enemy logistical build-up to the Tet Offensive. As a prisoner of war, he displayed another kind of courage and tenacity; his native intelligence, imagination, and verve often outwitted North Vietnamese interrogators, and, in the process, protected him and his fellow prisoners from unnecessary interrogation. During six years of captivity, he never lost his faith in his country or himself. Whenever possible, he used the otherwise wasted days and months of bleak prison to better himself. By the time Colonel Craner was repatriated, he had learned Russian from a Russian-speaking fellow POW. Two years after release, he graduated Phi Beta Kapa in Russian studies from Holy Cross College, having compressed a four-year course into twenty-two months. While studying at the Russian Institute in Garmisch, Germany, Bob Craner taught himself fluent Hungarian. After serving as an Air Attaché in Budapest, he was slated for advanced training and eventual general rank within the Defense Attaché program, but he died before he could enjoy this bright future.

Guy Gruters, who is now an airline pilot and businessman in Florida, cooperated fully with me at every stage of this project. I could not have written the book without his help.

Equally, Col. Glenn L. Nordin, USAF (Ret.) has been energetic and selfless in his support of the project; he has shown himself to be as determined and professional a researcher as he was a fighter pilot.

Lenora Monaco is now a bank officer in northern California. She generously shared with me her proud, painful memories of Lance Sijan.

Michael Smith, Sijan's close friend and academy roommate, was equally forthcoming.

Finally, the Sijan family, Jane, Syl, Janine, and Marc, have given fully of their time and of their cherished memories of Lance, their son and brother.

Prologue

Washington, Thanksgiving Day 1982

Carol and I decided to visit the new Vietnam Veterans Memorial late on Thanksgiving morning, hoping that the site would not be crowded then. But, when we arrived at the mall on that sunny holiday noon, we were surprised at the scores of families who had come out to the memorial.

Because of the slight rise in the ground, we did not at first see the entrance. Suddenly, as we moved along the damp path, the rolling lawn opened into a hollow and we saw the hard, dark lines of the memorial cutting into the earth. The black granite panels sliced down at a shallow angle, growing taller as they neared the vertex, 240 feet away. I had not been prepared for the sheer *scale*, the length and height of those dark wings.

There are almost fifty-eight thousand names etched on the stone panels.

Halfway down the ramp, I could still see the white marble of the nearby Lincoln Memorial and the bright shaft of the Washington Monument half a mile to the east. I began to recognize the genius of Maya Ying Lin, the young-woman architect who had won the design competition. The criteria had specified that the memorial be "reflective and contemplative in character; contain the names of all who died or remain missing . . . and make no political statement about the war."

The two wings are called the East and West Walls; they join at their point of maximum height—the central vertex—then cut away at diminishing angles. At the top right center of the vertex, the beginning of the East Wall, are cut the large numerals 1959. This marks the first Americans who died in Indochina. There are seventy panels of names marching away from west to east along the wall. The names are arrayed in alphabetical and chronological sequence all the way to the tiny wedge of black stone bearing only one name that marks the end of the East Wall; then the unbroken circle begins again at the narrow one-name wedge that marks the extreme end of the West Wall and continues as the panels rise in height to the tall slabs of the vertex. There, at the bottom of the last panel of the West Wall, are etched the large numerals 1975. This date marks the last official American casualties in that long war.

On these shining stone walls the names are linked line by line, panel by panel. The memorial brochure tells us that Ms. Lin intended them to form a sequence "as though the panels were pages in a book."

We retraced our way up the East Wall. About half the distance from the vertex to the final thin wedge stood panel 29 East. Lance's name was the level of my shoulder, at the right-hand, eastern end of the line.

LANCE P. SIJAN ◇

The small diamond after Lance's name meant that his death had been confirmed.

I leaned closer to the wall to read the names that followed on the left, below, line 63.

"Billy Templeton, Freddie L. Thomas, Jr. . . ."

I stopped reading. There were so *many* names. Each was a dead man, a unique individual who had done his duty, who had gone where his country had ordered him, to the red dust of the demilitarized zone, the hot gloom of the A Shau Valley, or the green velvet scum of the delta.

"Let's take a picture of Lance's name," Carol said softly.

"Would you like me to take both of you?" The young woman was about thirty, nicely dressed, alone.

"Thanks," I said, handing her the camera.

I stood beside Carol as the woman focused on us. "What name do you want to show?"

"Sijan," I said, pointing to Lance's name. "There . . . Lance P. Sijan."

She nodded, intent on framing the picture.

"Lance . . . Si . . ." The woman could not pronounce Lance's name.

I helped her. "Sijan . . . *Sigh-John.*"

"Was he a friend . . . a relative?" she asked, then snapped the picture.

"He was a friend of ours from high school," I said.

"Lance was a pilot," Carol began to explain. "He was shot down and he escaped. He was horribly wounded. . . ." Her voice trailed off. It was difficult to tell all this to a stranger, among the other strangers on this crowded walk.

"Lance Sijan won the Medal of Honor," I blurted out. Like Carol, I saw the difficulty of telling his story under these circumstances.

The young woman nodded somberly and glanced quickly toward the wall.

"He died in North Vietnam in 1968," I said, trying to answer her unasked question. "He was shot down in November 1967 . . . inside Laos. . . ."

As I spoke, I warmed to the subject. On either side of us, people were stopping to listen. I continued, my voice growing stronger, less tentative. I slowed the narrative, dragging up as many half-remembered details as I could recall. But even my vague version of Lance's story produced an obvious impact on the circle of listeners.

When I finished, women and men both had tears on their faces.

I felt a confused rush of shame eclipse my pride, as if I'd somehow grandstanded on Lance's story, as if in my re-creating his heroism, I was trying to share his glory. But I found the people on the walk not looking at me. Instead, they stared at the black granite panel toward line 62.

Back on the paved path at the entrance to the memorial hollow, a young family in matching jogging clothes strode toward us. The oldest of the two kids was a boy about ten who had the engaging, but difficult demeanor of a bright preadolescent.

"What *is* this dumb old place, anyway," he moaned with theatrical distress, "some kind of Civil War statute or something?"

We were face-to-face with the family now. The father must have seen the sadness in my expression. He took the boy gently but with a certain firmness by both shoulders to dampen his kinetic bounce. "This is the *Vietnam* Memorial, Craig," he said. "You settle down a second now. I'm going to tell you and Sheila something about this before we go down there."

I glanced around the sunny mall toward the monumental stone. That precocious youngster, I realized, was getting a history lesson. I was sorry only that he had not been on the path beside panel 29 East ten minutes before to hear some fragments of the story of Captain Lance P. Sijan, United States Air Force, Medal of Honor.

Perhaps one day he will read this book.

Part I

★

Combat
in
the
Air

Chapter One

★

Medal of Honor

A member of the American Armed Forces can merit the Medal of Honor in only one manner: by a deed of personal bravery or self-sacrifice, above and beyond the call of duty, while in combat with an enemy of the nation. The gallantry must be certified by two eyewitnesses, and be clearly beyond the call of duty. Moreover, it must involve the risk of life and must be the type of deed that, if not performed, would evoke no criticism of the individual.

General John D. Ryan
Former Chief of Staff
U.S. Air Force

The Vietnam war was this country's longest sustained conflict. Over three million young Americans served in the war zone. Two hundred and thirty-eight Medals of Honor were awarded for "conspicuous gallantry" in that protracted, unfortunate war. Yet the American public can name, at most, only a few of those who served their country with such distinction.

A decade after the fall of Saigon, however, America is slowly beginning to reexamine the nature of that divisive struggle and of the role played by its servicemen in Indochina. With the recent dedication of the Vietnam Veterans Memorial and the equitable settlement of the rankling Agent Orange dispute, the country seems to be finally welcoming home the men who—from professional pride, personal conviction, or family tradition—went to serve where they were ordered.

During the ten years of active American combat in Indochina, the news media brought home to the nation the horrible essence of modern wars of insurgency. Americans also learned a great deal about the brutalizing effect this warfare had on its servicemen. But we did not learn much about the nobility of spirit, the selflessness, or the astonishing bravery so many displayed in battle.

Reading the 238 citations for the Vietnam War's Medals of Honor is a wrenching experience. Over half the medals were awarded posthumously. The citations are often painfully brief, a few score words making up the stock phrases "extraordinary heroism" and "uncommon courage." In the spare text of the citation, the action of the honored individual is outlined. But there is no way the shorn, bureaucratic phrasing can convey the raw bravery, the triumph of will and faith, the suffering these young men endured and the incredible self-sacrifice they exhibited.

By any standard, one of the bravest and most selfless of these young heroes was an Air Force pilot in his midtwenties named Lance Peter Sijan.

Chapter Two

I Corps, South Vietnam

Autumn 1967

Two aircraft clawed through the sky. Climbing past broken stratus, they left the white beaches and green coastal plain and turned northeast toward an orbit point twenty miles out to sea from the Ben Hai River, the muddy stream that marked the center of the demilitarized zone.

They were F-4C Phantoms, hulking twenty-ton machines, almost sixty feet long and forty feet between the tips of their swept-back wings, mottled green and pinkish beige, the camouflage of the Southeast Asia theater. Beneath each wing, three long green bombs hung on pylons. As they snarled through the low turbulence on afterburner, their twin engines burned fuel at one-hundred gallons a minute.

Carbine Flight was a strike mission of the 366th Tactical Fighter Wing's 480th Squadron. Off afterburner now, they flew in fingertip formation at four hundred knots, *Carbine 2* only twenty yards behind the starboard wing of *Carbine 1*. It was just past ogoo on a hot morning, late in the dry season. Inland, the smoke haze was already bad; peasants who had not yet been driven off their land by the bloody large-unit battles in I Corps burned the stubble in their dry rice paddies in anticipation of the overdue northeast monsoon.

Looking back toward the landmass of Indochina, the pilots saw the narrow plain shimmer from a verdant band to a brown smear, then disappear into the backdrop of clouds hiding the spine of the Annamite Cordillera twenty miles inland. High ahead a single plume of cirrus cloud curled to the east. Otherwise the sky above was clear, aching tropical blue.

Each Phantom carried two pilots in separate, tandem cockpits. Normally the frontseat pilot was the aircraft commander (AC), a captain or major with several years experience as a rated jet pilot and months of intensive training in F-4s. The rear cockpit pilot was informally known as a GIB—Guy in Back. He was usually a young first lieutenant.

The crew composition of the mission lead, *Carbine 1*, was normal. But in *Carbine 2*, the pattern was reversed. The frontseater was a twenty-five-year-old lieutenant named Lance Sijan. The GIB in the cramped cockpit behind him was Major Glenn Nordin, Sijan's flight commander in the 480th, who at thirty-six was an experienced instructor pilot.

The purpose of this checkout mission was for Major Nordin to assess Sijan's potential for upgrade-in-theater from backseater to aircraft commander later in his tour. Also, Sijan's regular frontseater, Dick Hearn, had just been transferred down to Seventh Air Force in Saigon, and Hearn had recommended Sijan as the backseater for his squadron commander, Lieutenant Colonel John Armstrong. Before Nordin would officially second that recommendation or nominate Sijan for upgrade to AC, however, he wanted to observe Sijan's performance in the frontseat, on a moderately tough mission.

The morning's mission was a bombing strike against North Vietnamese Army artillery positions dug into tunnels and bunkers in the hilly scrub jungle of the DMZ, the de-militarized zone, just north of the Ben Hai River. For over a month, North Vietnam 130mm long-range guns and heavy mortars had been shelling the Marines' northern I Corps firebases strung out above the dusty track known as

Highway 9. The most forward outpost, Con Thien, had been especially hard hit. Only a few days earlier, the enemy had pounded the bunkers and trenches of Con Thien with over eleven hundred rounds of mortar, artillery, and rocket fire. Marine casualties had been high.

The American response to these artillery assaults was equally massive. Phantoms of the 366th struck suspected enemy batteries and support units day and night. Repeated heavy bomber, B-52 arc light missions had pounded the jungle hills above the river with thousands of tons of bombs dropped in carpet patterns that left the terrain denuded and overlapped with orange mud craters.

Today, *Carbine* Flight's detailed mission order gave the coordinates of a bunker-and-tunnel complex three-and-a-half miles north of Con Thien. Seventh Air Force Intelligence had evidence that these entrenched positions had been occupied by a North Vietnamese Army (NVA) artillery battery late the previous day and that this battery was about to renew the assault on Con Thien. If Intel's estimate was accurate, the flight's bombs would probably trigger a series of secondary explosions: if, of course, the pilots delivered their ordnance accurately on the target. A 750-pound bomb dug a deep crater and made a terrible noise, but it did little damage to a fortified NVA artillery shelter in the limestone caves of the DMZ unless the pilot scored a direct hit on the camouflaged position. But this would not be easy; intelligence reports also indicated there was at least one six-gun 57mm flak battery in the area, controlled by a Firecan radar fire-direction system.

The pattern of escalation and response, followed by counter-escalation and counterresponse, was now well established in Vietnam. The original war of insurgency of only two years earlier had quickly evolved into a large-scale conventional war, and that bloody struggle had, in turn, become a costly stalemate, a war of attrition.

These larger considerations, however, did not long preoccupy Lance Sijan as *Carbine* Flight climbed toward the white cirrus plume and their holding orbit, the Initial Point, from which they would receive clearance to assume their heading to the target from an orbiting Airborne Command Center with the radio call name Hillsboro. Sijan was flying his first out-country strike in the frontseat; he was absorbed with the complexities of his aircraft, with navigation, and especially with the visibility back over the coast. If the high false-monsoon cloud layer closed up any tighter and lowered into the haze of smoke and dust, he realized, target identification would become difficult. An F-100 fighter-bomber, *Misty* FAC was on hand to act as a fast-mover Forward Air Controller, but even *Misty* might have trouble identifying the low, fist-shaped knoll above the jungle valley that had shown up so poorly in the reconnaisance photos Sijan had studied before briefing.

Unless they could positively locate the target on the first pass, the flight would be obliged to make multiple passes, *Carbine 2* following its lead down onto the bomb run from the relative safety of the fifteen-thousand-foot orbit they had been assigned during the briefing. On such a multiple-pass profile, they would "pickle" only two bombs at a time and only if they were certain they had the target identified. It did not take much imagination to picture the reaction of the experienced antiaircraft gun crews when the Phantoms wheeled down out of the overcast on the steady, straight dive of the bomb run. Then again, and once more, at predictable speeds and angles. The NVA had Soviet advisers; these gunners knew how to lead a diving fighter-bomber as well as anybody in the world. In the past two years they'd had ample experience.

But, as Major Nordin liked to point out, the Air Force had not spent all that taxpayers' money on these bombs so that cowardly or incompetent pilots could dump them "somewhere in Southeast goddamn Asia." To get good bombs under these conditions, a man had to just swallow his fear for a little while and fly that airplane well, not simply ride along with it like an airline passenger. He had to *press*.

By this he meant that the bomb run had to be steep, fast, and relatively low. Given the physical laws that controlled ballistics, aiming bombs involved three basic factors: dive angle, speed, and bomb-release altitude. On a good clear day, with a large, obvious target, the bomb run could be accomplished with a shallow dive angle, at slow speed, with a reasonably high release point. But on a day like this one, they would probably have to go in there at sixty degrees, 550 knots, and not release until six thousand feet above ground level. During this attack, there could be no evasive maneuvers; jinking and dodging flak disturbed the laws of bomb ballistics.

Sijan tried to relax in the narrow ejection seat, to let his feet rest easily on the rudder pedals and his right hand lightly caress the plastic grip of the stick. Flying combat missions in a jet aircraft was as demanding as it was dangerous. One of the more humorous GIBs at Da Nang had described being on these missions in a letter home as being like a matador driving in a sport car race on the way to the bullring while he played blind chess over the radio. Another lieutenant who had just returned from a rough night strike on the heavily defended Rao Nay Valley had expressed his agreement to his friend's description. "I'll buy that," he said, then sucked down half a can of Blatz, both hands shaking. " 'Cept we're the bull, not the matador."

"*Carbine* Lead, Hillsboro." The voice of the Airborne Command Center cut through Sijan's memory. "You are cleared to ingress to target. Contact *Misty One Four* on three-three-eight point eight. Good luck." Control was being passed to Misty Forward Air Controller (FAC) in the de-militarized zone.

The rivets and access tabs stood out sharply on the metal skin of the lead plane, only sixty feet away. Sijan's fingers flipped across the radio console beneath the right cockpit sill as he switched his radio to 338.8, *Misty*'s frequency. He was flying his forty-fourth mission north. In the next fifteen minutes, they would reach roll-in orbit above the target, and *Misty* would go down first. Once the FAC had marked the target with white phosphorous rockets, Lead would roll in to the first bomb run. If visibility was decent, Lead would pickle all six and jink back up to orbit.

Then Sijan would roll in, following the FAC's instructions on the aiming point. By this time, of course, the flak batteries in the area would be wide awake and active. But there would be no evasive action possible as he hurled the plane down in its steep, fast dive. He would watch for the aiming point to appear in the reticle of his bombsight. He would monitor his airspeed indicator and his altimeter. And he would try hard not to be distracted by the glowing orange-and-red balls of the heavy tracers that would glide up to smash him. The number-two plane often caught more flak than the lead. But there would be no jinking until after bomb release. This was the way you flew these missions, the only way you got good bombs.

That summer, some of the GIBs in the Bachelor Officers' Quarters (BOQ) at Da Nang had circulated a rather breathless journalistic memoir entitled *The DOOM Pussy* that made reference to the colorful shoulder patches worn by the B-57 crews who flew night strikes up north. This patch featured a yellow cat with a pirate's eye patch holding in its jaws a small jet plane. Surrounding the patch was the embroidered Vietnamese phrase *TRONG MIENG CUA MEO CUA THAM PHAN,* which translated into English as "I have flown into the mouth of the cat of death."

Sijan had found the war correspondent's narrative a bit romantic, but he did appreciate the sentiments of the B-57 Canberra bomber pilots. In a letter home in which he tried to describe what it felt like diving into the low hills of scrub jungle in the Pack I target area or the steep limestone gorges of Laos as the candy-pink tracers floated up at you, Lance made direct reference to the expression. "I call this," he printed in his neat pilot's hand, "flying into the mouth of the cat."

"Carbine One, Misty One Four," the FAC called cheerfully. " 'Morning, gentlemen. We've got a nice one for you today."

The two Phantoms banked over into their roll-in pattern just beneath the lowering gray overcast twelve-thousand feet above the smeared browns and greens of the hills. They were already three-thousand feet beneath briefed orbit, but that couldn't be helped. Visibility was marginal with the haze, but the FAC went on to assure them he had the target taped.

Sijan set the two thick throttles at the 80-percent mark on the quadrant and briefly raised the nose to chop off fifty knots of air speed. Lead swung out ahead of him, then looped right into the oval orbit. Their pattern would form an elongated clockface in the sky, with *Carbine 1* and *2* maintaining positions six hours apart. Banking over ten degrees on the right wing, Sijan stared down through the tan haze at the flattened patterns of jungle hills and the valleys choked with elephant grass, searching for the characteristic knoll of the artillery position. There could be a couple of divisions hidden down there, he realized, and they wouldn't be able to see them through this haze.

But then he picked up *Misty,* a chunky camouflaged dart falling away from a lower orbit and plummeting toward the south. Smoke and yellow flame tore away from the F-100 as two marking rockets streaked ahead. The phosphorous explosions were tiny white pinwheels against the drab sunless jungle.

"Lead, *Misty,*" the FAC called up. "Right on the money." Then adding the official phrases for the benefit of Hillsboro, *"Carbine One,* you are cleared to attack the target as marked."

"Roger," Lead answered.

Sijan increased his bank angle so that he could watch Lead roll in from the opposite side of the orbit. The camouflaged Phantom was hard to distinguish against the hills below, but Sijan knew both planes stood out clearly beneath the gray cloud deck. The plane's exhaust plume went sooty dark, and he saw Lead had applied more throttle, then chopped back to idle before rolling over on the run.

"*Misty One Four,*" Lead called formally. "*Carbine One* rolling in."

The Phantom rocked onto its starboard wing, hung there for a moment, then fell, nose down, still banked steeply to the right. Vapor vortices streamed from Lead's wingtips as the plane pulled Gs. Two seconds later the Phantom was dropping fast, straight toward the marker smoke far below, at fifty degrees dive angle. Aside from the thinning chalk smear of the phosphorous smoke, there was no indication of a target down there. Ten seconds into the run and still no flak.

But Sijan did not have time now to think about the danger of the next few minutes. Still banked right so that he could watch Lead's bomb run, he reached forward with his left hand to the weapon select panel.

"I'm going to arming sequence now, Major," he said over the intercom. He hoped his voice sounded reasonably calm.

"You're the AC today, Lance," Major Nordin said. "I'm just along for the ride."

That was the Academy method. If a guy wanted to sit in the driver's seat, let him drive. But never forget: Command and responsibility were inseparable.

Three years before, Major Nordin had been a captain, an air officer in command at the Academy when Lance was a senior. There Nordin had had a reputation as a fair but demanding leader. Here in Vietnam, some of the GIBs in the 48oth called him the Mad Bomber. He definitely liked good BDA—bomb damage assessment —to put bombs accurately on target. If you're good, he'd say, if you learn how to really *press* the attack, it's one pass and haul ass *and* good BDA. But, as a few of Lance's friends had told him after flying with Major Nordin, that one pass could be quite thrilling. Nordin described his methods more frankly. "Cowards," he'd say, "don't like to fly with me."

Lance clicked the select knob to Bombs Triple Ejection and flipped the arming switch to Nose and Tail. "Bombs, triple," he intoned. "Inboard pylons, arm, nose, and tail."

This selection would show the Major he intended to salvo all six bombs from the triple ejection racks, that he meant to make one steep, fast bombing run, low enough to clobber the target on a single pass.

Major Nordin repeated the sequence, his voice devoid of emotion.

They still hung on their slow bank as *Carbine 1* continued to drop beneath them. He was almost at his bomb-release point six-thousand feet below, and his dive angle and speed had increased as he prepared to pickle. Then Sijan sucked in a lungful of oxygen, an involuntary reaction to the hot red balls of 57mm tracers that slashed across Lead's flight path. The guns were firing from two positions, one a thousand meters south of the target, the other on a cratered ridge further west. Just as Sijan was about to call out a warning, a green blip appeared on the small screen to the right of his panel. They, too, were being "painted" by the Firecan radar direction system of the flak battery. But only two guns of the full battery had shown themselves so far.

"Firecan on the scope, sir," he said. "That's who's shooting at Lead."

The glowing tracers streamed in hypnotic patterns, seeming to hook very close to the diving Phantom. Still, Lead did not break off his bomb run. A few seconds later, with the tracers about to converge on his nose, he pulled away in a savage high-G break left that must have put the two pilots close to blackout despite their G-suits. Dark specks, Lead's entire bomb load, continued the original trajectory of the pass, gliding through the thick tracer snake, falling straight toward the thinning rocket smoke.

Lead was jinking now, hard left, nose up. Then right, rolling down, afterburners blue and incandescent orange. Then dropping off burner. Now climbing left in a tight banking turn, his afterburners blazing. The tracer columns broke apart into confused, wobbling clumps of two or three shells as the Phantom's high-speed evasion overloaded the fire-control radar.

Sijan heard the nasty rattlesnake buzz from his own warning system in his earphones. Their own plane was now squarely in the middle of the Firecan's director beam. He had been trained for this contingency for months on the bombing ranges back at George. *"Misty One Four, Carbine Two* rolling in."

Without waiting for the clearance, he rammed the throttles up the quadrant, threw the stick hard right, and stood on the right rudder pedal. The Gs hit like an invisible piston, forcing him down into the hard cushions of the ejection seat as the bladders in his G-suit automatically filled with compressed air. Gray sky, then dull horizon spun past the canopy. Dirty green jungle smeared across the nose. Slowly he eased the stick forward, then reached blindly with his left hand to snatch the twin throttle knobs back to idle. Again the hazy horizon line crossed the canopy. Nose down forty-five degrees, the plane was in the ballistic swoop of its bomb run. His ears blocked as the cockpit pressure changed, but he was sure the snake buzz of the Firecan warning was gone.

He gripped the stick more lightly and extended his will into those braided, hidden thickets of hydraulic tubing and electrical cables that controlled the plane. For the next timeless swoop, there was no tangible separation between his body and the careening twenty-ton composite of aircraft, munitions, and fuel.

He did not have to calculate bomb release. The point was there when the reticle of the bombsight filled with the dusty target. His right thumb stroked once; the bombs were gone. He could think again, suddenly torn away from his mindless union with the airplane.

Tracers looped and sparkled through slow trajectories ahead of him. They seemed so far away, so soft, irritating but inconsequential, like flies outside the mess hall. But his reason returned with the chemical shock of adrenaline that came when the RHAW warning system snake buzz again filled his headset.

"Jinking, sir," he heard his voice announce.

The stick was against the green pouches of his survival vest, then hard left. Sijan jammed the throttles up through Military Power to Max. The afterburners knocked him back into his seat. He kicked rudder and threw the stick full right. Gray overcast and brown horizon spun and tumbled through his vision. His helmet banged the left side of the canopy, then the right. Sijan was six feet two inches, 195 pounds, a powerful athlete, but despite his tight seat harness, the violence of these maneuvers threw him from side to side like a stuffed doll. In training he had twice broken his nose this way, but that had been flying backseat on the other side of the world. This was the war. Clawing almost blindly, he found the throttles and dragged them back from Afterburner. The plane slid into a violent turn, and he let the airspeed drop as it yawed. Then he broke the turn and rolled left in a tight bank as he thrust the throttles full forward again with the heel of his left hand. The stick came back. Again the Gs assaulted him, but he knew the plane was streaking toward safety in a Mach 1 corkscrew climb.

"Watch the high-speed stall, Lance." Major Nordin's voice was slow and unemotional.

His distant fingers plucked at the throttle knobs. He centered the stick. The cleated rubber sole of his green jungle boot worked heel-and-toe on the left rudder pedal. Slowly the dim weight of the Gs dissolved. The cloud deck fell soundlessly past them. Lead was out there a mile or so ahead in a banking left turn. *Misty* was further off, also banking left.

"Good work, Lance," Nordin said. "No way a Firecan could track *that.*"

Sijan heard the voices of the other pilots talking in normal tones about the flak batteries below the overcast.

". . . Ah, I roger that one, *Misty,*" Lead said.

"Okey-dokey, *Carbine,*" the FAC said. "We'll get some . . . uh, other people on them *tout de suite.*"

"Thanks, *Misty,*" Lead called. "It's nice doing business with you."

The bombs were dropped. Neither plane had been hit. The only dead and wounded were on the ground. It was time for casual banter while the sweat cooled and pulse rates fluttered back toward normal.

"Nice bombs, *Carbine,*" *Misty* added. "*Carbine Two,* you clobbered them. You're as good as your boss."

"Thanks, *Misty,*" Lance said.

Sijan's forty-fourth mission to North Vietnam was almost over.

"The little guys in rubber sandals were pretty sharp today," Nordin said cheerfully, becoming conversational now that the main business was over. "They almost nailed us there at the end of the run."

"They *did?* I was too busy to notice."

"Yeah," Nordin said. "Well, you got damn good bombs, Lance."

Sijan smiled again. Major Nordin liked good bombs. He always said that the whole idea of a war was to kill the other guy before he killed you. Later, when the peace treaty was signed, there'd be plenty of time to be friendly. Major Nordin also knew damn well that the little guys in rubber sandals were some of the best trained, best equipped troops in the world.

Below them the altostratus broke up into a mackerel sky. Dusty valleys appeared south of the DMZ. Off the starboard wing, the jungle foothills rose steeply toward the long parallel ridges of the Annamite Range. The other side was Laos, and all the choke point targets of the Ho Chi Minh Trail. Northern I Corps unrolled directly beneath their flight path.

In eighteen minutes they'd be on high station about to enter the Da Nang traffic pattern. Then there would be plenty to keep Sijan occupied. Da Nang Air Base, with its two long concrete runways, had recently become the busiest airport in the world, averaging over sixty thousand takeoffs and landings a month. Landings there were fast and demanding because of the extremely steep glide slope you had to fly to avoid Vietcong and NVA ground fire from the surrounding jungle and swampy estuary.

The remaining scraps of low broken cloud burned away with the heat of the high morning sun. There would be no rain again that day. Everybody was talking about how late the monsoon was this year, how the NVA were taking advantage of this dry weather to move thousands of troops and thousands of tons of supplies south, some down through Tally Ho above the DMZ but mostly along the Trail in Laos. Normally the southwest monsoon disrupted infiltration routes in Laos and Cambodia from May to October; then the northeast monsoon swept in from the Gulf of Tonkin to wash out the feeder roads leading from North Vietnam over the spine of the Annamite Mountains into Laos. For several months this autumn, however, hazy, rainless overcast prevailed, giving the NVA the best infiltration conditions they'd had for years.

In the three months he'd been in Vietnam, Sijan had noticed a definite shift in the way people referred to the enemy. They used to say "the VC" or "Charlie." Now everybody talked about "the NVA." The term had a solider, more serious ring to it. Intelligence had identified the NVA 325C Division and the 304th Hanoi Guards Division moving into I Corps, besides the 320th just across the

DMZ. The Special Forces' deep recon teams that worked the Trail even had pictures of tanks moving south, fast amphibious Soviet PT-76 tanks. The Americans had deployed two marine divisions, two Marine air groups, and four army infantry brigades in I Corps, but even so, people were spread pretty thin on the ground.

Sijan stared down at the landscape as they began their descent southeast, toward Da Nang. No two fields were the same size or shape, and the crazy-quilt pattern was highlighted by the dark green tree lines and canebrakes that separated one peasant's land from another's. The scattered hamlets were overgrown jumbles screened by dense stands of lichee and citrus trees and tall bamboo groves. Where streams cut the plain and joined the meandering rivers, the brush again thickened to tunnels of scrub jungle.

In July, enemy troops had attacked Da Nang repeatedly after moving, undetected, across this landscape. It had been in sampans hidden inside these tunnels of vegetation that the NVA rocket units had penetrated the South Vietnamese defensive zone around Da Nang and blasted the airfield.

In his letters home to his high school friends and his family, Lance had tried to explain the complex nature of this war. But this was not an easy task. All summer he had read magazine reports and seen TV footage on the growing antiwar demonstrations in the States. Then the rioting in the urban ghettos exploded—Newark, Detroit, finally Sijan's home town of Milwaukee.

To some of the guys who sat around the Da Nang Officers' Open Mess—the DOOM Club—at night drinking beer, it seemed that the States were going straight to hell in a hand basket, just when MACV was finally getting on top of the military situation here in 'Nam. A couple even saw the sinister hand of the Russians behind the rioting and the antiwar demonstrations. But Sijan's letters show that he didn't buy that line. He realized that people were frustrated by the apparent lack of progress in the war and, of course, by the mounting casualties as the level of combat intensified. This was not World War II or even Korea. The issues weren't as obvious. The strategic goals were much less clear. People were bound to become confused and angry. It was a natural reaction.

Still, no matter how explicable the demonstrations and rioting back home were, it was hard on morale to pickup *Time* or *Newsweek* and see forty thousand people outside the Pentagon calling the

President and the men who followed his orders over here baby killers. In September, when the wing was flying its heaviest and most costly combat operations of the war so far, some wag had written a poignant message on the Squadron Operations blackboard.

"Grow a Mustache," the chalked message proclaimed, "and Protest the War in America."

The morning Sijan read that joke scrawled on the blackboard, he began to grow his mustache.

Chapter
Three

★

Da
Nang
Air
Base

November 9, 1967

All across the vast base, men worked in the stifling heat. To the west the green ridges of the Nui Mang piedmont and the beige scar of the Hill 327 fire base faded into the rippling mirage above the rice paddies. The winter monsoon had still not swept down from the northeast.

Inside the barbed-wire perimeter lay acres of metal huts, trailers, and prefab buildings. Bulldozers and graders worked in small storms of dust, scraping out new roads and foundation pits for large, ostensibly permanent, barracks and chow halls to replace the green pyramid tents sagging in the heat.

The massive American buildup of the previous two years had brought a blighted boomtown sprawl to the former French base. Chugging generators squatted on flatbed trucks close beside a plywood chapel with an incongruous white steeple. Modular surgical wards of the Med-Evac Hospital stood fifty meters from the greasy mud containment wall of a fuel dump. And among the pastel aluminum blocks of Wing Headquarters, mildewed tile-roofed buildings of the French *Armée de l'air* slowly crumbled under the annual cycle of monsoon and summer sun. The centerpiece of the base was the airport. Two long parallel concrete runways stretched north to south across the narrow Tien Sha peninsula from Da Nang harbor to the swampy Vu Gia estuary.

In certain ways the base was emblematic of the war itself. Events were moving too quickly to permit careful planning or serious self-assessment. But it was obvious that America was here in force, that it had deployed the whole panoply of its technological civilization, that it was committed, building for the long haul, for the duration.

Lance Sijan slept most of the hot afternoon in the air-conditioned BOQ that housed the backseat pilots of the 366th. His squadron was now on early-night rotation, with mission takeoffs scheduled between 4 P.M. and midnight. He was due to fly at 2000 hours as GIB to his new frontseater, Lt. Col. John Armstrong, his squadron commander.

In the previous month the wing's operations had shifted from the Tally Ho target zone north of the DMZ to the Steel Tiger area of Laos. On the Ho Chi Minh Trail, a massive NVA logistical effort was underway, the buildup for the rumored enemy offensive down south. The evening's detailed mission order had come in from Seventh Air Force while Lance was asleep. Such orders were called "frags": Air Force parlance for fragmentary order. When a crew was scheduled to fly a strike, they were said to be "fragged" for a certain target. With the NVA expansion came greatly enhanced antiaircraft defenses. Some crews that fall drew orders to attack the notorious 57mm batteries near the major NVA base area at Sepone in Laos. These frag orders specified that cluster bombs be dropped, in daylight, at low altitude, on "high drag mode" to assure maximum "suppression." Crews that drew such orders were said to have "gotten their ass fragged with a real winner."

The physical and psychological effects of this demanding duty showed differently on each individual, but on the whole, the combat pilots of the 366th seemed proud and confident. From photo reconnaissance and ground recon reports, they knew they were inflicting heavy losses on a regular NVA invasion force.

A few majors and colonels were on their second combat flying tours. Lieutenants like Lance would be rotated back to the States on completing a hundred counters up north. After a couple of years, however, if the war still dragged on, they could expect to be back in Indochina again flying another tour.

That was the grim, uncompromising reality Lance Sijan and the others faced. Their country was engaged in a seemingly endless and clearly unpopular war. Because of its limited nature, bombing enemy supply routes had acquired inordinate strategic importance. Thoughtful young officers like Sijan and his roommate, Joe Kosciusko, often discussed the obvious fact that it would have been more effective to destroy the docks of Haiphong and mine its harbor than to try to eliminate small clusters of trucks traveling roadways camouflaged under a triple canopy mountain forest.

But the President and the secretary of defense had decided against further escalation. The officers of the 366th Tactical Fighter Wing had no choice but to follow their politically acceptable frag orders. This was their duty, dangerous and thankless as it might be. And despite private bitching about civilian meddling in military operations, these officers believed strongly in the concepts of patriotic duty and civilian control of the military.

Years later, surviving pilots from the 480th still clearly remember the large and small events that marked the day and night of November 9, 1967. In letters and taped messages home and in their war diaries they note the dusty heat of the prolonged dry season, the seemingly inexplicable losses of two Phantoms in two days—victims of "golden B-Bs" on ostensibly milk-run bombing strikes.

Friends of Lance Sijan also recall that he was unusually subdued and apprehensive as he prepared for the evening mission. Lance had just returned from a five-day rest and recreation (R and R) in Bangkok that morning and had been greeted at the plane ramp with the news that his best friend, Lee Ellis, had been shot down the previous afternoon up in Package I. Normally Lance had an easy smile and a confident manner in the BOQ and the Mess Hall. But this afternoon he was quiet.

Sijan got up just after four. Briefing for the mission would begin at six; takeoff was scheduled for eight. As always, he prepared himself very carefully for a mission. Sijan was meticulous to a fault when it came to flying duties. Normally he went to the wing's intelligence facility in the command post well before the scheduled briefing so that he could carefully read the latest estimates of enemy activity and air defenses, not just in the area of his fragged target but across the wing's whole area of operations.

Flying as backseater to the squadron commanding officer was not easy. Colonel Armstrong was a West Pointer who had flown Sabres in Korea and was demanding and professional. He needed a backseater who could carry more than his half of the load because Armstrong himself was too busy running the outfit to spend extra time preparing. It was Sijan who had to work up all the complex premission material: the selection of maps, the latest Intel reports, changes in radio frequencies and tanker stations, and the myriad other details.

Lance took a long shower. This time of day the normally poor water pressure was even weaker. He shaved, then used foot powder. Lance was aware that he might have to depend on his feet and legs to save his life before this tour was over. In the past three months he had followed a rigorous program of weight lifting to toughen his muscle tone. He had been in combat since July and still had approximately four months of his tour to fly, forty-eight more counters. If he had to punch out over enemy territory, he planned to be ready.

Chatting through the open door of his room with the guy across the hall, Lance dressed carefully—clean cotton socks and shorts and a green combat T-shirt he'd bought at the Marine PX. A white T-shirt showing at the open throat of his flying suit would provide an obvious target. Lance had told his friends that were he ever shot down, he would do his damnedest to evade capture. Seemingly small details like the T-shirt might help in that evasion.

He pulled on his one-piece tropical cotton flying suit. This gray-green suit bore no unit patches or decorations. Above the left breast pocket was sewn a green rectangular name tag surmounted by cloth pilot's wings. There were numerous zipper pockets and sleeve pouches for pens and pencils. During his last leave home, Lance had persuaded his mother to sew additional hidden pockets on the inside legs of the suit. Into these pockets he methodically placed several nonstandard items of survival equipment: a multiblade pocketknife, a watertight metal tube of wooden matches he had carefully waterproofed, dipping the heads in melted paraffin, and a small prismatic compass to back up the one in his standard survival vest.

His pistol and holster would be at the squadron Personal Equipment Office with his flying gear. From his top dresser drawer he removed the long, curved bolo knife he had bought that summer from a Togali merchant outside the gates of Clark Air Force Base in the Philippines after he had completed jungle-survival school. The knife had a thick, keen-edged blade over ten inches long. The grip was of well-tanned buffalo hide. It was a knife capable of hacking down small trees or of being used as a savage weapon in close combat.

As was his habit, his premission ritual, Lance paused before his dresser. Arrayed in a neat row were framed family pictures: his mother, Jane, his father, Syl, Marc, his younger brother, and Janine, his little sister. Lance had always felt a special attachment to Janine and despite the complex demands of combat flying had maintained his unselfish role as her confidant and adviser through letters and taped messages. They were an unusually cohesive family, and Lance, the oldest child, had kept in close contact since he had left home seven years before. On each of his vacation leaves from the Air Force academy, he had come back to the family home on the bluff overlooking Milwaukee's South Shore Park and the blue expanse of Lake Michigan. He loved the summers in Wisconsin, the swimming and sailing, golf and baseball. Sijan was a physical person who enjoyed sports for the satisfaction of coordinating strength and dexterity. But mainly he came home simply to be with his family; they were his closest, most emphathetic friends. His father had once said, "Our family is one unit, whether we are together or apart."

Before a combat mission, his roommates report, Lance liked to spend a little time alone with his pictures. Often he would write a letter home or make a tape-recorded message before he flew. This helped ease the diffuse but yawning loneliness they all felt before going into combat. Now there were other pictures on top of the dresser. During the past four months Lance had been dating—if that domestic expression, evocative of peacetime adolescence, was applicable—a striking, quietly serious Continental Airline flight attendant named Lenora Monaco. She was in her midtwenties, small and fine boned, with long black hair and dark, expressive eyes. They had met on the charter flight that Lance took from Travis Air Force Base in California to Clark, near Manila, en route to Vietnam. Lance had been quite taken by her looks and quiet, intelligent manner. Lenora was older than many of the girls on the run and had a degree in art history.

Lenora now remembers that her first reaction to Lance's approach was to reject him out of hand. But, as in most undertakings, he was persistent. Before she left the flight at Wake Island, he had obtained her promise to have dinner with him in the Philippines on her next trip out. They met at the funny little hotel just off base where the commercial aircrews and the pilots attending jungle survival school were billeted. There, Lenora tried to renege on their dinner date: she had a personal policy, she explained, not to date guys who were going into combat. It was just too emotionally draining.

Lance had again persisted and, of course, prevailed. Lenora recalls that they ate the ersatz American food at the hotel restaurant, then sat out by the cracked concrete swimming pool and drank several iced bottles of San Miguel beer, talking softly in the candlelight, getting to know each other.

For the next several months, whenever Lance could manage a few days away from Da Nang, he would volunteer to fly aircraft "mod" flights, ferrying F-4Cs scheduled for modifications over to Clark. Lenora sent her flight schedule from California, and Lance tried hard to match her turnaround stops at Clark. Four times that autumn they were able to meet in the Philippines, sometimes able to spend several days together, on other occasions only a few hours. Between visits, they wrote. In October Lance telephoned Lenora in California to say he was in love with her.

In the intervals separating their time together at Clark, Lance flew combat missions north as far as Route Package VI, the well-defended Hanoi-Haiphong triangle, and into the intensive flak areas of the Ron River Valley and the Tally Ho area of Package I. His eyes acquired that hooded fatigue that Lenora says she had seen so often on other men who'd spent time in combat.

For her part, Lenora's profession was almost as bizarre as Lance's. Once every five or six days, she would leave her Los Angeles apartment and board a Continental Boeing 707 for the forty-hour trip to Tan Son Nhut, Cam Rhan Bay, or Da Nang. She would take her day off at Clark, maybe see Lance, then board a ten-thousand-mile flight carrying 120 or so lucky Marines or G.I.s who had just completed their in-country tours. Some of these young men had been in fire fights or under NVA artillery barrages only hours before they climbed aboard the plane home. She was a thoughtful, observant person, and she could plainly see what combat had done to them. Then, thirty hours later, she would report to Travis or El Toro for the next trip out.

Lance placed the colored snapshots of Lenora next to the framed pictures of his family. During their five days and nights in Bangkok, they had been inseparable. For the first time, with the new and intense physical intimacy, there had come an emotional bonding so strong that they had both been shocked by its power. Lenora realized that neither of them had been prepared for it.

Lance, hitherto outwardly stoic about the danger of combat and the pain he felt for his dead and missing friends, opened his emotional core to her. He admitted his habitual combat anxiety, his worst, unshakable premonitions about getting shot down. He told her he had cried for his lost friends. He talked angrily about the conduct of the war, about the disastrous results of unprecedented political interference in even the smallest operational details of the combat missions. This interference led to repetitive and predictable tactics that caused increased combat losses. If America continued to fight the war as it now was, he said, the effort was doomed to fail. And yet he still had half his tour to fly. And probably one more after that.

Lenora in return opened her heart to him. She clung to him in the narrow hotel bed and sobbed about her shared fear that he would be killed or captured. That, she explained, was why she had originally resisted getting too close to him. But now, and for several months, she had known how much she loved him, how much she wanted to share her life with him when . . . They had made an unspoken rule at Clark: Don't talk about after the tour, don't talk about the future. Now she was doing just that. She loved him and she wanted to marry him.

Lance spoke for the first time about marriage. His tour would probably be up in February or March. When he rotated back to California, they would fly out to Milwaukee to meet his family, then on to her family in Pennsylvania. They had made their commitment. And these optimistic, life-affirming plans did much to bolster both of them emotionally. The prospect of going back to war was nonetheless cruel.

Lance had left the darkened room in the Hotel Asia at four that morning to catch his bus out to the airport for the return flight to Da Nang. When he closed the warped plywood door of the room, Lenora remembers that his face and uniform collar were wet with a mixture of both their tears.

Following the premission routine that his friends all remember, Sijan stood before his small wall mirror, picked up his blue serge overseas hat, squared it on his head, and examined his appearance. He was singularly handsome, well over six feet, with a heavy, muscular frame, angular features, and dark, intelligent eyes. Other people, especially women, had always made much of Lance's looks. At the service academy prep school at Bainbridge, he'd been elected the king of the 1961 *Cruise* yearbook—a title never before given a cadet —as much for his good looks as for his ". . . Promethean amalgamation of dynamism, masculinity, and that certain intangible something which represents everything clean and decent in America. . . ." Not to mention his indefatigable pursuit of feminine company, the *Cruise* editors added sardonically.

The humid darkness of the parking ramp was cloying after the chill air-conditioning of the Command Post. It was after seven-thirty, and they were due to start engines in less than twenty minutes. As always, the detailed mission briefing had dragged on well past the one hour it was allotted in the flight schedule.

Sijan grabbed the narrow steel ladder clamped to the open rear cockpit and heaved his heavy frame onto the first rung. His cumbersome flight gear made him awkward. Over his cotton flying suit he wore the rubber-and-nylon leggings of his G-suit, his green-mesh survival vest with a dozen bulging pockets that sagged with emergency radio, signal mirror, flares, and first aid kit, his inflatable life jacket, and, finally, his thickly webbed parachute harness.

After easing himself gingerly into the cramped pit, he rested his helmet on the cockpit sill and switched on the inertial navigation system so that the gyros could warm up. Next he carefully entered the exact coordinates of the south taxi ramp of Da Nang Air Base and those of the primary target, the Ban Loboy Ford, a river crossing on the Ho Chi Minh Trail six miles inside Laos from the North Vietnamese border. The target was near a junction of main vehicle infiltration routes on the part of the Trail the Americans had designated LOC 101. It lay in wild, uninhabited, triple-canopy mountain forest, surrounded by sheer chimneys and towers of limestone called karsts that rose from the narrow jungle valleys.

On this mission the two-plane flight, bearing the call signs *AWOL 1* and *AWOL 2*, would work with a Forward Air Controller who would illuminate the target with flares and direct each plane's bomb run. Overall control of the mission would be maintained by a C-130 Airborne Command Center with the call sign *Lamplighter*. The FAC, *Nail 11*, flew a Cessna O-2 from Udorn Air Base in Thailand; his task was to identify the target positively and to verify that visibility was within acceptable limits for accurate bombing. The FAC would also act as a search and rescue coordinator should either of the *AWOL* crews be forced to eject.

In that event, a formal search and rescue (SAR) effort would be launched, with Jolly Green Giant rescue helicopters escorted by heavily armed, prop-driven A-1 Sandys converging on the scene at first light. While the downed crewmen talked to the Jollys on their survival radios, the Sandys would suppress any enemy ground fire with rockets, cluster bombs, and 20mm cannon fire. Then the survivors would pop their orange smoke flares and the big helicopter would drop a rescue seat—the jungle penetrator—by cable, and winch the pilots up through the thick canopy to the hovering chopper. In theory this was an efficient, almost foolproof search and rescue tactic. In reality the system worked well about half the time. Often the downed pilot was killed, smashing through the roof of the towering triple-canopy forest; sometimes he landed among enemy road security troops on the Trail and was either immediately seized or killed trying to evade capture.

Climbing back out of the rear cockpit to complete his preflight inspection of the aircraft, Sijan had to shift the long pistol holster strapped to his right thigh. Like many of the pilots, Lance had invested his own money in a heavier handgun than the standard-issue .38 revolver. His was a Smith and Wesson .357 magnum with a six-inch barrel; it was accurate and packed a killing blow in each round.

Lance had often told his friends that he did not intend to be captured. He was strong and athletic, fast on his feet. Since his freshman year in high school, he had played tight end on several championship football teams. At the Academy his rugged endurance and spirit on the football field were well known. Now, three years beyond scrimmages on chill Colorado afternoons, halfway through his first combat tour, when he told friends from the Academy that he was determined to evade capture, they took him seriously.

In the lower pockets of his G-suit he carried two additional smoke flares, a flashlight, and two plastic baby bottles of water. His squadronmates considered Lance a prudent, well-organized type when it came to survival gear. But he did not go overboard. Some guys carried so many extra items in the legs of their G-suits that the weight of the additional equipment ripped away the pockets during the tremendous stress of ejection and the equipment was lost in the cloud of debris streaming from the crippled plane. Lance was not an extremist, but he intended to stay alive.

During jungle survival training in the Philippines, he had proven himself to be one of the most adept and adaptable trainees. He had absorbed as much jungle lore as he could from his instructors, and he had made a real effort to read and analyze mission critiques of earlier successful and unsuccessful air rescue efforts in Vietnam.

After fifty-two missions, the lessons of survival school were no longer abstractions. Were he to parachute into North Vietnam or the mountains of Laos, he would be alone on the ground surrounded by a skilled and determined enemy who had been bombed around the clock for two-and-a-half years. He could hardly expect such a foe to show compassion. He would be hunted and forced to hunt like an animal once he was out on those forest slopes.

If he ejected, in a matter of seconds he would be separated from his complex, heavily armed airplane, which was capable of supersonic flight and of delivering twelve tons of bombs to a target hidden by darkness and forest canopy. In the short time it took him to parachute to earth, he would travel from the relative security of the twentieth century's most advanced military technology to a jungle where the rules and conduct of combat had not undergone any major alteration since Neolithic times.

Before leaving for Vietnam, Sijan had visited his academy roommate, Mike Smith, at Wright-Patterson Air Base, and they talked about what it would be like to face the enemy alone in the jungle. He and Joe Kosciusko had spoken of this, and he had shared his fears with Lenora on their last night in Bangkok.

As did every flier, Sijan had turned over his wallet to the supply sergeant before each mission. The only personal papers a pilot carried into combat were his Air Force identity card, his blood chit and inoculation record, and a laminated card with the Geneva Convention rules on the responsibility of prisoners of war. This last item was of little value; North Vietnam, although party to the Geneva Convention, refused to consider downed American airmen prisoners of war. Since no declaration of war had been issued by either side, they claimed, American pilots who bombed their territory were to be considered air pirates.

Sijan's next preflight task was to inspect the ordnance and external stores. Under each wing they carried three 750-pound bombs slung from the first pylon outboard from the centerline. These bombs were long steel cylinders painted gray-green, with bright yellow nose and tail cones where the inertial fuses were attached. Around each protruding fuse cone, an arming wire was secured; it led through eyelets back along the bomb casing and was anchored on the wing pylon. When the bombs were released, the arming wire would rip away the protective cone of the fuse, initiating the electrochemical timing mechanism of the bomb detonator. These particular bombs were fused to explode exactly six seconds after release at eight thousand feet so that they would safely pass through branches, bury themselves even in the concrete of the river ford, and throw up deep craters. This fuse system was new, a recent modification made necessary by the enemy's stepped-up infiltration effort in Laos.

The bomb-release clamps that held the ordnance to the pylons were each secured "locked safe" with a thick steel safety pin that trailed a bright red warning flag on which was stenciled Remove Before Flight. Lance inspected each bomb, its arming wire, sway brace, and the release-clamp safety flags, verifying that the number and type of ordnance as well as its method of fusing and position on the aircraft's weapons pylons were as specified in the frag.

Colonel Armstrong next proceeded through the remaining forty items of the F-4C Exterior Inspection Checklist, examining such disparate details as the rivets on the engine air intakes and the release doors of the drag chute used to slow the plane on landing.

At the top of the narrow steel ladder to the rear cockpit, Lance would have to lower his large frame carefully down into the padded vinyl seat. The rear cockpit was cramped, a tight nest of electronics consoles, instruments, and controls. Once in, he would snap the risers of the stowed parachute backpack into his harness, double-checking each quick-release buckle that connected him to the main body of his parachute, enclosed behind him in a protective fiber-glass shell. Clicked into his seat harness with his helmet and mask balanced on the canopy sill he would go to work.

He had to black out the most brightly illuminated dials on his instrument panel with bits of masking tape that were stuck to the sides of his helmet in a seemingly messy array. It was a typical Vietnam improvisation: the F-4 Phantom had been originally de-signed as a naval air-defense fighter, a fast missile-launching plat-form. In the Navy version of the plane, the F-4B, the backseater was a radar observer. There was no need for him to dim his instrument panel lights because he was not required to protect his night vision.

Now, however, the Air Force had adapted the Phantom into a day-and-night fighter-bomber in order to take advantage of the plane's superior ordnance capacity on a combat radius of over nine hundred miles. The F-4C's radar system, designed for air-to-air missile combat, was of little use when the plane was employed as an old-fashioned dive bomber. So Sijan diligently applied small squares and rectangles of masking tape to the lamps illuminating the vertical speed indicator, the airspeed dial, and each of the major cockpit instruments, with the exception of the altimeter, the artifi-cial horizon, and the magnetic compass.

Such compromises were widespread during the Vietnam war, and their necessity did much to embitter thoughtful young officers like Sijan. During World War II, a vital aircraft modification program would have been given high priority; the lives of combat crews depended on their equipment. But the Vietnam conflict was Amer-ica's first cost-effectiveness war.

After the masking was completed, he slipped a disc of transparent red plastic into the throat of his radar scope. Given the altitude and ingress route of the frag order, he should be able to get a rough radar bearing and range on the limestone karst formations in the target area during their approach to the Initial Point, where the FAC would take over. Other backseaters might not have bothered, but he was known as a good radar head, and he enjoyed the sense of control such radar work gave him. It helped alleviate the frustration of riding in the pit.

By the time Lance had completed this job, Colonel Armstrong had finished his own external preflight checks. Sijan and Armstrong each put on his dull green flying helmet and plugged in his intercom cord. From now until the end of the flight, they could communicate only through microphone and earphone. They began their long preflight and takeoff checklist, using the challenge-and-response method, with the backseater, Sijan, calling out the items from his clipboard and Armstrong, the AC, completing the required instrument or control setting and responding when it was completed. Slowly, methodical as any airline crew, they worked in the humid darkness.

The perimeter of the base was lit now by dazzling white parachute flares that drifted down from the scattered clouds above the swampy estuary. Every night the Spooky C-47 gunships flared the area, searching for NVA rocket teams. The marine artillery also fired illumination rounds over suspected infiltration trails, and when sampan traffic or unidentified troops were seen moving in unauthorized areas, 105mm guns or the Spookys cut loose. The airmen of Da Nang learned that to preserve their night vision they must avoid looking at the bright magnesium flares and the artillery flashes.

Although the noise of artillery came to them through the open canopies, Sijan could hear Armstrong's voice with perfect clarity. The backseater in a Phantom was perched behind and slightly above the aircraft commander, isolated in a separate pit of instruments and flight controls. After their canopies were snapped down and locked, they would be isolated from the outside world as well.

When the two huge General Electric engines were started and all the pre-taxi checks had been completed, Armstrong signaled his ground crew with a thumbs up. They pulled the wheel chocks and the big, squat jet trundled down the taxi ramp toward the Arm-Dearm area at the head of runway 35 Right. As it taxied, the humid heat seemed more like a breeze, carrying the smoke and mildewed fecundity of nearby swamps into the open cockpits. Off to the west, a Spooky gunship was working a target, and there was the occasional white flash and a slap of a Marine 105 shell landing a couple of klicks away. Choppers clattered overhead through the smoky darkness. Another typical night in the long war.

At the arming area, the big plane stopped neatly on the painted lines. Lance raised his hands and rested them on the top edge of the open canopy. Although he could not see the Colonel, he knew he was doing the same: safety procedure; while the ordnance men were down there pulling the safety flags from the weapon-release clamps, both pilots had to have their hands and arms completely clear of the weapon circuit panels. The ordnance supervisor signaled that they were clear, and Colonel Armstrong advanced the throttles.

Sijan closed his canopy and double-checked that the locking arm was down and the green closed/locked light was on. He snapped his mask on and adjusted the oxygen flow rate and double-checked the flow indicator. The plane was bouncing slowly over some rough tarmac now, nearing the head of the runway. In his earphones he heard the Colonel request and receive permission to enter the runway. A moment later they were given their takeoff clearance. Craning his neck, Lance looked at his rearview mirror to be sure their wing man, *AWOL 2*, was behind them.

They were working a high UHF frequency that in theory did not carry very far beyond the confines of the base. But they still kept their plane-tower communications to a minimum. Twenty miles offshore, in international waters, Soviet trawlers strung with all manner of antennae slowly beat up and down the coast, intercepting and analyzing American radio traffic. The Russian ELINT vessels maintained direct communication with the Soviet Military Intelligence Center in Hanoi; probably every American flight northbound out of Da Nang and the other coastal bases was monitored and reported to the NVA Air Defense network along the Trail.

The full extent of the Soviets' offshore ELINT coverage of American air operations, as well as the efficiency of the North Vietnamese antiaircraft crews in making use of Soviet technical assistance, was only then beginning to be understood by the tacticians of the Seventh Air Force. Once an American mission was airborne, the planes used fixed-channel communication frequencies. Furthermore, scheduled interdiction flights used regular, predictable call signs to identify the missions. Thus, the 2000 hour, two-plane strike from Da Nang was always called *AWOL;* if it worked with the airborne controller called Lamplighter and the FAC called *Nail,* the Russians could safely assume the mission was headed toward one of ten Trail targets in the Laotian panhandle between Sepone and the Mu Gia Pass.

The Soviet ELINT trawler would contact Hanoi, and the Soviet liaison officer would alert NVA Air Defense. On the ground along the Trail, the gun crews would receive a good twenty minutes' advance warning that American planes were on their way.

The deputy commander of the 366th Tactical Fighter Wing sent an urgent, secret message to his superiors at Seventh Air Force that autumn. "Aircrews in this wing," he wrote, had "observed evidence that the enemy may be monitoring our strike and reporting frequencies." He went on to recommend that henceforth all fragged strike flights should communicate using only their mission numbers, not their call signs. As the mission numbers changed each day, the enemy would have a harder time identifying fragged interdiction strikes. He ended his message with a strong appeal for "secure voice ciphony" radio scramblers to be installed on all the concerned aircraft and ground stations. These scramblers, of course, were expensive, and it was years before they were widely used by American strike aircraft.

In November 1967, very few American military leaders or politicians wanted to acknowledge publicly that the country had slid sideways, almost unawares, into a proxy war with the Soviet Union. But that, of course, was the reality of the Russian ELINT trawlers, their command center in Hanoi, and the radar-controlled flak guns along the Ho Chi Minh Trail.

Colonel Armstrong swung the Phantom smartly onto the centerline of the runway and locked the brakes. Ahead of him, the long line of amber lamps stretched away toward the distant strings of obstacle lights up on Monkey Mountain. It was 2009. Lance called out the final takeoff check-list:

"Flight controls."

"Free and unrestricted."

Lance sat in his seat, slowly reading the list to the last item: "Warning lights."

"Negative."

"Checklist complete, sir."

"Rolling," Colonel Armstrong said.

The engines howled to an overpowering, all-embracing roar. Lance was thrust back in his seat. From the sides of his eyes, he caught the runway lights streaming by. Peeling aside the tape on the airspeed indicator, he called out the knots toward V-1 and rotation.

They broke free of the ground and were climbing. The gear came thumping up beneath them, and Lance responded to the Colonel's call for reduced flaps. Below the right wing, fishing sampans, each with a flaring gaslamp, were strung out across the bay like a constellation in a black sky. Off to the left there were smoky fires burning. A chopper gunship circled, pumping tracers into some suspected enemy movement. They were climbing steeply at three hundred knots, up past the lights of Monkey Mountain, clearing eight thousand feet. *AWOL 2* was right behind them, tucked into a fingertip position near their starboard wing. Lance verified that he had visual contact with 2, and the Colonel continued his climbing bank toward their first ingress heading. Once they had cleared the approach boundaries of the base, both aircraft commanders extinguished their navigation lights. The dark, camouflaged planes were almost invisible in the weak moonlight.

At flight level, on the first ingress heading, Lance was able to verify their exact position and ground speed independently of the inertial navigator by taking a course bearing using the TACAN radio beacons at Da Nang and Phu Bai Air Base near Hue, thirty miles north of their course. The inertial system was operating perfectly.

He heard Colonel Armstrong talking to *Lamplighter*, announcing their estimated time of arrival (ETA) at the turning point and requesting clearance beyond that point for the northerly ingress leg, up the Laotian panhandle to the target. On this channel the communications were almost continuous but of short duration. The various voices of *Lamplighter* represented combat controllers on board the airborne command post working different flights of fighter-bombers, flare planes, and Stinger gunships.

Sijan's view straight ahead was blocked by the rear of the Colonel's ejection seat. To either side he had a clear and open view of the earth below, and three rearview mirrors gave him a good field of vision behind the plane. There was not much new to see tonight. The war of attrition was still going on in I Corps, of course. From this altitude, the fire fights, artillery fire, and gunship activity appeared like smoldering remnants of campfires. Occasionally the sky below would burst with a neon glare as a Spooky flared the area around a marine or South Vietnamese Army (ARVN) fire base. If he had been monitoring a ground-support radio channel, Lance would have heard the voices of young Marine officers directing the gunships against the concentrations of NVA troops outside the wire perimeter of the fire bases.

From intelligence reports Sijan knew that the NVA was licking its wounds. But the Marines, dug into bunkers and weapons pits, also suffered heavy casualties.

Often these casualties arrived on dust-off choppers at the Med-Evac Hospital on the other side of the 366th's flight line. Sijan and his friends had seen them and heard the hoarse sobbing and moans that even morphine did not quiet. Nights at the DOOM Club the men would watch these same bloody Marines on the wide screen of the TV set above the bar. Night after night, it seemed, the American networks concentrated on casualties, American, South Vietnamese, and civilian. Burned villages and ambushed American convoys also seemed popular. There were never, of course, any pictures of NVA tanks, artillery positions, or flak sites. That side of the war was impossible for the American camera crews to report.

AWOL 1 and *2* reached their turning point a minute ahead of schedule. Lance confirmed their position by inertial navigator, and Colonel Armstrong called out his new heading to *Lamplighter*. Now the ground was dead black below them. There were no fire bases or fire fights inside Laos. Now they were over the dark mass of the Annam Cordillera, the long mountains, which thrust up steeply to a sharp spine of jungle ridges six thousand feet above the narrow coastal plains.

Low-level flight among these ridges and exposed shafts of limestone formations, or karsts, was extremely hazardous; as Major Nordin put it, "the karsts can come up and bite you." The NVA had been known to lay out decoy lights, imitating stalled truck traffic, to lure American bombers into cul-de-sacs surrounded by hazardous terrain. Exact navigation was therefore of crucial importance.

At this phase of the mission Lance would have adjusted the radar set, switching the scanning mode from narrow search to a wider angle and the scanning range to forty miles. The sharp relief features of the mountain chain appeared in his scope in bright fluorescent bands beneath the pink plastic disc. If he adjusted the scale for sixty miles, the pie wedge of the search area would change shape in his scope. At the outer range of the search area, the rapid scan beam could pickup the ground pattern of the target area. The narrow river valley was bordered on the east and west by peaked ridges averaging four thousand feet in elevation. These showed as blurred abstractions, as if an artist had spilled a bottle of fluorescent paint on a black table. The darker areas between these electronic smears were the deep gorges and wider valleys, hidden in the radar shadows by the high ground. As the Phantom sped nearer, the familiar array of ridges would slip down the scan wedge of the scope, growing larger until the darker central area threw back some sharp, unmistakable echoes—the massive, freestanding limestone karsts ringing the Ban Loboy Ford.

When the flight was twenty-one miles south of the target, they were on the Initial Point (IP), where they were to orbit while *Lamplighter* spoke with the FAC, *Nail 11*, to determine if the target was workable. Ahead of Lance in the darkened jet, Colonel Armstrong was observing the target in his cockpit radar repeater scope.

"TACAN fix please, Lieutenant." The Colonel was a careful pilot; he wanted to verify their position before calling *Lamplighter*.

"Sixty-one slash one-oh-two on Channel Eighty-nine, sir."

They were sixty-one nautical miles out on the 102 degree radial from the Nakhon Phanom Air Base in Thailand.

Armstrong called out their position. "*Lamplighter, AWOL One*, orbit on IP. Painting target two-six-two positive at twenty miles."

"*AWOL One, Lamplighter.* Roger. Stand by."

The two Phantoms went into a banking, left-hand turn and reduced speed to 350 knots. They were 19,500 feet above the dark Ho Chi Minh Trail. As they turned, the two crews had a good view to the south where the other flights under *Lamplighter*'s control were working. Thirty miles down the Trail there were a lot of flares near the junctions of LOCs 610 and 611. At this distance, the flares were chalky pink. A heavy Stinger AC-119 gunship was clobbering a truck column down there. Even further south, where the valleys opened up, *Misty* FAC was directing a flight of Phantoms from Udorn in Thailand on a truck-smashing road reconnaissance near Sepone. To the north the Mu Gia Pass would catch it all night, with the weather so good.

They orbited, idle, while *Lamplighter* and the FAC discussed the current state of the Ban Loboy Ford. Within five minutes they might be on and then off the target, flying south again toward Da Nang, toward debriefing after an uneventful mission, toward the cool shadows of the DOOM Club, a couple of cans of Bud, and the late newscast on Armed Forces Vietnam-TV.

"*AWOL One, Lamplighter.*" The airborne controller was speaking. "You are cleared to target area. Handing you off to *Nail One One* on primary FAC channel. Good luck."

"Roger, *Lamplighter.* Thank you. Good evening." Armstrong's voice was cool, precise, as if he were an airline captain talking to a Federal Aviation Administration controller in the bright sunshine of peacetime America on the other side of the planet.

The four crewmen in the two planes switched their command radios to the primary FAC channel for Steel Tiger.

"*Nail One One,*" Armstrong called, "*AWOL* Flight inbound from IP for the two-six-two."

"*AWOL One, Nail One One.* Roger. Press on and call out high orbit."

The two Phantoms banked north again and gathered speed as they descended from the IP to the high-station orbit fourteen thousand feet above the target valley.

"*Nail Eleven, AWOL* Lead," Armstrong called. "Holding on high station."

"Roger, *AWOL.* Stand by for flares."

While the FAC dove on the target for his first flare pass, *AWOL 1* and *2* carried out their separation maneuver, with *1* turning south again on the downwind base leg of the flat orbit. *AWOL 2* S-turned and slowed his aircraft so that he would be on the opposite side of their invisible oval holding pattern. In each plane the crew carried out the bomb-arming checklist. Once the flares were strung out and the target well illuminated, *AWOL 1* would roll into his bomb run. By the time he had released his bombs eight thousand feet above the target and had pulled out in a violently evasive jinking climb, the FAC would clear *2* into the target. If *1* needed more than a single pass, *2* would simply stay in his high-station orbit, awaiting clearance in.

The rubber bladders of Sijan's G-suit inflated with compressed air as the Colonel added more throttle and banked toward the bottom of the holding pattern. He was being pushed down hard against the contours of his seat, his restraining harness keeping his limbs away from the flight controls. To the left the first flare burst. Then the second and the third dazzling magnesium parachute flares popped far below the port wingtip, casting deep wavering shadows from the karsts. As the glaring bowl of flare light filled the valley, the target area became plainly visible. Raw mud switchback roads and the bomb-splintered trunks of tiny defoliated trees stood out in gray detail, as if seen in a sharp black-and-white television picture.

"*AWOL* Lead," the FAC called. "You are cleared to attack the target."

Sijan swallowed to unblock his ears, tugged down smartly on his harness straps, and placed the gloved fingers of his right hand on his right knee, close to but not touching the rear cockpit control stick. The Phantom banked hard to the left, and the flare-lit valley seemed to tumble onto its side as the roll angle increased.

"*Nail*," the Colonel called the FAC. "*AWOL* Lead rolling in."

Sijan was thrust more evenly down into his seat now as the roll-in maneuver evolved smoothly into a thirty-five-degree dive at just over 450 knots. As the Gs increased, he would have steadied his head on his shoulders to keep his vision clear. There were no enemy tracers yet. The Colonel would jink violently as soon as he had pickled the bombs at the release point but would take no evasive action until then. The Phantom screamed down into the glare of the flares. This was the most dangerous moment of the mission.

Nail 11 was on a lazy one hundred-knot orbit at ten thousand feet and upwind of both Phantoms, midway between the high station and the bomb-release point. His flare pattern was holding well tonight, so all three planes were in theory protected from visual ground observation by the glare of the flares. He could just discern the brown silhouette of *AWOL 1* diving smoothly toward the target, bottom-lit by the flares and faintly highlighted by the setting moon. As the FAC reported later, he watched the attacking jet, noting that the dive angle seemed a little shallow and realizing that *AWOL 1* was probably laying on some more Gs to keep his speed down. But a few seconds later he saw that *AWOL 1* was diving at almost fifty degrees and rolling now, to the left. The roll maneuver blurred into a flat turn that broke the dive, and *AWOL 1* jinked hard left, now right, and was climbing fast into a left-hand bank toward high-station orbit. He had still been a couple of thousand feet above bomb release when he broke off his attack.

Nail 11, a prop pilot, caught his breath, as he always did watching big jets climb away fast from a night bomb run. If the jet pilot lost it for a moment and advanced those throttles all the way up the quadrant to afterburner, there would be hell to pay. Those afterburners were like big red-and-blue searchlights. Every flak battery down there would have an irresistible target. And it was an easy enough mistake to make; he had seen it happen several times. But *AWOL* lead knew what he was doing. He was on full military power, just shy of afterburner, getting away from there fast.

"*Nail One One, AWOL* Lead. Pass aborted. I lost my target reference."

"Roger, *AWOL* Lead," the FAC said calmly. "Do you want to have at it again?"

"That's a roger, *Nail. AWOL* Lead standing by."

The FAC rolled back to level flight, then banked slowly to the right, hanging on his wing as he gazed down at the flare pattern and the target. There had been no visible flak, and the two higher flares still had plenty of good burn time in them.

"*AWOL One, Nail One One.* You are cleared to attack the target."

They were on the base leg once more, about to roll in again on their second pass. Out of the left side of his canopy, Sijan could have seen that the flare pattern was still okay.

The plane rocked, then banked hard to starboard. The Colonel was attacking from the five o'clock position on the orbit now, as against the seven o'clock spot where he'd rolled in on the first pass. Good thinking; use any trick you could to confuse the enemy gunners.

Again the familiar, even pressure on torso and legs. Again the weight on head and neck. The Phantom screamed down toward the valley into the chalky glare. The Gs decreased as the roll diminished and they achieved their proper dive angle. Down, smoothly at 450 knots, into the flare light.

Nail 11 leveled off at twelve thousand feet. Beyond his starboard wing's leading edge, he saw *AWOL* Lead dropping fast toward bomb release. This pass was going to be a winner. The flares were spread perfectly to give good target reference and some dimension to the dark ridges and karsts below. A few more seconds and he'd pickle his whole load. Suddenly there was flak, two then three streams of orange 37mm tracers floating up from the dark valley.

There was something red, a spark of neon red. Then a massive, shocking explosion, an incandescent ball of flaming debris that cascaded down like a napalm burst all the way into the gray-black canopy of the forest two miles north of the target. He hung in his seat harness gazing down at the flaming wreckage of *AWOL 1* burning in the blackness below. Flares swung near the forest roof dragging darkness with them from the surrounding ridges. For perhaps thirty more seconds the wreckage burned, then went out.

The FAC adjusted his prop pitch, throttle, and mixture to conserve fuel, to extend his loiter time in orbit. He had seen no ejection seats fired from the crippled plane nor any orange-and-white parachute canopies against the dark jungle slopes below. But the explosion and streams of flame from the jet had killed his night vision.

He shook his head violently and called the other F-4C. "*AWOL Two, Nail.* Did you see any chutes?"

"Negative, *Nail.* But the fire was pretty bright."

Now the FAC asserted his assigned command role. "Roger, *Two.* Maintain high orbit. Carry out search and rescue procedure and make sure to squawk your IFF to Emergency. *Two* Alpha, monitor *Crown* Primary. *Two* Bravo, monitor Guard. Watch for pen flares. I'll contact *Lamplighter.* If you copy a beeper, try to get a fix on it."

Nail added throttle and climbed now to a safer altitude, well above the target. He was not sure *what* had hit *AWOL*, but whatever it was, he didn't want it to hit him. When he was ready to report, he would check in with *Lamplighter*, then with *Crown*, the C-130 airborne search and rescue command post that was orbiting above the Thai-Laotian border a hundred miles to the west.

His instructions to Major Fitzgerald and Lieutenant Jones—*AWOL 2* Alpha and Bravo—had been right out of the *Search and*

Rescue Guide, procedures both of the other pilots would have known by rote. It was a precise litany of command, of familiar procedure. Probably it helped erase the image of the exploding Phantom.

Lieutenant Jones now selected the Guard Channel on his radio console, 243.0 megahertz. This was the frequency of the RT-10 survival radios. If either Colonel Armstrong or Sijan had made it out of the plane alive and was now down there on those dark slopes, conscious and uncaptured, he would activate his beeper or try to make voice contact.

AWOL 2 Alpha, Major Fitzgerald, flipped the switch of his IFF transducer to the right, Emergency. Now his plane had become a bright electronic beacon fourteen thousand feet above the Ban Loboy Ford, winking out a Mayday signal that could be seen on American ground radar scopes all the way from Da Nang to Thailand. Within minutes the search and rescue headquarters at Tan Son Nhut Air Base outside Saigon would be alerted that an American aircraft had crashed inside Laos, and the preliminary rescue mission plans could be formulated.

Nail 11 had now climbed to sixteen thousand feet. He set his autopilot to turn him in a lazy orbit and made some quick notes on his knee clipboard. *AWOL 1* had exploded at 2039 local time, 1339 Zulu. Neither the FAC nor the wingman had seen chutes. The Phantom had impacted approximately two miles north of the target among rugged jungle slopes and naked limestone karsts. SAR procedures had been initiated. He was ready now to break the news to *Lamplighter.*

Below the orbiting planes, the long mountains were dark again. The flaming wreckage of *AWOL 1* had not burned very long, evidence that it had crashed on a steep rock slope that had dispersed the fuel. The FAC printed his precise notes on his clipboard while his aircraft flew itself through the starry night.

Below, there was only dark wilderness.

Chapter Four

Ban Loboy Ford, Laos

November 11, 1967

Dawn broke over the long mountains. Broken clouds clung to the ridgetops, but the day promised to be clear, VFR all the way from the Thai border up to Package VI. This Saturday—Veterans Day back in America—would see a busy bombing schedule in the North.

Now, a few minutes after sunrise, *Drill* Flight, consisting of two F-4Ds from the 8th Tactical Fighter Wing based in Ubon, Thailand, had just come off the tanker in an aerial refueling zone code-named Brown Anchor. The camouflaged Phantoms joined up again at twenty-eight thousand feet and wheeled back onto their first ingress heading for their target, the rail yards north of Hanoi. Aboard the two aircraft, the four young men were silent after the curt, tense radio exchanges of midair refueling.

Their planes were now each loaded with twelve tons of fuel, bombs, and missiles as they sped northeast toward the massed flak batteries and surface-to-air missile (SAM) sites that ringed Hanoi. Within thirty minutes these four pilots would be right in the middle of it, diving toward bomb release between the Red River and Thud Ridge, amid the heaviest concentration of antiaircraft defenses ever assembled. Now, in the pastel dawn, they still had a few moments of relative peace, time to enjoy the profound beauty of high altitude flight during the transition from darkness to day.

Drill Flight Lead heard the beeper first. A moment later his backseater called out a loud survival radio beeper on Guard Channel bearing seventy-four degrees true. Then *Drill* 2 called in the same bearing. *Drill* Lead ordered the flight into a long banking S-turn while the two backseaters got to work, refining their automatic direction finder (ADF) bearings on the Mayday beeper down there in the mountains and taking TACAN readings to produce their own position. As part of their mission Intel briefing, *Drill* Flight had been alerted that there was an F-4 crew from Da Nang, *AWOL 1*, who had been knocked down Thursday night. Now, possibly, one of the downed pilots was coming up on the survival radio.

When they had a decent fix on the beeper, *Drill* Lead called *Cricket,* the Airborne Command Center on station to the west over the Thai-Laos border. It was 0610 local time. *Cricket* ordered *Drill* to take up a high orbit and to talk to the survivor on Guard. The airborne controller then diverted *Nail 10,* a Steel Tiger 0-2 FAC, into a lower orbit and asked *Misty* FACs *21* and *11* to take up a medium altitude station in the area. Within minutes of the first beeper signal at dawn, four American jets—the two Ubon Phantoms and two Misty F-100s—and *Nail 10* were patrolling the sky above the Ban Loboy Ford.

Now *Drill* Lead assumed temporary command. Once the beeper signal stopped, he called down on Guard, asking the unseen pilot to identify himself. During this conversation, the other pilots listened intently to the voice rising from the mist-banded forest slopes below. The NVA were known to have some persuasive English speakers who used captured pilots' survival radios to lure rescue forces into flak traps. The man who answered sounded young, calm, plausibly Air Force. He said he was *AWOL 1* Bravo, that he was on top of a heavily forested karst about three or four miles north of

Target 262; almost in passing, the calm young voice concluded, "I'm hurt kind of bad . . . left leg broken, compound fracture. My head's hurt pretty bad, too. Can't really move around too well down here. I was unconscious all day yesterday."

"Roger, *AWOL*, copy," *Drill* Lead acknowledged. "Stand by."

He switched from Guard to Command and spoke with *Cricket*, who quickly passed him off to *Crown 1*, the C-130 search and rescue airborne command post that was now heading for the scene. With the approach of *Crown* toward high station, a formal SAR effort was under way. Radio traffic was switched off the normal command frequencies to 364.2 UHF; the orbiting FACs and fighter-bombers were now under the overall command of *Crown*. He, in turn, was under the command of *Compress*, the senior SAR commander working from the rescue headquarters at Udorn Air Base in Thailand.

As the sun rose higher above the rolling green ridges, the broken clouds began to burn off, exposing the deep valleys and white limestone karsts. The jets orbited at a safe altitude: No ground fire was yet reported. En route to the site, *Crown* spoke briefly to the survivor, advising him that an SAR effort was under way and asking for more formal identification.

"Sijan, Lance Peter," the cool, precise voice rose out of the jungle. "First lieutenant, United States Air Force." He recited his serial number, then crisply asked if *Crown* had copied his transmission.

"Copy, *AWOL*, stand by."

Crown had not only heard Sijan's transmission, the on-board commander had also satisfied himself that the voice down there was probably an American survivor, not an NVA soldier who spoke good English. In addition, the orbiting jets had been able to refine their radio fix on the signal while Sijan spoke. The transmission seemed to be coming from a massive, tree-covered karst formation about three miles due north of the bomb-pocket target zone at the Ban Loboy Ford. This would conform to the original shoot-down report from *Nail 11*, the night FAC. *AWOL 1* would not have been in his chute very long because the ejection occurred too low for either the FAC or the wingman to see a parachute.

Crown 1 now called *Compress*—Rescue 1 Command Post at Udorn —and was advised that an airborne rescue team was on the way from Nakhon Phanom Air Base, eighty-five miles to the west, just inside Thailand. This team consisted of two Sikorsky HH-3 Jolly Green

Giant helicopters to be used for the actual pickup, and two well-armed A—1E Sandys as escorts. The Sandys would arrive first and dip down over the survivor's suspected location to pinpoint his position and to troll for flak, flying low, slow turns to tempt any imprudent NVA gunner into firing and thus betraying his gun site. If they encountered ground fire during this maneuver, the orbiting fast-movers could be FAC'd in by *Nail* and the Sandys to clobber the guns.

The pilot of *Sandy 7* was the senior officer, so he would assume on-scene command, with *Sandy 8* as his wingman, once the two heavy old prop planes reached station. By the standards of the Vietnam War, these Sandy and Jolly Green pilots were veterans; they had many months of cumulative experience rescuing downed airmen from the Trail, and they knew the habits of the NVA gunners and road-security forces hidden down there under the dense, moss-like roof of the triple-canopy forest.

If the NVA decided to use the survivor as bait in a trap, *Sandy* lead and *Crown* could call upon almost unlimited aerial firepower to suppress the flak. As needed, *Cricket* would divert flights fragged into the Packages or scramble flights on alert as far away as Takhli and Korat in Thailand to Phu Cat and Da Nang in South Vietnam. Early on in the complex SAR operation, if it became clear that additional high-performance jet aircraft would be required to loiter on station, a Boeing KC-135 aerial refueling tanker would be sent in to orbit in the nearest safe area to the rescue site. Using the tanker, the jet fighter-bombers could extend their time on station to six or eight hours.

That spring the Jolly Green Giant helicopters had been modified so that they, too, could be refueled in flight. To accomplish this unlikely mating between a helicopter and a fixed-wing tanker aircraft, the *Crown* C-130 had been modified. It now could deploy long hoses from its outboard underwing fuel tanks; these hoses ended in small drogue cones that rode evenly in the big plane's slipstream. The Jolly Green had a collapsible hydraulic fuel probe that could be extended almost twenty feet from its nose. While the large command plane—throttled way back on full flaps—trundled along at less than one hundred knots, the big, ungainly helicopter would cautiously approach, its fuel probe extended to strike into and lock the hose drogue that was planing slowly back and forth in the turbulence from *Crown*'s four big propjet engines. This was a tricky maneuver, especially in rough, marginal weather. Wind shear or severe turbulence could send one aircraft careening into the other, with the Jolly Green being the most likely loser in the scrape.

But the refueling potential had extended the range and loiter time of the Jolly Greens so that they could now effect rescues deep inside North Vietnam or remain on station in Laos for hours while the Sandys and the fast-movers beat up the gun sites near a survivor. Again, American technology had been pitted against a stubborn, skilled, and resourceful enemy. But in the evolution of the SAR potential in Southeast Asia, a uniquely Western preoccupation with the value of the *individual*—in this case, a downed pilot—illuminated the vast cultural differences that separated the opponents in this long war.

To the Americans it was sound military doctrine to risk the lives of literally scores of airmen to rescue one downed pilot from capture. The value of the individual was high.

Obviously the Asian ethos of the North Vietnamese was not parallel. To them, individual casualties were lamentable but not a major factor in the outcome of a battle or campaign. When the collective group went into battle, part of the group was usually destroyed, but the collective survived. If a single NVA soldier found himself wounded and cut off in enemy territory, he would never expect his unit to send out a rescued party to bring him back. Buddhist fatalism coupled with Marxist dogma and bitter years of xenophobic struggle had shaped the North Vietnamese to the point where they found almost incomprehensible the Americans' preoccupation with hazardous rescue missions and elaborate medical evacuation from the battlefield. To the NVA, such operations were a sign of decadence. An SAR helicopter or a Med-Evac Huey were objects of contempt, worthy of nothing more than destruction.

By the autumn of 1967, the complex operational ritual of an SAR effort meant two things to local NVA road-security commanders. The People's Liberation Army might suffer casualties from the cluster bombs, rockets, and cannon fire of the rescue escorts, but such operations might also render more downed American aircraft and more American casualties. At the end of a hard day's fight out in the mountains, fifty People's Army soldiers might be dead or wounded, but, of course, the unit would have survived, and with luck, the smoking, shattered hulks of an escort plane and a rescue helicopter might have been added to the nearby wreckage of the original fighter-bomber.

Moreover, the NVA might have captured more American pilots: valuable pawns in the inevitable negotiated withdrawal of the Americans.

Now, as the sun pulled higher and the misty cloud remnants tore away from the silent green ridges, just such another long day's battle was about to begin.

While *Sandys* 7 and *8* and *Jolly Greens* 27 and 52 were inbound from Thailand, *Crown* contacted *Compress* to receive *AWOL 1* Bravo's secret authenticator questions. This information was kept on file at Rescue 1 for combat aircrewmen. In theory these questions contained personal information unique to the downed airman: the color of a child's eyes, the name of a pet, or perhaps his mother's maiden name. Each man also had a secret authenticator number randomly chosen by computer.

The questions Sijan had submitted for his authenticator file illuminated certain aspects of his personality. His primary question was "Who is the greatest football team in the world?" For Lance, of course, there was only one answer: the Green Bay Packers. He was from Wisconsin and felt a deep loyalty to the Packers. But, beyond that natural chauvinism, he had an abiding respect for the dogged, lonely determination, the stubbornness that Vince Lombardi and the Packers brought to the football field in good, lucky years and equally in bad, injury-hampered seasons. Sijan empathized with the Packers. They were not flashy, they worked hard, they drove themselves far past the norm, and they were intensely loyal to each other.

There was another, grimmer aspect involved in the choice of this question. If captured by the NVA and held, bound hand and foot with a gun to his head, obliged to give *some* answer when the authenticator question came over the survival radio, Lance could simply say the name of another football team, the Dallas Cowboys or the Chicago Bears. The battlewise lieutenant colonel sitting at the radio console in the orbiting *Crown* command post would know at once that Sijan was a prisoner.

Sijan's backup questions, also indicative of his interests, concerned the middle names of family members. For some young men the answers might be difficult to recall in the terrible excitement and fear gripping them on the ground alone, surrounded by enemy patrols. But Lance's closeness to his family had never wavered in his years away from home. In Da Nang he had known the details of his little sister Janine's eighth-grade report card and his father's plans for his restaurant as well as he did the TACAN channels and compass headings to alternate airfields from the missed-approach point at Da Nang.

On this cool, pastel morning in the mountains of Laos, Sijan lay on the steep slope of a limestone karst in a tangle of dead leaves and thorny, parasitic vines that covered the stony soil. Around him the smooth trunks of hardwood trees rose to a distant green canopy. The slope was acute and cut by gullies of raw, sharp-edged rock, and the roof of the forest appeared uniform in density, an interlocking skein of leafy branches that blocked all but a few splintered glimpses of the sky.

The forest canopy was almost two hundred feet above him. The hoist cable of the Jolly Green's jungle penetrator was only 250 feet long, and given the angle of the slope, the Jolly could hover no less than thirty or forty feet above the treetops . . . which meant that the helicopter would have to be *exactly* overhead if he were to reach the penetrator. To achieve such precision the Jolly would have to find Sijan's exact position on the mountainside, a position for which he had no landmarks to offer in guiding in the chopper. He certainly would not be able to walk to any gully clearing. Sijan had hit this karst in thick darkness, nearly blinded by the glare of his exploding airplane. The terrible forces of the explosion, of ejection and parachute deployment at five hundred knots, and the slamming collision with the hardwood trees and rocky ground probably would have killed anyone less muscular than Sijan. They had *almost* killed him; certainly he was severely crippled.

His memory of the explosion was jumbled. But the visual image was sharp . . . hot, white glare. They had been at the bomb-release point, and the Colonel called, "Breaking left!" just as he pickled all six. The next instant, the invisible fist of the Gs was crushed by the hot white rush of noise and fire. The plane ripped itself apart. There was fire all around them. Somehow his hand found the ejection trigger and fired it. The charge slammed his seat up through the dome of orange flame.

He was tumbling in the cold, dark wind. Then the chute. The noise was gone. He hung in the silence, rocking beneath his chute, his mind bleached to numb stupor by the explosion. Slowly rational thought returned. There had been some tracers far to the left. But the blast had ripped them to pieces just when Armstrong pickled. The bombs. Premature detonation of all six bombs. Over two tons of high explosive had erupted less than fifty feet from the plane.

The fuses, he realized. *Those new fuses were defective.*

In the weak moonlight, the valley swayed and wobbled up at him. He was being carried by a breeze toward the chalky smear of a tall, wide karst, a couple of miles north of the target. Off to the right he could see the pale scar of the switchback road, three, maybe four miles due east. Then, as always during other jumps, the last five hundred feet rushed up, and he knew that he was going into the black, dimensionless roof of the forest.

For most of the previous thirty-five hours, he had lain unconscious on the steep forest floor. His helmet had been torn off, his parachute canopy, rubber dinghy, and auxiliary survival pack ripped away as he slammed down through the trees. He had been unconscious before final impact with the limestone karst.

But when he had finally regained consciousness the day before, he had discovered just how badly injured he was. His left leg had still been numb, but he saw from the weird angle and position of his boot that the leg was broken below the knee. Fortunately, the heavy nylon web and rubber bladders of his G-suit had acted as a rudimentary splint and tourniquet, preventing further injury as he had thrashed about in semiconsciousness. His right hand was mangled, with the three smaller fingers dislocated and bent back at an awful angle. There were deep cuts under his bloody flight suit in the flesh of his forearm. But it was his head injury that gave him the most pain and anxiety that first day.

Delicately probing with his left hand, he tried to explore and assess the nature and extent of this injury. It felt bad. His blood-matted hair covered a wobbly, crusted crater behind his left ear. The swelling seemed grotesque when explored in this manner, but he knew from years of first aid instruction that he would not be conscious and lucid if he had suffered a really catastrophic skull fracture. But he also knew there was some bad damage to his cranium and that this damage had produced a serious brain concussion.

At some point during a lucid period of the previous day, he had partially unstrapped his G-suit and surveyed the injury to his left leg. What he found made him gag. The flesh of his shin and calf was swollen blue-black and the hair on his leg was dark with clotted blood. From the center of this swelling protruded two forks of dead white bone, each several inches long: a compound fracture, what he had been taught to identify as a "green tree fracture," a vertical splintering of the tibia.

This fracture had shredded the normal musculature and nerve pathways of his lower leg. Below his knee, the limb was powerless, uncontrollable. Luckily, there had been no serious artery cut, or he would have bled to death while unconscious. Working awkwardly with one hand in his near delirium, he marshaled as much strength and concentration as he could and proceeded to dress the wound, using sulpha powder and a sterile battle dressing from his medical kit. Then, with the pain coming in hot spasms, he bound up the leg with his blood-caked flight suit and laced the G-suit back as tightly as he could.

At some vague point during the previous day he had injected himself with one of the morphine syringes from his kit. And despite the concussion nausea, he had managed to drink ten ounces of water from one plastic bottle.

Now, a day and a half after his airplane had literally ripped apart from under him, he lay with his shoulders against the smooth, finbacked root of a hardwood tree, holding the cool metal and plastic of his survival radio near his burning face, willing himself to think rationally as he listened to the whine and snarl of jet engines in the distant sky.

Crown was there, a calm, faraway voice of a senior officer. This voice had said that SAR was inbound. It was only dawn; as far as Lance could see through the slits in the leaf canopy, the weather was good. They had all day to find him, all day to get the penetrator to him to lift him out. Twelve hours of daylight up here. It wouldn't be dark until after 1800. Twelve hours was plenty of time for the Jollys to find him. He must have realized that he had to get on top of his pain and dizziness and be ready for them. Nobody's work was going to be easy today, and he also knew that he had an especially hard job to do, trying to guide the Jollys directly overhead.

Fortunately, Sijan was lying on a steep karst. It wasn't likely that the NVA could get to him with either troops or flak guns.

The gloom of the forest floor paled as the morning rose. Sijan waited with his back to the gray-barked tree, holding his radio; the two smoke flares that had not been ripped away during ejection were arrayed neatly beside his shattered leg. His big pistol was cocked on his lap.

It was some time between Sijan's initial contact with *Drill* Flight at 0610 and the arrival on station of *Sandys* 7 and *8* at 0730 that the first mishap occurred. As often happens in the confusion and stress of combat, someone takes an action or gives an order for the best of all motives which has the diametrically opposite result to the one intended.

With at least six fixed-wing planes orbiting the karsts north of the Ban Loboy Ford and the Sandys still thirty minutes away, the high performance aircraft made a few passes over the survivor's general area to see if they could spot him. The problem with this maneuver, however, was that F-4s and F-100s—laden with various combinations of ordnance and external fuel tanks—were unable to fly low and slow, skimming the jungle canopy. Instead they carried out dry strafing passes across the karsts, throttled well back but still flying at over three hundred knots.

Whether Sijan in his injured and muddled condition misunderstood a radio exchange with one of the passing jets or whether a frustrated pilot wanted to speed up the rescue procedure is not known. What has become reasonably clear, however, is that Sijan expended his two precious smoke flares. The cloud of bright orange smoke that blossomed up from the steel tube he grasped above his head was dissipated on its way through the trees, so that only a few rusty wisps appeared above the thick canopy.

The jets, moving fast in tight turns under the surrounding ridge lines, were unable to get an exact fix on the smoke, on *AWOL*'s position. The pilots saw that he was down there *somewhere*, beneath the solid tree canopy, on that huge, table-shaped karst, but they could not be sure of his *exact* position.

When the fast-movers turned back for more passes, they encountered the first tentative ground fire. And thereafter the situation changed completely. This was no longer a relatively routine pick-up of a downed backseater in Laos. The SAR effort had become a battle.

Sandy 7 rolled into the twisting valley and banked north toward the big karst where the jets had reported *AWOL* was down. The Sandy pilot chopped his throttle and S-turned to slow his approach, even though he knew such a maneuver was an invitation to get smacked right in the teeth with a 37mm. He had solid contact with *AWOL* on Guard, and now he asked him for twenty seconds of beeper.

As the beeper pinged in, five-by-five in *Sandy* Lead's earphones, the compass needle of his automatic direction finder swung a few degrees north and held at 357. He kicked in a little left rudder and yawed over five degrees so that his heading needle matched the ADF. The beeper seemed to boom in his headset; he was flying straight toward *AWOL*. As soon as he overflew him, the beeper would null for a second and the ADF needle would swing back onto the recip bearing. He would have *AWOL* pretty well pinpointed. Then he would climb into a low orbit, with his detailed chart folded to the appropriate place on his map board, and ask Sijan to pop smoke. With the first big puff of orange smoke above the trees, *Sandy* Lead and his wingman would get good visual fixes on it, and they'd have the guy locked in for the Jolly's pickup.

In the Sandy's clear-bubble windscreen, the wide table of the karst grew larger. *Sandy* Lead could now see that the limestone slopes were splotched here and there by low scrub jungle in gullies. About halfway up the raw stone wall, the triple canopy took over. It was going to be dicey getting a guy with a broken leg out of that stuff. *Sandy* chopped his throttle more and dropped some flap, slowing the aircraft to ninety knots. Then he eased off the prop pitch at the same throttle setting, and the air speed fell to around eighty-five. *AWOL*'s beeper chimed loud and clear.

Less than a mile out from the karst, *Sandy* Lead saw the first automatic weapons tracers. The fire came from the dogleg in the valley, left of the karst's blunt eastern slope: green tracers, light stuff, certainly something to think about low and slow like this but not as bad as a quad ZPU or 37mm site. Then, closing on the karst, he saw heavier red tracers, spitting up from the other branch of the valley, on the southern slope. He jinked hard right, firewalling the throttle; in a blur of action, he retracted flaps and snatched the prop pitch back to full. That was a dual 23mm and it was tracking straight and fast. Whoever was aiming that thing was good and knew how to wait his chance.

As *Sandy 7* jinked away, wheeling low toward the south again; the beeper signal warbled in his earphones and the ADF needle swung away.

"*Crown One, Sandy* Lead," he called. "We've got *beaucoup* problems down here, and we're going to need some muscle."

For the next twenty-five minutes, *Sandy* Lead acted as FAC and directed *Drill* Flight down to work over the area from which the 23mm fire appeared to have come. They were carrying 750-pounders, which were not as effective as frags in that dense valley jungle. So, after the fast-movers made a few passes, *Sandy* lead and his wingman went in there with rockets, cannon, and a couple 250 frag bombs.

Meanwhile *Crown* called down that *Jolly Greens* 27 and 52 had arrived on station and were orbiting over the high karst country southeast of the target area. As soon as *Sandy* Lead was satisfied he had sufficiently suppressed the ground fire, the two Sandys should join up with *Jolly* 52 and lead him up to the survivor's position. *Jolly* 27 would high orbit in reserve.

Crown also announced that *Sandys* 5 and 6 were en route. At that time, *Drill* Lead asked about the availability of a tanker, and *Crown* passed him off to Lion GCI ground site for a tanker rendezvous. The SAR frequencies were getting jammed up now, so *Crown* ordered the Sandys to use their own channels and *Nail 10* to swing back into medium orbit and ask *AWOL* the authenticator questions. In the confusion and activity of the first flak suppression passes, the vital questions had been neglected.

Crown 1, however, was earning his colonel's pay today, and he did not get paid to forget little items like that.

At 0759, *Sandy 8* took some very bad hits, light small-arm rounds but also some solider stuff around the engine. Fire lights blinked on and he started to smoke. Banking back toward the orbiting Jollys, he calmly called out his Mayday, the rescuer now needing rescue, and proceeded to estimate he could stay airborne for about three minutes if he dumped his remaining ordnance. He then requested permission to jettison his bombs and rockets on Safe and to drop his large external fuel tank.

Sandy Lead advised him to dump it all, squawk emergency on his IFF, and head for the hills, the safe area to the southeast where the two Jollys were holding station.

In the middle of this tense exchange, *Nail* called Sijan and asked him the first authenticator question.

"*AWOL One* Bravo, *Nail One Zero.* Question number one. Who is the greatest football team in the world? Over."

"*Nail One Zero, AWOL One* Bravo," Sijan answered immediately. "The answer is the Green Bay Packers. Repeat, the Green Bay Packers. Copy?"

"Roger, *AWOL.* Stand by."

Nail switched to SAR Primary and asked *Crown* if the answer was right. *Crown* confirmed, then asked *Nail* to talk to the survivor for a while to keep his morale up while the SAR was temporarily diverted to the flaming Skyraider limping toward the southeast.

At 0806, *Sandy 8* ejected over the high forest karsts south of the Ban Loboy Ford; his shoot-down marked the first serious battle damage of the long day.

Crown asked *Compress* for more support. It was a bright, clear morning now, and the NVA gunners were obviously wide awake. *Crown* was advised that the call was out to *Cricket* for more F-4s to be diverted from fragged flights en route north. Another KC-135 tanker was also placed on reserve, and *Crown 2* was standing by to the west. *Crown 1* now advised *Compress* that he needed as many A-1E Skyraiders as he could get from the Air Commando Wing at Nakhon Phanom in addition to the F-4s. These prop planes would be able to offer the Jolly Greens "daisy chain" protection by flying slow circles around the helicopters. Also, the A-1 pilots were used to beating up camouflaged targets along the Trail. The slow-movers carried rockets and multiple racks of antipersonnel fragmentation bombs. This was the ordnance that *Crown* would need at his disposal if indeed more gun sites became involved with the developing battle. After a few moments *Compress* advised *Crown 1* that *Electron* and *Hobo* Flights, comprised of four A-1Es armed for road recce, were en route, and that *Sandys 1* and *2* were standing by on alert.

While *Crown* and *Compress* spoke on their Command channel, *Nail 10* talked to Sijan on Guard. Asked about his physical condition, Lance replied that he was "okay," except for his head injury, and, of course, a compound fracture of his left leg. His voice remained "cool and professional"; his phrasing was precise, accurate; he was a military officer seemingly in command of himself and his circumstances. Silently the expanding ranks of orbiting pilots who monitored Guard channel shook their heads in admiration for that poor bastard down in the jungle lying there helpless with a bone sticking out of his leg while the NVA cranked in one gun site after another to drive back the SAR forces. And he said that he was "okay."

Nail asked Sijan about his frontseater, Colonel Armstrong. Again the voice of the survivor was precise. He had no hard information about the Colonel. Lance did not see Armstrong eject, nor had he seen any parachute. But he thought that the aircraft had crashed on the south slope of the karst, so he suggested that the Sandys make a slow visual search of the area. *Nail* thanked *AWOL* for the tip and told him to hang in there.

Eight miles away, the pilot of *Sandy 8*, Major Griffith, swung slowly back and forth under his orange-and-white canopy parachute. His crippled Skyraider had just cleared a three-thousand-foot ridgeline when he punched out; the ejection was violent and loud, but now, he saw, he was coming down into a narrow side branch of the main valley. There was reasonably clear, level ground down there near the blue mountain stream. If he could reach that gravelly stream bed, there'd be room for the Jollys to make a fast pick-up protected by the surrounding ridges from the gun sites that ringed Ban Loboy.

As the major rocked under his chute, he reached down to check his legs and hips for injury. One knee was banged up pretty bad, and he had some cuts from hitting the canopy sill on the way out, but otherwise his body was surprisingly intact, considering that he had ejected from a burning, uncontrollable aircraft. Now, God willing, he could slip this chute down toward the flatter ground, and the Jollys would find him before the NVA.

First Lieutenant Platt thrust his control stick down and to the right and twisted open the throttle grip. The helicopter's huge five-bladed main rotor cut from hover to a coarser pitch as three thousand horsepower engaged the rotor shaft from the two whining turbine engines. *Jolly Green 27* wheeled out of orbit and charged up the steep jungle valley on a compass heading of ninety-six degrees true. Five miles ahead the valley narrowed to a tree-choked gorge that disappeared into the massive green wall of the main range.

Sitting close beside Lieutenant Platt in the cramped cockpit of the rescue helicopter, Lieutenant Sichterman, his copilot, was adjusting the directional antenna of the UHF homer. They had a good loud beeper from the Sandy pilot, and now as the Jolly clattered into the valley, Platt could see a white smear of *Sandy 8*'s chute, collapsed on some low scrub brush near a sharp bend in the stream.

Platt craned his neck to examine the surrounding hillsides for any band of red laterite mud that would indicate a trail, road, or gun site. The valley looked pretty clean; maybe, if they were lucky, they could snatch *Sandy 8* out of here without getting shot at.

Sandy 7 pulled up alongside now, throttled back with flaps down to match the Jolly's speed. Platt told *Sandy 7* he had the chute in sight, and *Sandy 7* said the valley looked clean. He would now swing ahead to troll for ground fire. If he got nothing on the first pass, he'd ask Major Griffith to pop smoke. At that point *Jolly 27* should get in there *tout de suite* and haul Griffith's ass out. Obviously there were NVA all over this general area, and they probably had people heading for those ridge-tops right now. If they could fire down on the rescue aircraft in this narrow valley, the fit would definitely hit the Shan.

At 0815 thick orange smoke appeared above the brush to the left of the stream bed. Three minutes later Lieutenant Platt sped up just over the treetops, and the big helicopter lurched into a hover, the downwash from the rotors shredding the smoke and flattening the domes of the trees. The bright yellow bomb-shaped probe of the jungle penetrator dropped straight down, and less than a minute later, Sergeant Negrette, the flight engineer who operated the winch, reported that Major Griffith was coming up. As soon as the penetrator was clear of the trees, Platt pitched up and right and the Jolly climbed fast out of the valley, the survivor still hanging below the loud ungainly aircraft like a fish on a line.

Lieutenant Platt was not playing cowboy when he undertook this maneuver. Hovering up here at almost three thousand feet elevation, heavy with fuel, was very hard on the aircraft; thermals or sudden downdrafts could cause a stall. Also, the longer he stayed in hover, the better target he was. They had been very lucky to find

Griffith and get him out so fast. But they couldn't start passing out the cigars yet. *AWOL 1* was still on the ground up there with a broken leg, somewhere on that jungle karst, surrounded by one hell of a lot of enemy guns.

Crown 1 now assigned *Jolly Green 52* a higher orbit, to the west of the main target area, with the newly arrived *Hobo* Flight of two Skyraiders as escort. *Jolly 27* was placed on orbit to the southeast once *Crown* had learned that Major Griffith did not require more medical attention than Sergeant Taylor, the Jolly's pararescue man, could offer. This potential medical assistance was actually considerable. The enlisted rescue men—known by their old designation of parajumpers, PJs—were probably the most diversely expert enlisted personnel in the American military. They were certified expert in parachuting, advanced first aid, scuba diving, small arms combat, karate, and survival under desert, swamp, jungle, and arctic conditions. As a group the PJs were tough, dedicated, and resourceful. During the long years of the war in Indochina, the parajumpers won more combat decorations than any other group in the Air Force.

Crown next passed *Sandys 5* and *6* down to *Sandy* Lead, so that the three aircraft could dip low over the big karst to get a fix on Sijan. Once they knew where he was, they could estimate which gun sites definitely had to be eliminated, and *Crown* could help choose the safest ingress and egress routes for the Jolly. *Crown* also had other tactics up his sleeve. Both the Sandys and the incoming Air Commando Skyraiders had CS and bomb live unit riot gas bombs aboard, as well as underwing rocket pods for producing a thick smoke screen. When *Crown* ordered the pickup, the A-1s would hit the known flak sites with gas and further blind the gunners with smoke. This tactic had worked well in the past during rescues in heavily defended areas.

But pinpointing Sijan was not going to be easy. It was now known that he had no smoke left, and the little .22 caliber pen-gun flares, difficult enough to see in open country, were almost useless when fired into the thick roof of the forest. His signal mirror, of course, was worthless, as sunlight did not penetrate to the forest floor. It was just possible that his high-intensity strobe light might have been visible from directly overhead, but the Sandys did not have the capacity to hover while their pilots gazed down through the jungle canopy. All this meant that they would have to locate *AWOL* by ADF triangulation of his voice and beeper signal. Flying a slow, circular orbit above the karst, the aircraft would take up the three, six, and nine o'clock positions and watch the needles of their automatic direction finders lock onto Sijan's radio signal as the Sandys swung around their orbit. If they weren't harassed too much by ground fire, they could probably get an accurate running fix on him.

This maneuver was risky, but *Sandy* Lead knew he had no options. He couldn't vector in the Jolly until he had a better idea where *AWOL* was, and he wouldn't know that until he got a decent bearing on him.

The three camouflaged Skyraiders jinked and rolled across the main valley, feinting toward the west, as if about to start another flak suppression run on the 23mm site. As they passed the survivor's karst, they peeled off and slowed. At almost the same time, four Ubon Phantoms, FAC'd in by *Misty*, dropped out of the sun in a steep dive-bombing pass and clobbered the area of the gun site with two 750s each. The smoke, dust, and shattered forest debris hung in a tan pall over the end of the valley.

The maneuver worked, at least for the first three or four minutes, adequate time to permit the skilled and disciplined Sandy pilots to get a decent radio fix on *AWOL*. He was on the steep southern slope of the karst, about a thousand meters into the triple-canopy forest that formed the pork-chop oval tabletop of the limestone formation. At three places, this oval mesa of trees was broken by secondary limestone chimneys that rose naked above the forest. These chimney karsts made low-level flight hazardous, especially for the fast-movers. To further complicate the problem, the southern slope of the main formation was cut by several seemingly identical deep, stony gullies that ran parallel to each other and perpendicular to the southern limestone wall. These gullies would give good access routes to the NVA who would even now be jogging up the personnel tracks that crossed the scrub jungle of the flat valley.

Sandy Lead realized that he would have to vector in *Jolly* 52 as soon as possible, before his opposite number, the local NVA commander, got his people up those gullies with AKs and automatic weapons. He made some fast, precise pencil strokes on his chart, then called *Crown* on SAR Secondary to relay his tactical plan. But before he could complete his message, he heard a hammering rattle on the belly of the plane and he knew he'd been hit by some light AW. At least he hoped it was light.

"Lead, watch your nine," *Sandy* 5 called, breaking into the channel. "You got tracers on your nine."

Sandy Lead jinked off to the right, away from his nine o'clock direction, from which a spatter of red and green tracers rose. The NVA were *already* up the gullies, moving troops and automatic weapons into position to surround the survivor as best they could. Jinking up to the left now, *Sandy* Lead sought a higher orbit, two thousand feet above the karst. But the aircraft was not responding well to stick and rudder. One hydraulic-system warning light snapped on, and he immediately switched the selector to the backup system. But the second warning light lit, and he felt the controls getting mushy on him.

He had no choice; his only option was to Return to Base (RTB) while the aircraft was still flyable.

"*Crown One, Sandy* Lead," he called on Primary so the other aircraft could hear. "My hydraulics are shot out and I'm RTB, but *Sandy*s 5 and 6 have got a lock on *AWOL.*"

Crown acknowledged the transmission and designated *Sandy* 5 the new on-scene commander. He asked *Sandy* 7 if he needed escort back to Nakhon Phanom. The Sandy pilot calmly replied that it was better not to disperse the SAR forces any more than they already were; he would be all right, flying alone, in a crippled aircraft across ninety miles of jungle mountains controlled by the NVA and their Pathet Lao allies. Perhaps on a less busy day, in a less desperate and difficult operation, at a less active time of the war, such bravery would have received wide attention. But this was November 1967, the most intense period of the air war; the SAR forces were flying this kind of mission almost daily.

Now *Sandy* 5 took charge and FAC'd in the *Hobo* Flight to rocket and strafe the narrow gullies leading down from the flat table of the karst. While the Hobos were beating up the front of the karst, *Sandy* Lead swung out to the northwest and escorted *Jolly Green* 52 across the back of the formation. The Sandy pilot gave clear instructions to Sijan: Transmit thirty seconds of beeper, then wait for instructions from the Jolly, with your survival radio in the Receive mode. If no instructions were sent, transmit thirty more seconds of beeper.

Sijan acknowledged the order and added that he had his compass ready to help guide the Jolly in. He would be able to hear the heavy thump of the rotors when the helicopter was close, and he would then direct it to change heading as the noise approached from above.

It was just after nine in the morning, and Lance Sijan had been talking to various aircraft for over three hours. He was feverish from his wounds and still dizzy from his concussion. Although he had eaten no food for thirty-six hours and in that time he had only drunk ten ounces of water, Sijan now had to be ready to carry out a demanding exercise in navigational direction, guiding in the Jolly Green by sound alone and transposing the magnetic compass bearings, distorted by local variation, into the reciprocal true headings of the Jolly's gyro compass.

The words he spoke into the plastic mouthpiece of the survival radio would draw his fellow airmen close to him but perhaps also close to a hidden enemy machine-gun site. Certainly, he knew, the Jolly could not stooge around in a hover up there for hours, not this close to the heavier flak sites up on those ridges. Listening on the Guard Channel, he had learned that one Sandy had been knocked down already and that *Sandy* lead had been forced to RTB with battle damage. The Jollys were nowhere near as solid as the chunky, well-armored old Sandys. Automatic weapons fire that would hurt a Sandy would almost certainly kill a Jolly Green.

He sat with his back against the tree root, holding his radio in his good hand, making sure that the telescoping antenna was completely extended and well clear of the vines and the massive pillar of the tree trunk. Good as they were, these radios had one Achilles' heel: the antenna. In order to transmit a signal on beeper, the long antenna had to be fully extended and not in contact with any obstacle. Also, the antenna was relatively vulnerable; it was basically an automobile-type device, and as every teenage gang member in the States knew well, a car's radio antenna could be snapped off with a well-timed flick of the wrist.

High above him, in the first gallery of the triple canopy, the monkeys and birds began to chatter and call again. They had gone silent when the Sandys had made their last flak-suppression pass down the valley to the west, but now the forest animals were returning to their normal wilderness existence. Sijan had bound the laces of his G-suit very tight across his left thigh in the hope that he could pinch the nerves leading down to his shattered lower leg and prevent serious debilitating pain. But the pain was coming hard despite his precautions, and he knew that he could not risk using the second of his morphine syringes.

There was also a pinching tingle around his neck and under the right sleeve of his flight suit. He had learned in survival school that this discomfort was caused by leeches. Earlier he had seen the small green parasites crawling toward him across the mulch of fallen leaves on which he lay. Somewhere in his survival vest there was a head net and strong insect repellent that he might use to keep the leeches off his body. But that would have to wait; now he needed all the dexterity of his one good hand and of his mind to help the Sandys and the Jollys find him.

The skipper of *Jolly* 52 had a loud beeper signal from *AWOL* in his headset and a solid ADF bearing on the panel. To his right, the copilot reached up with both hands above his head to work the knobs and switches of the UHF homer, an instrument that gave the range and bearing of the beeper. They were flying pitched down five degrees, on full blower, indicating just over 140 knots airspeed. Out ahead of them, the flat tree canopy of the karst formed a two-mile oval; from this direction it looked a paler green against the steep wall of the main ridge. Those slopes were still in the shadow of the bigger summits to the east which formed the border between Laos and North Vietnam.

Out there *Sandy* 5 was banked steeply in a tight orbit above *AWOL*'s approximate position. In ten more seconds *AWOL* would switch from Beeper to Voice Receive: and the Jolly skipper could talk to him. When good voice contact was made, the Jolly would throttle back and begin a slow, straight-and-level approach toward the spot *AWOL* guided them. Then, with the helicopter in hover, *AWOL* would shoot up a couple of pen flares, and with luck, they'd have his position fixed.

Behind the flight deck, the PJ and flight engineer hunched at the open port and starboard doors, training their M-60 machine guns down at the forest roof that raced by two hundred feet below the chopper.

The beeper stopped, and the Jolly pilot punched the transmit button on his control stick.

"*AWOL One* Bravo, *Jolly Five Two.* We're coming in. Can you hear us yet? Over."

Sijan answered at once. "*Jolly Five Two, AWOL.* Keep that heading. I hear you fine, and you're getting louder. Over."

"Roger, *AWOL.* Outstanding."

Jolly 52 dropped down fifty feet closer to the dense canopy and reduced speed to seventy knots.

"*AWOL, JG Five Two,*" the helicopter pilot called a minute later. "We're painting you right down there on ADF. How do we sound to you? Over."

There was a pause. "*Jolly, AWOL.* You are up there at my seven o'clock position. Come ahead toward your one or two." Sijan now switched back to twenty seconds of beeper.

As the Jolly Green moved slowly forward in a creeping hover, the copilot watched the range dial of the UHF homer. They seemed to be moving *away* from the beeper. Either the instrument was off calibration or *AWOL* was getting sound distortion, an echo effect from those trees and the nearby limestone chimneys.

The Jolly pilot went into dead hover again and spoke with *AWOL.* Sijan said that the rotor noise was closer but he could not see any downwash moving the branches above him. *Jolly 52* dropped thirty feet lower, so that the circle of rotor blast slashed and riled the thick forest roof for fifty yards around.

Sijan called up that he could still see no rotor wash on the trees. After consulting with his PJ and flight engineer, the Jolly skipper told Sijan that they would commence a short box-pattern search even closer to the treetops and that Sijan should sound off as soon as he saw the trees move. At that point the Jolly would hover higher and Sijan would fire a pen-gun flare and light off his strobe. When they got a fix on him, the PJ would ride down on the penetrator and conclude the search on foot.

Sijan acknowledged that he understood; *Crown* and *Sandy* concurred that the plan was sound. Once again the SAR forces were showing skill and determination.

But the North Vietnamese soldiers down in the nearby gullies and the main valley now displayed their own skill, courage, and stubbornness. As the Jolly Green crept ahead at the start of its box pattern, red tracers flashed up from at least three directions. The helicopter was slammed by several 14.5mm machine-gun rounds.

Jolly 52 broke off the search and banked away at full throttle toward the north, away from the firing. But the chopper did not stay at full blower very long.

"*Sandy* lead, *Jolly Five Two*," the pilot called. "I'm losing oil pressure in my number two and I've got wounded people on board here. We're going to have to RTB."

Crown acknowledged the transmission. Aboard *Jolly 52*, the intercom was jammed with conflicting voices, the desperate exchange between the two pilots trying to safely shut down the crippled turbine engine before it tore the aircraft apart and the moans and gasping of the seriously wounded crewman back in the cargo bay.

It was 0956, and the NVA gunners had just disabled the third aircraft of the morning.

Crown now came back on frequency and ordered a Hobo aircraft and the orbiting *Jolly Green 27* to RTB with *JG 52*, the Skyraider as armed escort and the undamaged Jolly to act as rescue bird should *JG 52* have to crash-land.

Now there were no more rescue helicopters available on the scene. Reluctantly, *Sandy* lead informed Sijan of the situation. Sijan acknowledged and added that he was standing by.

The sun rose higher. The valley echoed with the snarl of aircraft. A little after 1000, *Crown* advised the rescue forces that *Jolly Greens* 53 and 15 were ETA in thirty minutes. In the interim the Sandy and Hobo Flights should try to locate and suppress the ground-fire positions. It was not an easy assignment. The Skyraiders' slower speed made them better close-in bombers than the jets, but they could not evade as well as Phantoms or Super Sabres. Pulling out from a rocket or strafing run, a high-performance jet fighter-bomber could effect a jinking climb at over eight hundred knots on afterburner, while a propellor driven Skyraider could pull out at less than half that speed. This meant that the Sandys remained within the range of a 23mm gun for over a minute and within 57mm range for almost four minutes during the pullout maneuver. The heavy, solidly built Skyraiders carried a fair amount of armor to protect the pilots and engines, as well as double redundancy on most vital control systems. They could take more punishment than the sophisticated jets, but they also got hit by considerably more ground fire than the fast-movers.

For the next thirty minutes, the Sandys' job was to troll the edges of the tabletop karst, trying to locate the gun sites and mark them with rocket fire so that the jets could be brought in to dump their heavy ordnance.

At 1034 the two new rescue helicopters, *Jolly Greens* 53 and *15*, arrived on station from Nakhon Phanom. *Crown* sent them up to high orbit to the southwest of the target zone. Two minutes later, at 1036, *Sandy 5*, the on-scene commander, was slamming up a narrow gully at full throttle, about to pickle his rockets at an AW site hidden in the trees, when he was hit by a stream of 23mm tracers fired *down* at him from a nearby ridge. As he broke off his pass, loading the plane with high Gs, his left wing began to shudder with an alarming, noisy vibration. The aileron had a jagged rip over three feet long in the green metal; it was amazing that the wing itself did not rip apart.

Sandy 5 chopped his throttle and continued rolling left, then nosed down in a neat evasive maneuver and leveled off just above the tree-tops. The 23mm site continued tracking left, and *Sandy 5* escaped with his aircraft still under control. But then the usual warning lights popped on, and the flight controls started to mush up. His hydraulic system was shot out.

"*Crown One, Sandy Five,*" he radioed, "I'm RTB with some heavy battle damage. Please alert Channel Eight Nine I'm inbound with hydraulic problems."

Grimly, *Crown 1*, mission commander, acknowledged the message and accepted the withdrawal of the fifth aircraft of the morning.

Obviously, the NVA had their guns well dispersed down there; they had discovered approximately where *AWOL* was hidden, so the gunners knew where to train their weapons to intercept any incoming Jollys or their Skyraider escorts. So far they had not used anything heavier than a 23mm, but Intel had reported multiple 37mm batteries down there. It was highly likely that the NVA were saving the heavier stuff to cut loose once the actual pickup was underway.

Now *Crown* had another problem to worry about. *Sandy 5* needed an escort back to base, and his wingman, *Sandy 6*, was the obvious choice. But, with their departure, there were no more Skyraider pilots on the scene who knew the position of the survivor, *AWOL 1*. Therefore, the whole difficult and frustrating business of pinpointing Sijan for the new Jollys would have to be carried out by the new Skyraider flight, *Fireflys 13* and *14*.

But the purpose of this entire exercise was to extract one wounded American pilot, so *Crown* had no choice. For the next ninety interminable minutes, the new Skyraiders cruised above the karst, using their direction finders to triangulate the voice and beeper signals from Sijan's radio. *Electrons 501* and *502*, Air Commando A-1s from Nakhon Phanom, now linked up with the slow-mover team. *Sandys 1* and *2* arrived and took on the flak suppression task while *Firefly* worked on pinpointing Sijan.

Up on high station, the original Ubon Phantom flights had been joined by more F-4s from Ubon and Da Nang. The valleys and rugged karsts now echoed almost continuously with the sharp smack of bombs and the roar of aircraft. Wheeling in out of the sun, lines of F-4s dropped thudding high-explosive bombs on suspected gun sites.

But still the ground fire rose up to harass the slow-movers and to threaten any eventual helicopter pickup. The SAR effort had been in progress for six hours, and the rescue forces were no nearer to getting Sijan off that karst than they had been at the start of the mission.

At 1245 the *Firefly* Flight had expended its ordnance and was low on fuel. They RTB'd, and *Crown* passed on-scene command to *Sandy 1*. He felt that he had an adequate fix on *AWOL*, so he climbed to midlevel orbit and brought with him *Sandy 2* and the two *Electron* Flight A-1s for a battle-tactics conference.

They decided it was too risky to let the Phantoms work on the karst itself trying to suppress the light ground fire that seemed to be coming from all around Sijan's position. Instead, the Sandys would lay down a smoke screen, blinding the gunners and shielding the approach of *Jolly Green 53*. At the same time a stream of sixteen F-4s would swoop down, one at a time, and plaster the base of the karst with heavy ordnance and rockets, causing such terror and confusion that the NVA would be thrown off for a few minutes, enough time to snatch Sijan out.

As the Skyraiders were having their conference, *Compress* called *Crown 1* and ordered the big C-130 command post to descend and carry out a midair refueling of *Jolly Green 15*. This maneuver was difficult enough in a safe, uncrowded airspace. But the sky around the Ban Loboy Ford that afternoon was hardly safe or uncrowded. *Crown 1* would have to meet *JG 15* twenty miles to the west, over a relatively empty stretch of jungle near Ban Dong Pang that Intel had designated as a safe area. They would rendezvous at eight thousand feet, out of the effective firing range of light flak but still within the killing radius of 37mm and 57mm guns. Although this area was away from the main axis of the Trail, there were known NVA and Pathet Lao base camps in the region. Where there were base camps, there was often flak. The ungainly, perverse coupling of a thirty-five-ton transport with a six-ton helicopter, carried out straight, level, and slow for a minimum of five or six minutes, would present a memorable target to the NVA.

But, again, *Crown* had no choice; he needed that second Jolly, refueled and back on station to pickup survivors from the other SAR aircraft in the very likely event there were more shoot-downs. So reluctantly *Crown 1* wheeled off toward the green ridges to the west, followed at a slower speed by *Jolly 15*.

Crown 2 took up high station now and assumed overall mission command. The stage was set for *Sandy* lead's audacious, coordinated effort to finally pull *AWOL 1* off the karst.

At about this time, *Gunfighter* Flight, three pairs of F-4s from the 366th, arrived on high orbit, led by Major Glenn Nordin. When Nordin had received his briefing from *Crown*, he was overjoyed to learn that the survivor down there was *AWOL 1* Bravo, Sijan. The major asked *Crown* if it would help Sijan at all if he spoke to Sijan on Guard while the other aircraft were getting their ducks lined up for the big push. *Crown* explained the long hours of tense frustration that the injured young pilot had already gone through and concurred. Sijan needed his spirits lifted and his flight commander from Da Nang was the obvious person to do the job.

"*AWOL One*, this is *Gunfighter* lead, Glenn Nordin. Lance, how you doing, boy? Listen, you just hang in down there. There's a lot of us here now, and by God, we're going to stay here until we get you out of there. Copy?"

"*Gunfighter* lead, *AWOL One* Bravo," Sijan answered with warmth now. "Thank you, sir. I'm okay. I'm hanging in there. I'm standing by here for the Jollys."

"Lance," Nordin called, breaking temporarily with formal radio procedure, "we're going to get you back to the base and get you patched up. You don't worry about that. We're lining up this gaggle now, and we're going to have you out of there."

In the green shadows of the forest, Sijan held the cool metal of the survival radio close to his battered head, his eyes clenched against the pain, while Nordin's high-pitched, confident voice washed over him.

But then, after Nordin had signed off, Sijan heard another sound that was as terrifying as the major's voice had been reassuring. From down the slope to the left came the piping toot of a whistle, sounding at a distance like the whistle of a Lionel train on a faraway Christmas morning. Now, downslope and to the right, another tooting whistle answered the first.

He instinctively clutched the survival radio to his chest to muffle any transmission on Guard. Somewhere down in the trees below him, two NVA patrols were climbing in his direction. They were keeping in touch with whistles, a primitive but effective way to maintain contact in this thick wilderness.

Working gingerly, he found that he could use the swollen thumb and forefinger of his right hand if he took care not to touch the grotesquely bent, dislocated fingers. He reached across to his left leg and worried loose the restraining strap on his bolo knife. Next he broke open the action of his big revolver and blew hard through the breech to clear the barrel of leaf trash that had partially jammed the gun.

The Jollys were on their way, and the Sandys would take care of the NVA. All he could do was wait.

Petrol, Gunfighter, and *Honda* Flights were stacked between twelve and sixteen thousand feet, orbiting in a left-hand traffic pattern, ready to roll in to pound the foot of the karst. *Misty* FAC made one fast pass across the valley and fired several smoke rockets at the gullies leading to the upper limestone slopes. One by one, the Phantoms flew to the base leg of their orbits and rolled in on their bomb runs. They screamed down at high speed and steep dive angles, straight toward their bomb-release points. Dark clusters of 750-pound bombs tore away as the Phantoms pulled out, vortices of white condensation streaming from their wingtips.

The southern slope of the karst was battered with incandescent shock waves as the bombs struck. Domes of dust and forest debris cascaded up. More bombs hit, and the dust cloud swelled. On the eastern and western slopes of the karst, Sandys swung in low at full throttle, firing their 20mm and loosing an occasional rocket. As they neared the southern face, they rolled back onto the reciprocal heading and laid down their screen of dense gray smoke.

To pilots climbing back to high orbit, the combination of exploding bombs and the smoke screen created the illusion that the karst
had caught fire and was now engulfed in a smoke dome, illuminated
by the red flashes of exploding ordnance.

Jolly Green 53 headed down from the north at full blower, flat out
and straight for the south side of the karst. Right on schedule the
lumbering, camouflaged Sandys wheeled in to form the protective
daisy chain circle around the helicopter. It was 1325, and *JG 53* was
getting good voice contact with *AWOL* on the ground.

This pass looked like it would be a winner. Just behind the
cramped flight deck, the PJ crouched with the stock of the M-60,
tight against his shoulder, ready to return any ground fire. As soon
as they got into a hover above *AWOL*, the PJ would ride the penetrator down, strap that poor bastard to the seat, snap his own carabiner
to the cable, and they'd hoist them both out of there. Then it would
be RTB all around and time for a few cocktails at the club.

The Jolly's commander heard the M-60 cut loose to starboard;
then the portside gun joined in. His flight engineer's voice filled his
headset, drowning out Sijan's beeper.

"Sir, we're getting tracers from both sides . . . sir! we just took
some hits. Sir . . ."

The last words were shredded away as the front of the ship was
hit. The impact sounded like someone was standing outside the
cockpit, slamming the hull with a crowbar. The noise was terrible.

Out ahead, perhaps five hundred feet, the pilot saw a Sandy take
three solid AW tracers right through the tail section. Another
stream of tracers snaked up harmlessly off to the right. He clutched
his control stick and steadied his feet on the jerking rudder pedals.
Then, glancing down at his boots, he saw slimy orange hydraulic
fluid sloshing across the aluminum deck. The aircraft shuddered
and bucked and yawed hard to the right.

Automatically he kicked some rudder and eased back the stick.
They began turning left, and he gave her some right rudder. The
Jolly continued the left turn, climbing by itself up and away from the
forest roof.

"Sir," the engineer called on the intercom. "We just took something bad in the rudder section."

"Get your chutes on back there," the pilot yelled, then switched
to SAR Primary. "*Crown, JG Five Three.* I've got hydraulic fluid up

to my ankles and my rudder's shot out. Can only make left turns. Request permission to RTB, and I'm going to need some kind of escort."

Grimly the distant voice of *Crown* acknowledged. Aircraft number six had just been disabled.

On the ground, Sijan heard the news from *Sandy 1*. The Skyraider pilot told him that the forces were regrouping and that he should stand by with his radio on Receive.

Sijan acknowledged; for the first time his voice seemed less than fully confident. It was 1350, and he had been waiting for rescue for almost eight hours.

Crown 1 finished refueling *Jolly 15* at 1356. As soon as they were both back on frequency, *Crown 2* informed them that *Jolly 53* was hit bad and RTB. *Crown 1*, himself low on fuel, would escort the crippled chopper back to Nakhon Phanom, then RTB to stand by at Udorn should he be needed later in the day.

It was now the turn of *Jolly Green 15* to attempt the pickup.

But before the new Jolly Green could be vectored in, more effective measures were going to have to be found to deal with the ground fire surrounding Sijan's position.

All day the NVA had taken a real beating out in the main branches of the valley. Skyraiders working low and slow after the Phantoms had completed their passes had reported 23mm guns completely blown away with direct hits. The enemy was paying a heavy price for the damage they were causing. But they were far from knocked out of action. Up on the karst, green tracers from AKs and light machine guns had now replaced the red tracers of heavier automatic weapons and the smoking red balls of the 37mms that had been seen briefly earlier. Obviously, the NVA commander down there was saving his heavy stuff for the finale. But even his light-caliber antiaircraft fire was too much for the Jollys. The karst had to be cleaned out, and only the slow-movers could work close without endangering the survivor.

The long afternoon wore on. From out of the blinding sky, the *Sandy* and *Electron* Flights dove onto the karst with repeated strafing and rocket passes. After almost an hour the Electrons had to

RTB for fuel and ordnance. Another Sandy was hit and the pilot slightly wounded; he was forced to RTB with the Electrons as escort.

Out in the main target zone of the valley, new flights of Phantoms screamed down out of the sun to pound the suspected heavy-gun sites that *Misty* FAC had marked with smoke rockets.

Just before 1500, *Sandy 3*, the new on-scene commander, led *Jolly 15* toward the survivor; on this pass they tried swinging in from the southeastern corner of the karst to throw off the enemy riflemen firing from the lower brush of the jungle-choked gullies. Still a thousand meters from the hover point, *Jolly Green 15* was hit by a burst of AK fire and had to pull back, trailing a pale mist of fuel from a punctured outboard tank.

The Sandys and Air Commando Skyraiders now redoubled their flak-suppression efforts. Wheeling back and forth in steep, banking turns, they strafed the roof of the karst with their 20mm cannons and repeatedly hit the slopes of the jungle gullies with cluster bombs and 250-pound frags. The smoke, noise, and boiling dust clouds were impressive. But there was still small arms and light AW fire rising up from around the survivor.

Apparently the NVA was willing to expose small groups of infantry to the massed aerial firepower of the rescue force, but they were keeping their valuable Soviet flak guns hidden.

These were good tactics, and the mission commander in *Crown* was temporarily stymied by his Vietnamese counterpart on the ground. *Sandy 3* called up to say that he was pulling off the slow-movers again to evaluate the situation. While the Skyraiders were conferring, *Crown* handed off four new Phantom flights to *Misty* FAC so that the jets could beat up the edges of the karst and keep the NVA pinned down. These new flights had been scrambled expressly for the SAR effort, and they carried multibarreled Vulcan 20mm cannons in external pods as well as rockets and high-drag cluster bombs. Rolling in one at a time, *Dallas, Wedge, Locust,* and *Title* Flights pounded and strafed the edges of the karst, blowing down massive hardwood trees and shredding the scrub jungle of the gullies.

Meanwhile a new *Firefly* Flight of four Skyraiders had been scrambled at Nakhon Phanom and was ETA in twenty minutes. This incoming flight was carrying CS gas, smoke, and cluster bombs, and would bring the slow-movers backup strength for another concerted pickup attempt. It was almost 1600, and Sijan had been waiting for rescue for ten hours.

By now the pain of his wounds had almost overpowered Sijan. Even though no direct sunlight reached him, his fever produced uncontrollable thirst. He struggled to open his second water container, using his right bicep to grip the plastic bottle while he twisted off the tight cap. In a lower pouch of his survival vest, he had a folded plastic water bag—the "elephant's rubber"—which was, of course, empty. If there had been any streams nearby and if he had been able to walk, he could have secured himself a good supply of drinking water in the five-liter bag. But there were no streams on this stony karst, and he could not walk. He sucked down his second ten ounces of stale, tepid water and waited.

Somewhere up in the forest canopy, his parachute and inflated rubber life raft had torn away. In the raft's survival kit there were four pint cans of water, foil pouches of fortified survival biscuit, and an extra radio; most important, there were also four more smoke flares. But the raft was gone, snagged and unreachable in the thick roof of branches, over a hundred feet above his head. It was better not to think about the raft.

The sun was getting lower now, and long shadows reached out from the karsts and ridges. *Jolly Green 27* called in from orbit to the south; after dropping off the day's first casualty, *Sandy 8*'s pilot, Major Griffith, Lieutenant Platt had refueled his helicopter, replaced the medical kit with a fresh one, and headed back to Ban Loboy. He and his crew snatched a meal of cold C-rations as they flew. Over the command set, they could hear how poorly things were going, and they knew that they'd be needed.

The other helicopter, *Jolly 15*, had fuel problems again. They were losing a steady stream of JP-4 from the starboard drop tank, and there seemed to be a slight leak in one of the inboard, self-sealing tanks as well. Approaching bingo fuel, their only options were to mid-air refuel from *Crown 2* or RTB.

With deep reluctance, *Crown 2* chose the first option. But the big C-130 was the mission command post and radio relay link back to

Rescue 1 at Udorn. He could not retreat to a truly safe area to refuel *JG 15;* the operation would have to take place quickly over a nearby ridgeline, partially hidden from the obvious NVA gun sites on the valley floor but still within range of any heavy caliber stuff they might have dug in up on the passes.

Crown banked sharply down and leveled off at eight thousand feet. The AC chopped his throttles and dropped full flaps to slow the big transport to a near stall at ninety-four knots indicated air speed. The two hose-and-drogue arrays were trailed from the outboard fuel tanks, one to act as a fuel pipe for *Jolly 15,* the other to balance the aircraft and help create a smooth, uniform slipstream. In level flight, two miles astern, *Jolly Green 15,* approached at 110 knots, then throttled down to match speed with *Crown.* The fat, clumsy-looking helicopter floated gracefully on the invisible carpet of prop blast from *Crown's* four engines.

Inching ahead now, the Jolly's pilot extended his fuel probe and nosed it sharply into the floating cone of the hose drogue. The union was made, and a rush of fuel flowed at over a hundred gallons a minute. No thick red 57mm tracers rose to interrupt the mating of the two strange aircraft.

There were other problems. As the sun fell lower, clouds were forming on the high ridgetops, producing moderate turbulence at this altitude. After six minutes of swaying, jerky flight, *Jolly 15* broke away from the drogue. He had been able to take on over two thousand pounds of fuel, enough to extend his orbit until sunset, if necessary.

The spectacle of the two aircraft linked in their aerial dance obviously caught the attention of the NVA. A few ineffective streams of light-caliber green tracers rose in the general direction of *Crown.* But his altitude was beyond the range of automatic weapons.

Lieutenant Platt, however, seized advantage of the diversion to make a quick pass over the karst. The Sandy escorts undertook an additional diversion by forming a slow, circular strafing pattern across the valley. The jets that still had ordnance on board also carried out slow trolling on the opposite end of the valley.

Jolly Green 27 skimmed in fast, just above the trees. Green tracers flashed up, and he took several hits. He broke the pass and pulled away to the north to check for battle damage. The only serious problems Platt had were some holes in the outboard tanks. Now he, too, would have to link up with *Crown* to refuel. And the weather was definitely beginning to close in for the night. It looked as if there'd be a broken overcast later, with nimbostratus forming to sock in the higher ridges and flood some of the valleys. Nobody was going to be flying up here tonight.

Crown 2 climbed up to ten thousand feet to await *Jolly* 27. They had been lucky with the first refueling in this hostile area, but now they were stretching their luck to the limit.

A little after 1600, *Sandy* 3, the on-scene commander, FAC'd in the last of the fast-movers on their bomb runs into the valley. Now most of the jet aircraft were sent back to their various bases. But *Misty* FAC 25, an F-100, remained on station, and Gunfighters 1 and 2, Nordin and his wingman, stayed at high orbit to act as ResCap; they had sidewinder and Sparrow missiles on board to deter any North Vietnamese MiGs that might have been attracted to the day-long battle. Nordin and his number-two aircraft had just completed their third midair refueling of the day. They had enough fuel to orbit until dark.

The *Firefly* Flight of Air Commando Skyraiders now rolled in over the valley, and *Firefly* 15 assumed on-scene command. He did not waste any time but began talking directly to Sijan and homing on the Guard Channel signal. *AWOL*'s voice was louder and faster now. For the first time in ten hours of radio contact, the pilots overhead could hear obvious strains of pain and fear in Sijan.

Firefly dispersed his forces over the karst, and they went to work with delayed-action cluster bombs, fused to penetrate the canopy and airburst with devastating effect.

Issuing curt, precise commands, *Firefly* ordered *Jolly Green* 15 over the karst. There was still some light ground fire, but *Firefly* told the helicopter pilot that he had the survivor pinpointed.

When the helicopter wheeled in across the treetops, however, he took small arms tracers from the gully he had just crossed.

"*Jolly*, break left! break left!" *Firefly* ordered. "You went up the wrong valley there. Fall back and stand by. I'll lead you in."

Speaking nervously, the Jolly Green pilot acknowledged. Although he had not been seriously hit, he had come very close to a disaster a minute before. Now he watched the *Firefly* Flight string out in line formation and S-turn over the karst to take up a low daisy chain orbit at the far end. A Sandy flashed past him on the right to strafe and rocket the gorge from which he had just taken fire.

"Let's go, *Jolly*," *Firefly* called. "Come on in here now."

The helicopter made its fast approach and leveled off just above the slashing treetops. In his headset, the Jolly pilot had a cacophony to deal with and interpret: the loud beeper of *AWOL*, the voices of his own PJ and engineer, *Firefly* talking to *Crown*, and his copilot calling out altitude above the trees.

Suddenly the voice of *Rescue 1* at Udorn boomed through to order a general withdrawal of all SAR forces. The overall commander had decided that deteriorating weather, impending darkness, and continued enemy resistance had combined to make the dangerous mission untenable.

Crown 2 was quick to answer. "*Rescue One, Crown Two.* We've got a Jolly in a good hover right over the survivor now. The Sandys have the ground fire dampened way down and Jolly's not taking any hits. I advise against RTB."

Rescue 1 considered this transmission. After a brief pause, he sent his reply. "Have at it."

The radio traffic fell off to a minimum of exchanges between *Jolly 15* and Lance Sijan.

For the first time all that long, grueling day, Sijan could see the rotor blast of the rescue helicopter on the canopy. He could not be certain of the Jolly's exact hover position, but he knew the helicopter was very close.

"Drop the penetrator," he called, fighting to remain lucid and coherent through the pain and dizziness.

"*AWOL*," the Jolly pilot called, "I'm going to send my PJ down to find you."

"Negative, *Jolly!* Negative! There's bad guys down here close. Just drop the penetrator."

The two helicopter pilots stared at each other. Here was a poor bastard who'd been down there all day long, through all that shit, lying in the jungle with a broken leg, and now he refused the help of a rescue man. It was difficult to fathom that kind of courage and discipline.

"*Jolly, AWOL.* Look . . . I can see the penetrator. It's close. Stay in your hover. I'll crawl to you. Just stand by there. I'll crawl to you."

"Roger, *AWOL, Jolly* standing by." The pilot checked his panel clock and his watch, then made a quick note on his kneeboard. It was 1703. The shadows were long across the valley.

Around the helicopter, the A-1s had formed up in a tight daisy chain. Occasionally a burst of light tracers would squirt up at the Skyraiders, but no fire came near the hovering Jolly Green. The two young helicopter pilots sat sweating in their flak jackets, their fingers inside damp leather flying gloves lightly gripping their controls, their eyes fixed on the engine instruments, watching for any sign of overheat or power loss that might warn of a stall. Behind the vertical racks of electronics that separated the flight deck from the cargo bay, the PJ and flight engineer crouched at their machine guns, staring intently down at the treetops that slashed and tumbled in the rotor wash. The thin steel cable of the penetrator stretched straight down into the green shadows below the canopy.

Both crewmen had removed the green nylon safety harnesses they had worn to prevent them from falling out the gaping doors should the helicopter lurch or roll and replaced them with backpack parachutes.

The yellow snout of the jungle penetrator lay against a humpbacked tree root, twenty feet to the right. Sijan rolled carefully onto his right side and tried to worm his way across the vine-choked, stony ground. He kept his injured right hand free of the rocks and clutched the survival radio in his uninjured left hand.

This maneuver was not going to work. As soon as he put pressure on his right arm, the pain shot through him like an electric current. If he tried to balance his body by moving his left leg, the hot spasms of pain were even worse. And the thorny vines snagged his flight suit and tangled in the protruding pockets of the survival vest and the straps of the parachute harness. Squirming from one side to another, he banged the vulnerable antenna of his radio against roots and tree trunks.

In lucid moments between the pain, he saw that he would have to collapse the radio antenna, put the set back inside the pocket of his vest and use the bolo knife in his left hand to hack a path through the low tangle of vines. Before he attempted this, he had to make sure that the Jolly stayed in orbit. If they moved the penetrator, he'd be lost.

"*Jolly, AWOL,*" he called, the words echoing hollowly in his head. "Just hover. Just hover there. I'm going to crawl to you."

On the Jolly's flight deck, the two pilots again stared at each other. It was 1715, and *AWOL* had said almost the same thing twelve minutes earlier. What the hell was going on down there?

Sijan slid the telescope antenna back into the green metal top of the radio and placed it snugly inside the largest pocket of his vest. The pain was coming in waves now, and he realized that he could only function between the spasms.

He had his knife out. Then he was down on his back, reaching over his good shoulder to hack at the springy vines. His right knee was up, and the cleated boot sole bit into the moldy leaf mulch to give him leverage. Rising on his hips, he hurled himself backward, into the thorny tangle he had just attacked with his knife.

He rose, hacked, then fell away again. A moment later he lurched backward, deeper into the vines, closer to the gray tree trunk and the yellow bullet of the penetrator.

Far above him in the green gallery, the rotors of the helicopter thumped and tore the sky apart.

At 1736 the aircraft commander of *Jolly Green 15* asked *Firefly* lead for advice. The survivor had not answered the last two radio transmissions, and *JG 15* had been hanging here in a hover for thirty-three minutes. The valley was completely covered with shadow now, and the surrounding ridgetops were in cloud. Out on the A-1s' daisy chain, a few bursts of automatic weapons fire had just come up with light AK tracers.

Firefly Lead instructed *Jolly Green 15* to contact the survivor and ask him to repeat his authenticator number.

"*AWOL One* Bravo, *Jolly Green Fifteen*," the pilot called, using formal radio procedure. "Transmit your authenticator number. Repeat, transmit your authenticator number. *Jolly One Five*, standing by."

The rotors tossed the forest roof. The cable hung straight, disappearing into the gloom. There was no reply from *AWOL*.

Firefly Lead waited several minutes for an answer. *AWOL* was silent. The on-scene commander's instructions were clear in a case like this. "All Flights," he said, trying to speak calmly. "This is *Firefly* Lead. RTB. Repeat, RTB. Let's climb on out of here for egress."

In the starboard door of *Jolly Green 15*, the engineer hit the winch switch, and the penetrator cable came humming up at high speed.

Fifteen seconds later he reported that the yellow probe was clear of the trees. The helicopter banked away, still squired by its two Sandys.

As the clot of circling A-1s and the big camouflaged helicopter began to disperse, ground fire cascaded up from the edges of the karst and the dark floor of the valley. On the higher ridges to the east, 37mm batteries cut loose. The sky was ripped by streams of heavy red tracers. There was ground fire from all directions, green tracer small stuff but also lots of dual 23mm and several batteries of 37mms.

Two Sandys were hit, but somehow the Jolly Green managed to swing and stagger out of the flak trap with no serious mishap.

In the snarl of vines and dead leaves, Sijan heard the rotor pitch of the distant chopper change; then he saw the penetrator snap up through the branches. Twigs and pieces of ripped branches tumbled around him.

He collapsed backward into the vines, his chest hard with frustration and terror. His pulse was drumming in his head. The pain surrounded him like a skin of fire.

Desperately he ripped at his survival vest to extract the radio. As he tore at the snaps, he heard the echoing pop and spatter of the flak guns firing from all around the valley. He understood then why the Jolly had pulled away.

Up on high station, it was still bright daylight. Glenn Nordin banked hard left and stared down at the shadows in the valley. Even from this altitude, he could see the hot tracers. He had just heard and acknowledged the recall order. His throat was tight with rage and frustration, at the enemy, at the Jolly crews, at the Sandys. At his own impotence.

His right hand jumped across his radio console. "Okay, *Two*," he told his wingman, "let's go down there for one pass to show Lance he's not alone."

The two heavy Phantoms rolled out of the sunshine and dove into the darkening valley at over six hundred knots. Nordin flattened out just above the treetops and roared across the long jungle valley, directly toward the karst.

On Guard Channel, Sijan was calling for the Jolly. His voice was no longer calm and professional. He sounded young, badly hurt, and terrified.

"Lance," Nordin called as soon as the channel was clear. "This is *Gunfighter*. Do you copy?"

At the sound of the familiar voice, Sijan regained his composure. "Roger, *Gunfighter*, copy. Please advise mission status. Over."

"Lance, listen now. We're coming back to get you tomorrow."

The two Phantoms screamed across the roof of the karst and banked sharply for another pass.

"Lance," Nordin repeated. "We will *definitely* be back at dawn. You understand? We're coming back to get you in the morning."

"Okay, sir," Sijan said, his voice thin, exhausted now. "I copy that. Thank you, sir."

The two jets flung themselves through one last tight circuit of the valley, then climbed out, jinking into the pink clumps of sunset cloud.

Down on the forest floor, Sijan dragged himself backward in the opposite direction, toward his original tree-root resting place where he had dropped his water bottles and pistol. It was almost night down in the vines and roots. He could not risk a flashlight, so he pulled his body blindly backward, the pain from his leg a constant. He could not see the limestone sinkhole behind him, half-covered by thorn creepers and fallen leaves. His left hand plunged into the void first, then his shoulders. He dropped several feet through thorns before his injured head struck the sharp stone.

The pain stopped. The world stopped.

Part II

★

Struggle on the Ground

Chapter Five

The Mountains of Laos

November 1967

In the predawn chill of Sunday, November 12, 1967, the crews of twenty-three aircraft ate an early breakfast in the dining halls of Da Nang, Nakhon Phanom, Ubon, and Udorn air bases. They were the search and rescue group scheduled to arrive over the Ban Loboy Ford at first light in what everyone hoped would be a successful attempt to pluck Lieutenant Lance Sijan from the well-defended karst on which he lay, hidden beneath the forest canopy.

Crown 6 from Udorn, with an experienced senior rescue officer on board, would be the airborne command post. The first two Jolly Greens from Nakhon Phanom would be led by the base's SAR detachment commander, Lieutenant Colonel Warner Britton. From Ubon and Da Nang twelve F-4Cs would provide ResCap support.

Their pilots had been chosen to include aircraft commanders and backseaters who knew Sijan well and who could, if necessary, discern from the tone of his voice and the nuances of his language if he were talking freely or if he were somehow being forced by NVA captors to speak on his survival radio and lure the rescue forces into a flak trap.

Those who knew Lance discounted out of hand the possibility that he would cooperate with his possible captors in any way, but they considered the addition of Sijan's personal friends in the Res-Cap crews a prudent precaution. After the agonizing frustrations of the previous day's long effort, no one wanted the second attempt to fail for lack of intelligent preparation. Indeed, unit commanders at the various bases involved had worked late that night, coordinating their plans for the optimum combination of aircraft and ordnance and to guarantee the availability of reserves of properly armed planes and experienced crews. The men who had flown through the savage ground fire around the karsts the day before were disappointed, shaken, and exhausted by their long effort, but many of them volunteered to return this Sunday morning for the second try. They would be needed to help pinpoint Sijan's position.

Crown 6 was the first plane of the rescue force to reach the target area. While the crews at the fighter bases in Vietnam and Thailand were still washing down their soggy scrambled eggs with scalding coffee, the big C-130 wheeled through the darkness in a high orbit, its radar homing and warning gear probing the dark mountains below for any indication that the NVA had moved up radar-controlled guns or possibly even mobile SA-2 antiaircraft missiles during the night. Other direction-finding antennae aboard *Crown* were tuned to Guard Channel. As soon as the main body of the rescue force was airborne, *Crown* would make its first call to Sijan. Once contact was made, *Crown* would ask for twenty seconds of beeper, and the specialists aboard the plane would use their sensitive homing equipment to reestablish a reasonably accurate fix.

Major Glenn Nordin led the *Gunfighter* Flight from Da Nang. The six Phantoms flew north up the Laotian panhandle at thirty thousand feet to conserve fuel, in a loose radar-trail formation. They were armed with flak suppression ordnance: cluster bombs, rockets, and Vulcan 20mm gun pods. They had already heard enough about the SAR effort of the day before to realize that the Ban Loboy Ford would be very well defended today and that the fixed-wing aircraft would be called upon to work relatively low and slow among those jagged karsts once the operation got cranked up. The NVA on the ground undoubtedly knew that the American would be back for another try. The day was clear, offering good visibility equally to the rescue pilots and the NVA gunners.

At 0630, the main body of the rescue force arrived on station and the aircraft took up their assigned orbits. The two Jolly Greens and their escorting Sandys circled above the steep, forested karsts to the northwest of the main valley, ten miles from the "safe area" orbit site the Jollys had used the previous day. NVA road security units were known to be fast on their feet and could move their accurate and deadly 12.7mm machine guns many miles in a single night. Therefore, it was quite likely that they had already staked out the ridges near the Jollys' former orbit area southwest of the valley.

Sandy 3 was the on-scene commander. He had flown the previous day's mission and knew well the flat-topped, pork-chop oval karst where Sijan was hidden. Rolling into the valley from the half-light of the western ridges, the Sandy pilot jinked and feinted toward the karst formations north of the river. Ahead of him, the five-thousand-foot summit of Co Ta Roun caught the first sun above the bomb-cratered Ban Kari Pass.

Crown made his first call to Sijan. At various altitudes, in a variety of fast and slow aircraft, the pilots of the rescue force heard the call on Guard and anxiously waited to hear the reply from *AWOL*.

"*AWOL One* Bravo, *Crown Six*. Do you copy? Over."

There was no response.

Crown repeated the call. Sijan did not reply.

Sandy 3 roared in fast across the forest roof of the karst, his throttle wide open and the big four-bladed prop at full coarse pitch. The noise of the Skyraider echoed off the limestone walls of the surrounding karsts.

"*AWOL One, AWOL One,*" the Sandy pilot called. "This is *Sandy* Low Lead. If you copy, please acknowledge."

Sandy 3 banked and jinked back south for another pass across the top of the karst. In his headset there was delicate static, pips, and faraway strangled whistles, but no voice or beeper.

On SAR Primary Channel, *Crown 6* next asked *Gunfighter* Lead, Glenn Nordin, to call down to Sijan.

"*AWOL One, Gunfighter* Lead. Lance, this is Glenn Nordin. How you doing? We're back to get you. Come on up on Guard now. Over."

Nordin rolled over onto his port wing and gazed down at the green ridges twenty thousand feet below in the pastel dawn.

Sijan did not answer.

Back on low station, *Hobo* Flight of four A-1s from Nakhon Phanom joined the two Sandy low aircraft and all six Skyraiders now made repeated treetop passes above the indented oval karst. It was 0650, and the valley was now fully light and clear of mist.

After each low pass, *Sandy 3* asked *AWOL* to identify himself by either voice or beeper.

Sijan did not answer.

For the first forty minutes of the effort, there had been no ground fire. But at 0712, one of the Hobos saw automatic weapons tracers rising from a clearing near the road, four miles east of *AWOL*'s karst. It was inaccurate stuff, just a squirt of red tracers tracking far to the right of his flight path.

For the Sandys and Hobos, however, the ground fire provided a tangible focus for their frustration at not raising Sijan on Guard Channel. The Skyraiders jinked across the karsts to lay down a savage barrage of rockets, cluster bombs, and cannon fire on the roadside clearing. The display of aerial firepower was impressive and heartening to the pilots orbiting the Ban Loboy Ford. Beating up a gun site broke the tense monotony of holding orbit. These men were here to rescue one of their own and, if necessary, to fight the enemy to effect that rescue. Now, as the Sandys engaged that AW site across the valley, it was almost as if the spell of silence had been broken and the other half of the mission—the rescue—could begin.

The day before, the pilots had learned, 108 aircraft and four ground radar sites had been involved in the unsuccessful effort to pull Sijan off that goddamn karst. Everyone involved had given it their very best shot. Today the SAR forces were back again, better equipped and better organized than the day before. For many of the pilots—certainly for an optimist like Glenn Nordin—failure of this mission was unthinkable.

But, of course, failure was inevitable if Sijan did not answer on Guard Channel. To the senior SAR commanders in the lead Jolly, in *Sandy 3*, and orbiting high above in *Crown 6*, Sijan's silence indicated a variety of possibilities.

He could be dead. For sixty hours he had lain on the side of that karst with a compound fractured leg. Such a wound, by definition, was accompanied by hemorhage. Even with a tourniquet in place, he might have bled to death in the night. Sijan had also mentioned a head injury, a concussion. he might now very well be dead from the wound. Or he might simply be unconscious.

It was also possible, the SAR commanders knew, that his radio had been damaged while he crawled across the rugged karst to reach the jungle penetrator hanging from *Jolly Green 15* during the last futile pickup attempt the day before. In that event, he was just as isolated as if he were dead or unconscious. Without smoke or flares, he had no means of being seen. Given the terrain and the proximity of the enemy, no reasonable commander would allow a PJ rescue man to descend through the forest roof this morning to search the general area from which Sijan had last reported by radio the day before.

The most dangerous explanation for Sijan's silence was that he had been captured by an NVA patrol in the night. During debriefing, the Sandy and Jolly Green crews who had been involved in the last pickup attempt had reported that small arms and automatic weapons fire had been coming from within five hundred meters of Sijan's position on the top of the irregular oval karst. Even though the gullies leading up to the karst roof were almost vertical where they abutted the main formation and the thick tree canopy indicated a trackless forest, an energetic patrol of NVA road security troops who knew the area well could have climbed to the top after dark, hacked their way through the undergrowth, and captured Sijan.

If the enemy had managed to seize him, they might well have also taken his survival radio intact. And they might now be waiting for a sign that the vulnerable rescue helicopters were in the area before activating the beeper. Certainly, if the NVA had a good English speaker down there the day before and they had been able to monitor Guard Channel, they would have learned considerable information about the survivor: his name and rank, the fact that he was an F-4 backseater well known to the *Gunfighter* Flight, which was, in turn, known to come from Da Nang—*and* that a second rescue effort would be made at first light Sunday.

Even without an English speaker who could translate the various exchanges on Guard Channel, however, the local Vietnamese commander would have realized by the large, complex, and ultimately unsuccessful rescue effort that the Americans would be back a second day. It was probable that the enemy was keeping his 37mm guns and dual 23mms in reserve, waiting for the inevitable helicopters to appear or, even better, waiting for the prime target of a helicopter refueling from the *Crown* command plane within range of the heavier guns dug in along the ridgetops.

During the thirteen years since the French debacle at Dien Bien Phu, NVA doctrine had continually stressed the importance of well-structured and organized antiaircraft defenses: "flak traps," which took advantage of Indochina's steep terrain, from which skilled gunners could bring cross fire to bear on aircraft forced to fly slowly through narrow valleys. The advent of fast ground-attack jets capable of accurate night dive-bombing had done much to make this NVA doctrine obsolete, but the tactics developed to defeat the airborne logistical armada supporting the French garrison in the ridge-encircled valley of Dien Bien Phu now worked equally well against vulnerable American helicopters and search and rescue prop planes flying among the karsts and ridges of Laos.

One hour and twenty minutes into the mission, *Crown 6* ordered the low-station Sandys and Hobos to troll the edges of the karst, to fly slowly up the side valleys and steep gullies from which so much automatic weapons and small arms fire had come the day before. Maybe Sijan was semiconscious, unaware of his surroundings or that the SAR force was back. It was possible that his radio was not even switched on or, perhaps, that it was not on Receive mode. If the Skyraiders could provoke a little ground fire, then expend some ordnance around the foot of the karst, the explosions and shock waves might snap Sijan out of the stupor of his wounds.

But the trolling planes could not raise any ground fire from the base of the oval karst, and it was too risky for them simply to shoot up the area because Sijan might have somehow moved in the night.

After a series of very low passes, *Sandy 3* tried calling Sijan once again.

There was no response.

By 0825, the two orbiting Jolly Greens were running low on fuel, and a crucial mission decision would soon have to be made. Within twenty minutes they would be down to bingo fuel: enough to RTB, provided, of course, that they weren't hit by ground fire and develop leaks from their tanks. But if they remained in orbit longer than twenty minutes, they would have to rendezvous with *Crown* and carry out the tricky midair refueling maneuver, again over enemy territory, again within the range of the heavy flak guns the NVA were known to have.

The dilemma now faced by the mission commander was emblematic of America's wider dilemma in Vietnam. America's technologically advanced and democratic civilization could produce superlative weapon systems and large numbers of skilled, well-motivated, and aggressive fighting men. But this powerful military assemblage could not alter the geological and climatic imperatives of the Indochinese terrain. The steep jungle mountains of the Annam Cordillera and the central highlands were ideally suited for ground combat, especially ambush, but the forest, ridges, and gorges rendered air power almost impotent. Obviously, mechanized warfare in these tropical highlands was impractical except with light amphibious armored vehicles like the Soviet PT-76s. The terrain of the Ho Chi Minh Trail infiltration route was a paradise for the light infantry of the NVA.

The mission commander in *Crown 6* was well aware of the advantage held by his NVA counterpart. In the previous three days alone, NVA road security units had sprung two deadly flak traps on SAR forces along the Trail. Two nights before, in a valley across the Laotian border from Khe Sahn, the NVA had used a trapped special forces recon patrol as bait, luring in ARVN and U.S. Army helicopters to a well-coordinated cross fire. Two choppers were destroyed in the first pickup attempt, and later that night one SAR Jolly Green was badly shot up and crash-landed, and the other Jolly, riddled with machine-gun fire, exploded attempting to lift off with wounded survivors. In the follow-up rescue attempt, several other aircraft received damage.

And here at the Ban Loboy Ford, of course, the toll of battle damage from the previous day's mission had also been serious. Only a miracle had saved the two most badly damaged Jollys and the three seriously hit Sandys. The word was probably out among the NVA units along the Trail: Hold your fire and select your targets when the enemy comes to pickup survivors. A large-scale rescue effort in Laos gave the NVA the chance to really hurt the Americans.

After a final series of futile calls to *AWOL*, the mission commander called *Rescue 1* at *Compress* and recommended that the effort be canceled. *Rescue 1* briefly considered *Crown*'s request and, at exactly 0830, issued the general RTB order.

Immediately, Glenn Nordin called *Compress* and requested permission to remain in high orbit with his six Da Nang Gunfighter Phantoms. It was still possible, he reasoned, that Sijan might come back on Guard Channel during the day. He wanted to make sure that there were friendly forces in the area to help if Lance were still alive and uncaptured. *Compress* agreed and passed off *Gunfighter* Flight to *Cricket*.

In order not to alert the enemy to a general retreat and thus trigger the suspected flak trap, the Jollys and the low-element aircraft departed the area one at a time by different routes. Each Skyraider first climbed to a medium orbit to act as protective cover for the planes still down in the valley. When the second Jolly Green and its escorting Sandy had wheeled off to the west, however, the NVA realized that the SAR forces were pulling back without attempting a pickup.

Light automatic weapons fire rose from several sites near the oval karst, and heavier 23mm tracers looped down from camouflaged positions on the surrounding ridges. Rolling and jinking wildly, the remaining Sandys managed to leave the valley without suffering battle damage. They joined up with the Jollys and vectored west toward Nakhon Phanom. By 0900, only Nordin's Gunfighter Phantoms on high orbit remained in the area.

The *Gunfighter* Flight now separated into a wide, circular formation at eighteen thousand feet and throttled back to a lazy three hundred-knot left-hand orbit. Within fifty minutes they would each have to depart for the Thai border to refuel from the Brown Anchor KC-135 tanker out there on station. But now, with the bomb-scarred valley again empty of any visible human activity, all they could do was ease their backs in their cramped seats, monitor their instruments, and call down to Sijan on Guard Channel every few minutes.

"*AWOL One* Bravo, this is *Gunfighter* Lead. Do you copy?"

"*AWOL One* Bravo, this is *Gunfighter* Lead. Lance, do you copy? Over."

The sun climbed the sky. The shadows shortened toward midday. There was no answer from the ground.

Weeks later, before he slipped into terminal delirium, Sijan was able to recount the vivid details of his long evasion to his fellow prisoners, Guy Gruters and Bob Craner. From these accounts and from the nature of his injuries, as well as from studying detailed aerial and satellite reconnaissance photographs of the Ban Loboy Ford target area, it is possible to reconstruct accurately the major events of Lance Sijan's heroic effort. Although he was horribly debilitated when he finally encountered Craner and Gruters, Lance was still able to relate with precision the key elements of his lonely struggle: the battle with pain, the periods of confusion stemming from his concussion, the search for water, the brutal encounters with the thorn vines, limestone, and sinkholes on the forest floor.

Pain and thirst brought Sijan out of the darkness. His face and neck were clammy, but his lips were so hot and parched that the tip of his tongue was glued to the dry flesh. A fire was searing his scalp, deep into the bone. There was also pain down below his belly . . . to the left, another fire. He rolled his head, and the flames rolled inside his head. When he drew up his right hand to cradle his face, the fire spread to his forearm and wrist. A moan, a snarl of unreasoning hurt was stifled in his cramped chest. His lips would not separate to emit the cry of pain.

Darkness came again.

Thirst and pain returned. He opened his eyes and saw the delicate green tendrils and hard green barbs of a thorn vine. There was fire below and above him, but for the moment, he could think before the flames again touched his flesh. It was pale daylight. He was sitting in a squashed heap down inside some kind of sewer pipe, a broken concrete sewer pipe. He had fallen into an old abandoned French latrine out behind the wing. . . . The construction guys were always digging them up with their bulldozers. What a stupid goddamn place to fall and get hurt so bad.

He had to find a doctor, had to call the medics from the hospital. His head was hurt, his leg was broken, and his hand was bent backward and cut with this rotten dirty old concrete from this sewer pipe.

Now the fire came again, and he managed to scream.

Green light, vine-and-leaf light. He opened his eyes. The fire was low. Sijan stared at the narrow hooks of the vine thorns. The grunts called them wait-a-minute vines out in the bush. They did not grow on the base. . . . He was *not* on the base. He had not fallen down the sewer of an old French latrine. He was in the bush.

Sijan moved his head, gingerly. Daylight. Green daylight with the forest canopy brighter to the left than the right. Morning or afternoon? Time. *Time*... How many days had he been in this sinkhole? He opened his eyes and breathed in the fetid stench of the hole, the odors of his own horribly wounded, immobile, but living body.

With memory came thirst. With the thirst, the pain rippled back into his limbs. With the pain, time became elastic, then splintered, unpredictable. He closed his eyes, willing the fire to fall away. He opened his eyes and watched a blue-and-yellow beetle prance along a thorn vine. It was day, but he could not know what day. He pushed his right boot down and strained to rise on his right leg, thrashing above him with his uninjured left hand. The sinkhole, he discovered, was only a few feet deep.

Pain exploded behind his eyes, then blew away like the smoke from a phosphorous rocket. As he threw himself backward from the sinkhole, bile rose in his throat. He found himself sprawled on his back between the gray fins of the tree roots. There were creepers and vines, springy beneath the thick nylon web of his parachute harness. Under his hips the limestone of the karst was broken, jagged lumps.

Now the pain in his mangled limbs was pulsing up again, through his belly and throat, into that red-hot place behind his eyes. With his memory intact, he did not try to resist the pain. He forced open the dry, sour tube of his throat and howled, leaning into the hot agony like some circus daredevil.

According to his parents and academy classmates, Sijan knew pain from years of heavy sports, from all the long endurance runs on the stony trails of the Rampart Range above the Academy campus seven thousand feet high in the Rockies. The cadets had slogged along in combat boots, slung rifles cutting their shoulders, under the weight of the August sun, in the slashing December wind. He also understood pain from the stadium locker room. Pain lay coiled inside the cool stainless steel of the trainer's bench when they worked tenderly above him, snipping away the tape on the puffy red bruises of his damaged knees.

As he often told his friends, pain was not invincible. It was a powerful force but one he knew well. Pain could be managed, manipulated. He had learned this valuable lesson young. He had also learned that he could absorb pain much better than many of his friends and fellow athletes. His body was tough, stronger than most. His mind was tougher. This was a fact about himself that he accepted with neutral assurance, just as he had always quietly accepted his good looks. Physical toughness, endurance, and the mental determination to carry on . . . raw stubbornness, formed a large part of his self-perception.

Sijan had come to realize in late adolescence that he had reserves of strength and willpower that most other people did not have. He also recognized that this combination of physical endurance and emotional intensity could be focused, as one focused the lens of a camera.

During the last days of Cadet Summer Basic in August 1961, his flight of trainees was subjected to an especially difficult physical workout by the second-year cadets who were the trainees' absolute masters. Five-mile runs with rifle, combat boots, and packs were ordered almost every stifling afternoon. For Sijan, who had trained year-round for football during the previous five years, these endurance runs were hard but not completely debilitating. But for the younger, weaker cadets, some barely seventeen years old and lacking athletic experience, the runs through the dust of the Trails was agonizing.

Sijan's academy roommate, Mike Smith, still remembers one especially arduous run. Sijan and Smith, who was also a trained athlete, fell back to help the stragglers at the tail of their formation. Several smaller cadets in their flight were staggering behind the main group, their helmets banging against their noses, their rifle slings dragging down off their shoulders. These stragglers were within a few yards of collapse. With collapse might well come more hazing and, eventually, terminal discouragement. Such cadets were in imminent danger of washing out, even before they began the rigors of their first academic year.

So Sijan and Mike slid back to the stragglers and took the smaller men's rifles on their own shoulders. Then each gripped one wavering zombie and began to guide him back to the sheltering anonymity of the main formation.

At this point in the run, with only a thousand yards remaining, the upperclassman cadet in charge of their group caught sight of Sijan and Smith helping the stragglers. The senior cadet was a tall, imposing blond from the Midwest whom many of the Doolies feared. Unlike the trainees, he wore gym shorts and sneakers and was not burdened with helmet, pack, or rifle.

He trotted over to Sijan and pushed him and the smaller cadet *hard*, with both hands. "Give that man back his rifle and let him run by himself," he shouted.

Without warning Sijan spun around and delivered a heavy shoulder block to the center of the senior cadet's chest, sending him sprawling.

The upperclassman was pale with shocked rage. "Mister," he screamed, "I'm going to have your *ass* for that."

Still gripping the smaller cadet's shoulder with his right hand, Sijan gazed calmly into the blond's eyes. "You touch one of our people again, man, you won't be able to have *any*body's ass."

The senior cadet jogged along, his face loose with disbelief at the words he was hearing from this Doolie. He was about to call in his fellow upperclassmen for a real discipline session when Sijan spoke again, his voice still amazingly calm and precise.

"If you want to see who can run where with boots and rifles," he said, "you get your boots on and get your rifle. . . . then we'll come back out here and I'll run with you as long as you want."

The upperclassman, as it is told, must have become aware of an unusual intensity in Sijan. In any case, he was incapable of replying to this big, hitherto quiet Doolie. The upperclassman simply slowed to a walk and let the gasping, staggering formation continue up the long gravel ramp toward the brown lawn of the main athletic field and the finish line.

Later that afternoon, the upperclassmen convened to decide what punishment should be meted out to Sijan for this blatant breach of discipline. Those senior cadets who had already observed Sijan at close hand during the hard weeks of the summer training apparently knew they were dealing with an exceptional young man. The result of that afternoon's meeting was unusual: The upperclassman was reassigned to another flight, and Sijan received no punishment for having publicly braced his senior.

Heavy jets growled high above the green forest canopy. Sijan raised his face from his shoulder and stared up at the distant foliage. Time. There was something wrong with the way time was moving up here.

Now the light on the treetops was much further to the right than it had been only a few moments before. Or had he slipped away again to the warm darkness for several hours?

And the day. Was this the second day, or had he been gone longer? His watch was smashed on his wrist, the hands stopped at 8:39. There was something about that time that was important, something about the shoot-down, about the ejection. But now he could not remember. The fire inside his head was falling, but now there were loose pieces of some dark, heavy substance shifting within his skull. For hours that first day with the Sandys and the Jolly Greens just overhead, he had been able to fight the dizzy shifting rocks inside his head. But now the concussion had come back and was swelling behind his eyes to make clear thought impossible . . . so *slippery*, like time.

He watched the light on the forest canopy. He listened to the snarl and rumble of the jets far above. Time would come back in focus in a little while. Then he would talk to the jets on the radio. Now he just had to wait while the dark shapes rolled and ground over the fire inside his head.

When he opened his eyes, there was only darkness. A mosquito whined near his right ear, and automatically he raised his right hand to brush it away. The pain shot through his brain. Night. He swallowed, then managed to lick his cracked and swollen lips. With his left hand he gingerly touched the side of his face, his left and then his right cheek. The beard was wiry, stiff with dried sweat. How many days? Three, maybe four. Thursday, Friday . . . Saturday the Jollys had come. Sunday? Was that what . . . yesterday? He had no way of knowing the day or date, not that those bits of civilized data had any use out here. But it was important for him to know if he had been unconscious through the second day of the SAR effort.

Again he probed his beard with the fingertips of his left hand. The darkness around him was absolute. No light from stars or moon worked through the roof of the forest. Monkeys and night birds whined and hooted. Down here, smell, touch, and hearing were all he had at night. It would be stupid to try to move in the darkness. If there was one sinkhole on the broken, jagged floor of this karst, there had to be others, probably some a lot deeper than the one he had fallen into.

Reaching carefully to the left, he stroked the smooth bark of the tree. This would be a good backrest. In three dragging jolts across the sharp limestone, he was there and slid his back against the high slab of the root. Rancid odors of urine, blood, and fever sweat rose from inside his flight suit. He shook his head. How many days had he been lying here delirious with concussion?

However long he had lain in that hole, it had been long enough for the NVA patrols to have crisscrossed the top of the karst. If they had come near, they certainly had not found him. In the morning he could look for tracks or the blazes of their machetes. He had to be sure the enemy wasn't near when he called in the Jollys. But time had broken. He did not know how many days he had been up here.

There was no way to know the time until he was rescued. And the only way he could get the Jollys back was to call them. Working carefully in the dimensionless dark, he tentatively explored the dislocated fingers of his right hand with his left hand. The pain was almost gone, but the three fingers farthest from the thumb simply would not move. They were still bent far back, almost touching the hard, swollen top of his hand. But he could use the thumb and forefinger. The forearm was badly gashed and swollen. In the morning he would have to clean and dress that wound as best he could.

And, of course, there was his leg. But now, in this impossible darkness, he would not attempt to explore that wound again. When it was light, he would have to change the dressing and use the last of the sulpha powder. Then, if the pain was not too bad, he would try to make some kind of splint to protect the broken bones and keep the lower leg immobile. If he had been able to fashion a better splint for his leg that first day, he realized, he might have been able to crawl to the jungle penetrator.

Sijan sighed loudly and pursed his swollen lips. Twenty feet. He had been so close.

But there was nothing at all to be gained from brooding about that. Nothing. He had to think about tomorrow, about rescue. Even if the SAR team had been back yesterday and hadn't been able to raise him on Guard Channel, he knew there were flights up there right now with whom he could speak. And there would be a Night Watch Crown somewhere along the Trail which the fighters would call in as soon as they heard his beeper and voice.

Working with great care, he unsnapped the lower left-hand pocket of his survival vest and slid out the cool metal block of the radio. He could not trust his right thumb and forefinger to extract the antenna, so he used his injured right hand to jam the radio against his chest while he pulled out the telescoping antenna with his left hand.

Around him in the mildewed night large insects chirped and buzzed. The high-pitched voice of an unseen lizard cackled, "FUCK YOU . . . Fuck You . . . fuck you." When he had first heard stories of the Fuck You lizards from the marine officers at the club on Monkey Mountain, he had thought they were putting him on. Now, sitting here in this primitive, unbroken darkness, he realized that small forest geckos *did* produce an uncanny replica of that common obscene insult. Wait-a-minute vines and Fuck You lizards . . . trees two hundred feet tall. This was the real bush. He was a long way from the air-conditioned rooms of the BOQ or the Naugahyde comfort of the DOOM Club.

Only a handful of crazy Special Forces recon teams ever penetrated this deep into enemy territory. He knew that even the fabled LRRPs of the 101st and 173d Airborne never got themselves this isolated, this surrounded, this *alone* among NVA units in their Laotian base areas.

Calling in the SAR forces again would mean exposing the Sandys and helicopters to that concentrated ground fire he had heard booming up from all around this karst and from the surrounding ridges. The first day, one Sandy had gone down and a couple of the Jollys had been badly hit. Men had been wounded . . . trying to rescue him. Asking those same men to come back again was not fair. The NVA had this place locked up tight.

There might be another way. If he could make contact with *Crown,* he might be able to set up another pickup attempt at the northern edge of this karst. That first day, he'd heard them talking on Guard, describing the size and shape of the karst on which he lay. It was shaped like a pork chop, covered with trees, and he was on the southern edge of the formation, near a steep face of naked limestone cut by jungle-choked gullies. Now that his memory was coming back, Sijan was able to think more clearly, to form a plan.

He lowered the radio. In order to crawl half a mile or more through this forest, across the sharp, broken limestone, he would have to make some kind of solid but lightweight splint that would protect his leg. That wouldn't be too much of a problem. In the various survival schools he'd attended since leaving the Academy, he had learned the important principle of improvisation. The bladders of his G-suit and the inflated flotation compartments of his life vest, as well as the thick nylon webs of his parachute harness, could be combined with cut saplings to make a workable splint. He might also be able to make some crutches if he could find decent saplings. Hell, then he could *walk* . . . or at least hobble, out of here.

He still had his compass . . . actually *two* compasses, and his bolo knife. He also had a cloth survival map that showed North Vietnam and Laos in fairly good detail. If he were lucky, he could even find the karst on which he now sat and choose the best route across it.

An undulating wave of pain swept through his body, and he rolled with it. *That* was going to be a real problem. If pain like that hit him while he was trying to pick his way through this vine-choked undergrowth, he might just fall down again and reinjure his arm and leg. And the underlying limestone beneath the vines was so razor-edged and broken that any movement across it was agony. Still . . . he could learn to handle it, to feel the worst pain coming on and brace himself. There definitely were ways to get on top of most bad situations if you were able to use your head. He breathed in deeply and tried to control the weakness brought on by his thirst and fever. At least the concussion was almost gone. Now he had a plan. He would contact *Crown* and arrange a pickup on the north side of the karst. It was from the north that each of the Jollys had approached; that side was clear of guns. There was no way to guarantee that the NVA wouldn't move guns up there to block the north, but trying for a pickup on that side was better than running a replay of that first day, with all the SAR aircraft exposed to the guns down in that main valley.

Sijan again willed himself not to think of water, not to acknowledge his thirst. He had used such mental exercises for years, since the last semesters of high school when sports, his hectic social life, and all the extracurricular activities of clubs and student government piled up on him to seriously impair his study time. At some point he simply decided that he would function with less sleep than other people. He knew that he was physically stronger than the other kids; now he was going to see if he were mentally tougher. To defeat the normal adolescent need for eight hours' sleep so that he could continue his rigorous schedule of sports and social activities and study late at night while other people slept, he had to first learn to defeat fatigue by sheer willpower. He had to convince his body and his mind that he really was not tired.

To his surprise and pleasure, the system worked. He found that he could lead a full schedule of classes, football practice, student government meetings, and social club events, not to mention some pretty heavy dating, then come back to his room overlooking South Shore Park and sit down at his desk to study until two or three in the morning. Alone in his room, with the door closed and the gooseneck lamp bent to light the pages of his chemistry or history book or the thick Shakespeare anthology, he willed his brain to not recognize the fatigue that was flooding his body. He focused his mind away from the tight ache in his neck and shoulders, the heavy sagging in his back and legs. Slowly at first, but more quickly as he practiced the technique, he found that he could concentrate in such a way that the bruises and pain of football practice and the fatigue of the long, boring student government and club meetings simply went away to a distant part of his body and he could fill his mind with only the text that lay before him in the hot circle of lamplight.

At the Academy prep school at Bainbridge and throughout the first three years at the Air Force academy, Sijan had employed the same habits and techniques of concentration. It was during that third year, however, that the imperatives of the real world caught up with him. The academic washout rate was high at the Air Force academy in the early 1960s. Cadets were required to perform in an extremely demanding curriculum that combined hard laboratory sciences and rigorous humanities courses, as well as military science and history. These cadets were also required to take part in at least one interscholastic or intramural sport each quarter and to carry out a leadership role within their cadet squadron.

Sijan had attacked these challenges in typical fashion, by trying to do it *all* to the best of his ability. Football, however, the game he loved the best, and Electromagnetic Physics, the course he most dreaded, combined to teach him a valuable lesson about his own human limits. He was a tight end on the junior varsity team and he had a deep, almost unquenchable longing to play on the first-string varsity during his senior year. Unfortunately for Sijan, not for the Academy, the Falcons had been able to recruit during those years a very talented line which had a redundancy of fast, tough, and agile ends and linebackers. Sijan was a very good tight end. In Milwaukee, a town that produced good high school football teams, he had been an all-city end, the captain of Bay View High's champion team. But he was not quite good enough to play first-string varsity during his third year at the Academy.

He knew, however, that if he worked hard at his game all season, his chances of making varsity his senior year would be good. And, of course, to Sijan, working hard meant giving it everything he had. Six nights a week that cold fall, Sijan would return to his room in Vandenberg Hall, utterly exhausted, bruised and scraped from hours of scrimmaging against the varsity on the frozen mud of the practice field. According to Mike Smith, Lance would sleep like a dead man for two hours, then rise, shower, and sit down at his desk to attack his physics book in that hot circle of lamplight until he had completed all the next day's assigned problems. On most nights he would not extinguish that light until three or four in the morning.

During this same period he was a cadet officer in his squadron, the photo editor of the *Talon* magazine, an officer of the Sky Diving Club, and whenever he had time, he sang in the Glee Club. Despite his intense determination to succeed, to buck the odds and win, to do it *all* well, Sijan was brought down. By spring he was flunking Physics and badly behind in two other science courses. Although his humanities grades were excellent, his weak performance in the hard sciences threatened to wash him out.

He was called before the faculty's Academic Review Board and presented with a chance to continue as a cadet. But this opportunity included some hard choices. He could remain that summer at the Academy and repeat the physics course, thus missing the chance to take one of the coveted overseas summer cadet tours. This was a relatively minor sacrifice. But the next choice was harder. The board felt that varsity football took up too much of his time and far too much of his mental and physical energy. If he were to achieve an acceptable grade point during his senior year, he would have to devote more of himself to his classes, especially his science courses. For an Air Force officer, athletic prowess and recognition as a football player were attributes much less important than a solid foundation in the theoretical sciences.

Sijan was shocked. A self-proclaimed product of the New Frontier, he had come to equate athletic ability and competitive drive, when linked to intellectual flexibility and mental toughness, with the vigor that John Kennedy and his family had so epitomized for Sijan's generation. Now he was being asked to voluntarily give up varsity athletics, just when he finally had the chance to prove himself and receive the acclaim for which he had worked during three hard, anonymous years on the JV team.

But the board had made it clear to him that the choice was his. He knew, of course, that they were right, and that by leaving the choice to him, they were testing his character. He thanked the board for their concern and for having presented him with options. The next day, he said, he would return with his decision.

That afternoon he consulted Coach Jim Bowman, his friend and mentor on the junior varsity team. Bowman was a former center at the University of Michigan and had been trained as a B-47 bomber pilot. He knew about the pleasures and pains of football and he knew about decision making in the Air Force. Coach Bowman also recognized in Lance Sijan one of the toughest, most dedicated young athletes he had ever encountered as either a player or a coach. Obviously, voluntarily giving up football represented a bitter and difficult decision that would require unusual maturity. But Coach Bowman recognized, as had the officers on the board, that the decision must be made by Sijan alone.

At the end of their meeting, Lance announced that he would not be coming out for the varsity team that fall. He had made up his mind. And, Coach Bowman realized, when Sijan made up his mind, the decision was final.

The night jungle, as he told Guters and Craner, was anything but silent. It twittered and pulsed with animal sounds, insects, taunting lizards, and, high overhead, the occasional squabble of unseen monkeys. Sijan held the radio beneath his face, between the battered pincer of his right thumb and forefinger, while he probed in the darkness with his left fingers to turn the recessed function knob from Off through Stnby and Trns/Bcn to Trns/Vce. Closing his eyes, he tried to envision the sequence of positions as the knob clicked through its circle. In survival school they had taught all the aircrew about the danger of accidentally exhausting the battery on this RT-10. If the knob were inadvertently turned to either of the Transmit modes with the antenna collapsed, the battery power would be used up without a coherent directional signal escaping.

Now, sweating with concentration as he clicked the switch, Sijan felt the hot edges of panic. He couldn't be sure, but it seemed as if the knob only clicked ahead one position until it reached its stop at what should be the Transmit Voice position. If that were true, it meant that he had accidentally turned the knob to Transmit Beacon when he had jammed it back in his vest that first day after he had spoken to Major Nordin. How many days had the radio been beeping away impotently inside the green nylon pouch of his vest? How long did those nickel-cadmium wafer batteries really last?

Deliberately he snapped the function knob full right to Trns/Vce. "Mayday, Mayday, Mayday," he called into the plastic mouthpiece. "Calling any aircraft. This is *AWOL One* Bravo calling any aircraft. Does anybody copy?"

He clicked back to Standby and waited with the tiny plastic grid of the speaker near his ear. The static on Guard Channel was faint.

Again he switched to Transmit Beacon and let the beeper work for a minute of slow one-thousand-one, one-thousand-two counting. He clicked back to Standby and waited for a call. The background static seemed even weaker.

His chest was filling with hot breath; his throat was tight. Now he realized the full extent of his situation. Somehow either the radio had been left on beeper with the antenna collapsed, or the fragile set had been damaged when he had fallen into that sinkhole. In either case, he was in bad trouble.

With the uncontrollable panic mounting inside him, he clawed down the inside of the pockets of his survival vest for the foil pouch of spare nickel-cadmium wafer batteries. Then the full memory of that first day came swooping back. In midafternoon of that long heartbreaking day when the Jollys had come so close, he had changed batteries from the original set to the spares. This relatively simple task had taken all his dexterity and tolerance of pain as he worked with his chin, his battered hand, and his uninjured fingers, afraid of dropping the shiny discs of the fresh batteries and losing them in the vines and sharp, broken rock beneath him.

He hefted the radio in his good hand. The batteries in this set *were* the spares. If they were worn out, the set was dead. He swallowed painfully. If his radio were dead, he was damn well as good as dead himself.

Sagging against the fin-blade of the root, he let the pain, the thirst, the terrible loneliness of his situation combine to press him down into a black depression. He was dead; he would never get off this karst. He would never see the sun again or taste water . . . or see his family. Or Lenora.

Time became loose now. Monkeys clacked and hooted up in the canopy. The tiny lizards mocked him. At some point, Sijan later reported, he distinctly heard a small dog barking like a spirited terrier at some intruder. He realized that his mind was going away again with the thirst and the concussion.

Finally the roof of trees began to slip from black to a deep, undersea green. Day was coming. The feisty little terrier barked three times, quite close by, just to the right.

He raised his face, half-expecting to see some bizarre hallucination. Thirty feet away a delicate russet deer, no bigger than a cocker spaniel, stood on spindly, dappled legs, staring at him. Sijan's mind returned, and he laughed out loud, a full, rich sound which sent the animal bounding away through the undergrowth.

"Barking deer," he said to the green morning.

In jungle survival school they had talked about barking deer up in these mountains. Don't get spooked by their barks, they'd said. The little bastards sound just like dogs but they're good eating if you can catch one in your snare. Also, he'd been taught, barking deer used game trails, low, narrow tubes through the underbrush that provided cover for a man crawling and often led to water.

He had his prismatic compass out of its pouch and was taking a bearing on the point where the small deer had last been visible. Eighty-five degrees magnetic. With four degrees west variation up here, that made it almost ninety due east. There was some kind of a low track that ran east and west on this karst. That meant he could possibly move to the eastern end of the formation, away from this southern slope where the NVA had positioned their mobile automatic weapons.

Move? Crawl through that underbrush dragging his broken leg across razor-sharp limestone? Who the hell was he trying to kid?

He stared down at the twisted length of his leg. The G-suit was stained with ochre blood, the flight suit leg was shredded, his boot lay at a sickening angle to the shin. Dragging that mess through this brush would kill him. The splintered bone would slash around and rip an artery, and he would bleed to death.

He tried to lick his lips. How long had he been without water . . . three, maybe four days now. With these wounds he would go into shock and die if he didn't get water soon, in a couple of days maximum.

The problem, the choice, was clear. If he dragged himself along that rocky, narrow game trail, he might find water, but he also might die of shock or hemorrhage before reaching a stream or spring. If he stayed where he was, just . . . waiting, he would definitely die of thirst and shock in a few days, a week at the most.

He let the cool morning air fill his lungs. Breathing deeply in and out, Sijan began to form his plan. First, make a workable splint for his leg. . . . No, first put away his radio, wrap it back up in its protective cover and stow it inside his vest. Then recover his pistol and other gear and make the splint. Once he found water, he could fill his five-quart water bag, his "elephant's rubber" that was stowed in the bottom of his vest. With that much water, he could crawl to some open country . . . off to the east in the main valley. There he could use the sun or build a small fire to heat the batteries enough to give him adequate power for one last transmission on beeper or voice. He could call out his position, then use his signal mirror and his strobe, maybe even a smoky fire of burning parachute harness to guide in the Jollys.

It was a wild damn plan, but it could work. The alternative, sitting up here until he died of thirst, was nonsense. That was what a loser would do, and he had never thought of himself as a loser. He was a soldier, a professional fighting man in a war. Giving in to desperation was not very professional.

Without coming to any palpable decision point, Sijan found himself wrapping up and stowing his radio. Then he was down on his back again, using his good right heel, his uninjured left elbow, and the muscles of his buttocks to propel himself backward across the jagged stone, through the vines, to the left, toward the spot he had dropped his empty water bottles, his pistol, and his strobe light the afternoon of the first rescue attempt.

He stopped under a net of thorn vines. There was, of course, another alternative to dying of thirst or killing himself by crawling through this jungle: He could somehow attract the NVA soldiers down in that main valley and surrender to them. The pistol . . . that would be how to do it. If he fired a series of volleys, evenly spaced to signify that it was obviously a coherent attempt to make contact, the NVA patrols that had missed him the first day would find him.

Again he tried to move his tongue over his cracked lips. They had water. They had food. They had medics to treat his leg and arm. His pistol was just there; he could see it now, lying where he had dropped it into the leaves that first afternoon. He had thirty-six rounds of ammunition in his bandoleer and six in the gun. He could fire eight five-round volleys. They would find him easily. If they got close and still couldn't see him, he had his own whistle, a shrill police-type whistle to call back to their piping little tooters. They had water, food, medics. . . . In the jungle, down along the roadways of the Trail, the NVA had built rest camps. He'd seen Intel pictures of them taken by the Green Beret recon teams . . . crude bamboo dispensaries . . . open-sided field kitchens. There'd be big green canvas water bags dripping with condensation, steel bowls of hot rice, some kind of meat sauce or fish. They ate a lot of dried fish. Tin cups of cool water. Tea, maybe, cups of hot, sweet tea.

He shook his head, and pain brought him back to the floor of the forest. Out of his feverish pain a memory came: the last conversation he'd had with Mike Smith. It had been in June, during Lance's final leave before coming overseas. Mike was at Wright-Patterson, working on weapon systems, on the new smart ordnance for the night interdiction bombing, on low-light TV and infrared sights. Lance had just completed F-4 training and final staging through his Replacement Training Unit. His next stop would be Vietnam.

He and Mike had played golf one weekday afternoon when the base course was not crowded, a cool, cloudless Midwestern day in mid-June. Mike had asked him how he felt, about to go into combat. And, for some reason, it had all come pouring out . . . Lance's unmanageable, unbreakable premonition that he would be shot down, that he would be chased through the jungle like an animal by enemy patrols.

They were toward the end of the first nine, and suddenly Lance, the competitor par excellence, was no longer even interested in playing out his ball on this hole. He and Mike sat down on the grass in the shade of a big elm tree and Lance unburdened himself. From the senior pilots he'd flown with during training at George Air Base and during his final tactical F-4 exercises, he had gotten a pretty fair, unvarnished idea of what the bombing war was really like. These pilots had shared with him their frustrations about the circumvented strategy that produced inflexible, unimaginative tactics out in the combat theater. Because of publicly announced no-bombing zones around Hanoi, Haiphong, and the northeast railroad in Route Package VI, flights hitting the standard targets almost always ingressed and egressed on the same routes; each night interdiction strike along the Trail in Laos had to be approved all the way up to the Joint Chiefs. Air Force bureaucracy churned out standard frag orders right down to standardized daily call signs. . . . all this inflexibility caused disproportionately high casualties. A *stupid* way to fight a war.

And, he told Mike, he had an unshakable premonition that he would be one of those casualties, that he would be shot down. It wasn't so much that he feared the actual combat, he said, strange as that might sound. What he was most afraid of was being captured, of becoming a POW to be brainwashed, tortured, broken, and paraded around like a goddamn zombie.

Sitting under the elm tree on a sunny June afternoon, on an empty golf course in the Midwest, Lance spoke with a mixture of quiet apprehension and deep sorrow about the American prisoners of war whom the North Vietnamese had exhibited to foreign press and television reporters that spring. These were senior Navy officers, veteran carrier pilots, tough, dedicated, professional officers. Yet the North Vietnamese had managed to force them to bow like zombies before the TV floodlights, somehow forced them to read long, detailed confessions in which they admitted to genocidal bombing and assorted other war crimes.

Lance had been particularly shaken by the much-publicized war crimes confession made by Lieutenant Commander Richard Stratton, a Skyhawk pilot from the USS *Ticonderoga* who had been shot down over North Vietnam that January. In early March, only two months after his capture, Commander Stratton had appeared before foreign reporters in Hanoi, walking like an automaton, wooden, lifeless. He was seated before the hot floodlights to read a five-page confession in which he admitted to taking part in many air raids that had been carefully, deliberately planned to inflict maximum casualties by dropping fragmentation bombs among the innocent civilian population of North Vietnam's cities. To end his bizarre confession, Stratton assured the reporters that he had been "humanely treated" by his captors. He asked forgiveness from the North Vietnamese people for the unjust, genocidal war America had unleashed on them.

Mike and Lance had been close friends since that first grueling cadet basic course six years before. They had shared a lot of good and hard times; they had always been utterly honest with each other.

Now, on the verge of his departure for combat, Lance was again open with Mike Smith. "If I go down," he said with quiet finality, "they are not going to capture me. They won't turn me into some kind of a zombie like that poor son of a bitch."

He told Mike that he was going to buy a big handgun, either a Browning .38 automatic with an extended magazine or a .357 magnum with a six-inch barrel. He was going to spend hours with that gun on the firing range, until he was satisfied that he could kill an enemy soldier before he himself was killed. If it ever came to a shoot-out in the jungle, Lance said, he did not intend to go down easily.

"I am not going to let them capture me, Mike," he repeated. "They won't get me alive."

Daylight flooded the forest floor an aqueous green. Sijan dragged himself back to his original resting place and recovered his pistol. After checking the breech and action, he snapped it back into his spring holster on his right thigh, then adjusted the leg thongs so that the holster rode on the top of his leg, out of the way of the ground and handy, should he need the gun in a hurry.

Now he got to work on the splint. As he stripped off his vest, parachute harness, and inflatable life jacket, he allowed himself to think once more about surrender. With a direct task at hand and the daylight washing away the lonely chill of the night, he could reason more clearly. Also, he realized, the loose confusion of his brain concussion had finally left him. For the first time in several days, he was fully rational. And the most rational option before him was obviously to surrender to the NVA troops down in that valley. His leg was already infected; so was his arm. The bones in the back of his right hand were probably also broken, judging from the swelling.

If he played John Wayne up here, dragging his ass through the jungle in a long-shot attempt to find open country where he could call the SAR forces back, his leg and arm might become so infected that he'd lose them to gangrene. His broken hand would knit and probably never be the same again. By following the Code of Conduct and evading capture as long as he could, he was probably condemning himself to life as a cripple, very possibly as a double amputee who would never again fly an airplane, run, or enjoy any sport.

Surrender might bring some initial mistreatment, but it would also mean food, water, and medical care. The North Vietnamese had Soviet medical supplies and East European doctors. Once they got him up to Hanoi, they'd give him antibiotics, then they'd lock him up for the duration. The North Vietnamese were well-indoctrinated communists in the middle of a long and bloody war of attrition, but they were not animals. They would probably torture him for military information and propaganda purposes. The instructors at survival school had been very clear about that point. But the NVA would keep him alive.

How long would it be, though, before the war was over? With the bombing campaign steadily escalating, soon there would be no more protected targets. Once the election was over next year, the Navy would mine Haiphong and blockade the coast. Then the army would put a couple divisions into Laos to cut the Trail around Sepone. The Americans were winning this war. It would be stupid to surrender now without even trying to evade capture.

He fingered the green nylon webbing of his life jacket harness and stared through the tree trunks toward the lighter underbrush which marked the slope to the main valley and the NVA positions. There was another reason to evade the NVA. Those enemy soldiers down there had suffered badly during the long SAR mission that first day. From the sounds of the ordnance, the Sandys must have plastered the area with cluster bombs, rockets, and 20mm, not to mention old-fashioned 250 frag bombs. The fast-movers on ResCap had dumped tons of bombs all around that valley, trying to knock out the gun sites. No doubt a lot of North Vietnamese soldiers had been killed and a lot more had been wounded . . . because of him.

Sijan had heard enough stories of what marine and army grunts did to NVA or VC prisoners they flushed out of tunnels and bunkers after ambushes where the Americans had suffered heavy casualties. When you see your buddies blown away by an invisible enemy and there's nothing you can do and then, all of a sudden, you have one of these bastards in your hands . . . The MACV orders were to take prisoners and to treat them humanely. But orders did not always work out in the bush.

There was no reason to believe that the enemy soldiers down there were any more disciplined or understanding than young American grunts in South Vietnam. If the NVA caught him, if he drew them up here by firing shots, they might just put the barrel of an AK to his head and blow his brains out. Soldiers were a lot alike, he realized. The NVA troops would not want to lug some crippled 190-pound American pilot down off this karst through all that undergrowth. They'd take one look at his leg and his arm and decide that this guy was not worth saving, and besides, this American pilot was the one who had brought down all those cluster bombs and phosphorous rockets on them. He was the reason their friends had died.

Surrender, Sijan decided with final determination, was out of the question. He would evade capture. He would try to use the hidden game trails to crawl east, off the karst, first to find water, then to locate some open ground where he could again try to contact the SAR forces and bring the Jollys back to pick him up.

There was a vicious, uncompromising war being waged here, and he could not expect compassion from the enemy. They loathed the American airmen with a deep-seated hatred. He could understand and accept that. War was absolutely the most brutal of civilized human enterprises. And he was now completely engaged in war. He was in enemy territory, and capture—at least by the enemy soldiers in this valley—probably meant execution. His job, his military duty, was to escape, to evade capture, even if he died in the attempt. But beyond any formal military duty, he owed it to himself and to his family to stay alive, to get out of this horrible place and come home.

And, he recognized, as a wave of fever chill swept over him, he could not afford to wait any longer. He had to make his splint and be on his way east, toward water, toward the open valley and the slim chance of survival and freedom.

Chapter Six

★

Da Nang Air Base

November 1967

Both Lenora Monaco and Joe Kosciusko retain a sharp memory of the anguished encounter that occurred on the hot tarmac of the Da Nang Air Base shortly after noon on Monday, November 20, 1967. In emotional interviews years later, they were able to recount in vivid detail the painful circumstances of their meeting.

The big Continental Boeing was on final approach to Da Nang. As always when they landed at a coastal base, the captain had the aircraft in a steep, fast descent that would have sent the FAA up the wall back in the States. In the passenger seats, 165 young marines stared anxiously out the windows to catch sight of Vietnam. Lenora Monaco was strapped tightly into her jump seat in the aft galley, trying to control the raw excitement she felt. It was Monday noon, Vietnam time, and she had finally been able to get a trip into Da

Nang. If she were lucky, she'd have an hour on the ground with Lance.

In Bangkok ten days earlier, Lance had told her that he'd be flying night rotation, so she was sure he would be at the base.

She leaned forward and caught a glimpse of the bright green coastline cutting past the small window in the emergency exit door. They were almost down, and there'd been no reports of ground fire to provoke a last-minute diversion to another field.

Lenora was pleased with herself for managing to get this trip. It had meant some complicated juggling of schedules, with her turning around once at Guam and doubling back to Clark, but the chance to see Lance again so soon after their time together in Bangkok was worth the effort. Once again she hoped that he had gotten the special delivery letter she had sent from Los Angeles. The post office clerk had assured her that he would, so she was confident that Lance would be down there at the foot of the stairs when she swung open the rear exit door and the humid heat of Da Nang flooded the plane.

Only when the door was open and secured and the stairs were properly locked in place, did she allow herself to look down at the tarmac. Lance was not there. Instead she saw a tall, hawk-faced young officer with pilot's sunglasses and a sweat-stained green flying suit. There was something in this young man's gaunt, sunburnt face she recognized . . . of course, Joe Kosciusko, Lance's roommate. That was so typically Lance. He probably had duty officer or something, and he had asked Joe to be sure to be here to meet her flight and to take her over to where he was working so they wouldn't waste time.

Because Joyce, the head flight attendant, was going to cover for her on turnaround and boarding, Lenora just had to wait while the marines from the last twenty rows of seats exited; then she could go down and greet Joe and be whisked off to meet Lance. Finally the last tired, somber young marine clomped out the door, blinking in the heat and midday glare, and Lenora grabbed her shoulder bag and trotted down the stairs. She had a little care package of Stateside delicacies wrapped in foil inside her bag, Wisconsin cheese and sausage, all of Lance's favorites.

As she came down the hot aluminum staircase, she slowed, noting the pinched and stricken expression on Joe's face. But the meaning of his strange look did not become immediately clear.

"Well," she said warmly, "we're here. I finally made it to Da Nang when Lance is here. Hi, I'm Lenora, and you're Joe Kosciusko, aren't you?"

Joe stepped forward and gripped her hand. "Oh, my God, Lenora . . . you don't *know*. They didn't notify you."

Lenora's heavy shoulder bag dragged down off her shoulder. "Notify me . . . what? Isn't Lance here?"

Now Joe's shoulders sagged inside the flying suit. "Lenora . . . Lance was shot down last week, right after he came back from R and R."

Lenora's bag dropped to the greasy tarmac. She swayed in a tight circle and reached out to grip the handrail of the boarding stairs.

"*No . . .*" she screamed. "No . . . no . . . *no.*"

Ahead of her, just at the end of the port wing, 165 sun-darkened Marines with young faces and the eyes of old men stood waiting in formation to board the airplane back to the World. They gazed in embarrassed fascination at this good-looking stewardess with long black hair as she screamed and shook her body in violent denial.

For a moment she tried to pull herself together in front of these boys who must have seen so much suffering and agony in the past year. But she was not able to control her emotions for long.

"Oh, God, Joe . . . *where* was he shot down?"

"In Laos," Joe said quietly, "up in Laos, at night."

Again Lenora thrashed and shook her head. "No," she said adamantly, "no . . . we're not *bombing* in Laos. . . ."

"Yes, Lenora, I'm sorry. We are bombing inside Laos." He was having a hard time with her. There was really nothing much he could say.

"Look," he finally asked, "is there anyone in the squadron . . . any of Lance's friends you want to speak to about it?"

Lenora's head snapped up. "Let me talk to Lee Ellis."

Again, Joe Kosciusko's rawboned shoulders sagged. "Lenora, I'm sorry. Lee was shot down two days before Lance, up in Pack I, while you and Lance were in Bangkok."

Lenora leaned against the boarding ramp. Up in the door of the plane, two stewardesses stared down, suddenly realizing what news had so affected her. She pulled herself up straight. "Please take me to see Colonel Armstrong."

Joe sighed and shook his head. "Lenora . . . the Colonel was flying frontseat with Lance. . . ."

"Oh, my *God,*" Lenora sighed, the tears coming now through the shock. "They're gone. They are *all* gone."

Out in the thick heat of the tarmac, the young Marines with old men's eyes watched with silent understanding.

Chapter
Seven

★

The
Mountains
of
Laos

Winter 1967

Sijan thrashed out with his left hand, blindly, behind his head in the half-light. He had discovered that the crooked-finger hook blade of his parachute knife was his best tool for cutting through the thorn vines that arched over the narrow tube of the game trail. The big bolo knife was useful for chopping through thicker brush, but this little hook, designed for cutting away tangled parachute lines, worked perfectly on the cloying wait-a-minute vines.

These thorns were a problem. He'd lost his gloves in the ejection, and now, after several days of dragging himself across the jagged rocks of the karst top through these vines, the back of his left hand was badly slashed by the green thorns. He could live with the thorn scratches, but the deeper slashes from the sharp-edged chunks of limestone were getting serious. His shoulders, his lower back, and the thick muscles of his thighs were now cut raw, badly scraped by the constant dragging across the broken rock. By loosening and adjusting his parachute harness and G-suit, he gained some protection but not enough to prevent more slashes.

That afternoon he had stopped and chewed some of the bitter ferns that grew among the sharp limestone at the edges of the narrow trail. There was not much juice in the leaves, but they gave the feeling of moisture in his mouth. After he had rested, he cut away the cuff from the right leg of his flying suit to bandage his left hand and protect it from the thorns and broken stone.

Piece by piece, he was cutting up his clothing and equipment to fashion bandages and makeshift protection for his injured body. If only this game trail were a *little* wider and the covering vines and brush were not quite so low. If only the ground were more even, not crazy, tilted slabs of smashed-up, overgrown rock, the edges sharp as coarse wood rasps . . . Then he could actually make some speed across the ground. But the Trail had been opened by barking deer, forest rats, and bush pigs. None of these animals was bigger than a medium-sized dog. Their path through the brush, up and down this broken terrain, was half as wide as Sijan's shoulders. He had to squirm and hack his way through the tangle of vines and branches to make any progress. Several times he slipped headfirst into trench-like depressions and it took painful hours to climb out the other side.

If he had been able to stand upright and use both his hands, he could have moved at a more normal pace, climbing and chopping away the waist-high foliage with his bolo knife. But standing was not possible. He had tried it only once, after he had made his splint using inflated life jacket compartments laced tight against his injured leg with the cutaway right leg of his G-suit as a protective sheath. The splint gave him adequate horizontal support but no vertical rigidity. Trying to stand upright would only worsen his wound and incapacitate him with pain.

Pain, of course, was constant. Beneath his back the ground was broken limestone cleared of leaf mulch by animal hooves. The improvised protection of the chute harness and G-suit waist would not protect his hips and shoulders very long unless he found smoother, more level ground. After seven days and about six hundred yards' progress toward the east, his back was a bleeding mess. It did not take much imagination to realize that eventually the nylon mesh backing of his survival vest and even the thick straps of his parachute harness would wear through and his full back, not just his shoulders and hips, would be cut badly.

He was nearing the eastern edge of the karst, and he would be able to follow the thread of a game trail down a gully to softer ground. And to water. There had to be water lower down. This porous limestone of the karst top, pocked regularly with sinkholes and slashed by fissures, retained no standing water. But lower down, there was dirt, actual soil, there had to be. And there would be streams, clear mountain streams of cold, flowing water.

Until he found that water, no other human need, no other aspect of his evasion plan had any meaning. His thirst was reaching the point at which rational thought was impossible. The bitter ferns seemed to help a little, and he had also discovered that he could eat the squirming green leeches he jerked from his wrists and legs. Several times he had found fat white beetle grubs in dead wood nearby. But these were foul, incomplete substitutes for water. He had to find a stream or spring soon, or he would die. So he had no choice. He had to drag his scraped, bleeding body east.

Sijan stroked blindly with the hook blade of his knife, cutting away thorny vine tendrils. He dug in his right boot heel and his left elbow, clenched his buttocks on the sharp rock, and threw himself backward. Another yard of progress.

Again he thrashed above his head to cut vine. It was late afternoon, judging from the green light on the forest roof. Tonight he would not stop. He would push himself until he could not move. Then he would sleep. By forcing his body to the point of absolute exhaustion, he knew, he would be able to slip into unconsciousness and actually get some rest, despite the pain from his wounds and scraped flesh, despite the crushing presence of the thirst.

His grasp on time had slipped again. Day and night were very much the same. But now, at night, it was cold, and he shivered when he stopped moving. The night chill did bring a few drops of dew to the ferns. He found that he could lean over and lick the leaves before he tore them away to chew. The dew that he drank amounted to less than a few ounces each night, but the moisture kept his mouth and lips from drying up completely.

At night there were flares over the valley and the smacking thud of bombs hitting at the target zone around the ford. Flak guns and automatic weapons answered from the roadway and ridgetops. The glaring flares and the sounds of the bombing gave him a good sense of direction, and he didn't have to continually verify his route with his compass.

Sometimes at night he caught the muted roar of truck engines below the karst. The war had not stopped. He was still a soldier, alone in enemy territory. Blindly he dragged his crippled body east, toward the edge of the karst. Toward water.

The vine tore away, and he felt his shoulders drop. Instinctively he tried to cradle his head with his hands as he fell through thorn vines and tangled brush, down the stony chute of the gully, hitting first one side of the vine-covered wall, then the other. Thorns snagged at his cumbersome splint, wrenching his leg. His mangled hand was caught in a skein of branches. His head hit sharp stone.

The world exploded once again. Darkness.

Daylight. Green shadows. Pain and thirst. Flies, leeches. He lay, head down in a steep jumble of vine-choked limestone, hanging from his splint and chute harness. Slowly he worked to free his body from the web of thorns. Too late he saw that he was going to fall again, tumble down the near-vertical lip of the gully. His face smashed jagged limestone. Darkness.

The world returned with water on his face. Flies, leeches on his hands. *Water.* He opened his eyes to the pain, then ran his tongue across the cratered edges of his mouth. There was gray sky above the gully, the first sky that he had seen in ten days. Rain fell softly from that sky, a misty, trailing rain that beaded on his face, on the broken, stony ground, on the broad leaves of the scrub jungle brush choking the gully.

He licked. He licked the rainwater from his own exposed flesh, from the shiny nylon of his vest and parachute harness, from the leaves, from the stones. The rain trailed down in a fine, cool mist, and he lay on his back, his head tilted, his mouth open, letting the living fluid of the rain fall into the dry confines of his body.

Time moved. Night. The rain fell harder, in cold drops now. He ripped away a piece of his rancid T-shirt and spread it open to soak up the steadily falling rain. When it was sodden, he held the cloth above his mouth and squeezed out the water.

Time was slow, ebbing in strange ways in the wet darkness. All night he squeezed the cloth into his mouth. When the gray sky grew light again, he could hear trucks rumbling along unseen roads to the right of this steep gully. But there was another sound that he had thought he would never hear again. Water, running water, trickling over stones, a stream.

He carefully placed his T-shirt water rag in a pocket of his flight suit, then dragged his body down the jumbled, stony tube of the gully toward the sound of water.

The stream was no more than a wet depression in the vines and smooth interlocking roots. But there were several inches of transparent water gurgling over the mossy stones. Twisting on his mangled limbs, he lay belly down over the stream bed and thrust his face into the water. He drank for a long time. His stomach and esophagus burned. Again he drank. The sky clouded over more darkly, and rain pelted down onto the low jungle trees filling the gully. He drank, then rolled onto his back and slept.

Day again. Then chill night. Rain and bands of frozen, distant stars in the black sky. Wind in the trees. Cold. Bombs smashed into the forest to the south and east. Flares. He drank water and slept.

Another gray morning. He struggled to fill half his water bag. But exhaustion swept over him and he slept.

Night. The leeches woke him, on his throat, on his wrists and ankles. He gouged them away and managed to mash them between his teeth. The moss of the stream bed was tasteless, the cress and grasses at the edge of the stream were strangely salty. He dragged himself down the stony bed of the stream, harvesting moss and cress, water bugs and grubs.

There was daylight, sometimes sunshine. There was chill night, usually with dripping rain. He moved in broken spasms down the slope of the gully under the interlocking roof of scrub jungle that had blocked out all view of the sky. His compass told him he was traveling east, northeast. He had no idea of how fast he was moving, but he did realize that it took most of the daylight energy to rip away enough moss and springy green cress to partially fill his stomach.

This slow, Neanderthal gathering of greens and insects to eat was hampering his progress. In the cool light of one morning, he consulted his sodden cloth survival map and made his decision. From now on, he would not stop to gather food. He would move continually ahead, as he had that first week, day and night, pausing now occasionally to drink. He would drag himself for as long as he could until he dropped. Then he would rest. After he had slept, he would eat whatever he could easily reach and start to crawl again.

The weather was closing down. Although the main mountain ridge, six miles to the east, formed a barrier to the solid overcast of the northeast monsoon, every few days clouds did boil up through the Ban Kari Pass from North Vietnam and fill this valley. Soon there would be more days of low ceiling than periods of VFR. The Air Force interdiction efforts would shift further south, and few planes would come up here under the cloud deck. If he were going to find a way to heat those batteries and coax a few minutes of transmit time out of them, he had to have clear weather to use his signal mirror and strobe as a follow-up signal.

But there was not much clear weather remaining up in these mountains. Now that he had water and a relatively open route to crawl down off the main body of the karst, he had to push himself again. Food and sleep would have to wait. Water would keep him going. Thirst was behind him. Now he had to focus all his intense concentration and really drive himself.

Sijan folded his survival map and returned it to the upper pouch of his vest. Once more he used his compass to verify that the stream bed led east to the open valley floor. He tied his jiggling water bag securely across his chest, braced his mind and body for the inevitable shock of the pain, and scurried backward down the stony stream bed.

Chapter Eight

Milwaukee, Wisconsin

December 1967

For Lance Sijan's family, the news of his shoot-down had come in a series of telegrams and telephone calls from the Air Force, replete with phrases such as "deep regret" and "sincere condolences." Their initial shock quickly gave way to anguished uncertainty, especially after they received the first fragmentary reports of the unsuccessful search and rescue effort. During long, emotionally wrought interviews sixteen years after those terrible months, the Sijans could still clearly recall the days and nights of that bleak winter.

Sylvester Sijan sat at the mahogany desk in his living room holding the pen stiffly in his muscular hand. A split log burned in the fireplace nearby, and Laddie, the family dog, was curled at his feet.

Outside the window a cold wind blew off the gray lake, churning up leaves in the park. It was early afternoon on the first Monday in December. Lance's plane had been shot down twenty-four days before.

Syl was alone in the house. Marc and Janine were at school, and Jane was at the supermarket. He had chosen this time to compose the first letter to Lance from the family. Once they had read and approved his message, he would complete the Red Cross form which would accompany it, and then he would take it to the post office, register the envelope, and the letter would be dispatched . . . like a note in a bottle, like a child's message tied to the string of a helium balloon at the state fair. The letter would be sent into a void of uncertainty, into the darkness of the war in Asia.

He waited, the pen just above the untouched paper. It was suddenly so difficult to write a letter to Lance, to his beloved son who had disappeared into the jungle mountains of Laos. Syl Sijan knew with absolute certainty that Lance was still alive. But he was absolutely uncertain of Lance's status. Was he already a prisoner? Was he still out there in those mountains, hiding with his broken leg? Had they already taken him to Hanoi to be paraded through the streets like a circus animal?

He waited in the warm, silent room, alone, trying to feel a thread of human connection that would stretch all the way from this comfortable home in the center of America to the stinking shadows of that Asian jungle.

The Air Force had been very considerate with details, and the officers in Da Nang had provided as much information as they could about the loss of Lance's plane and about the heartbreaking, unsuccessful rescue attempt. Syl Sijan knew his son very well. He realized that Lance would not give up easily, and he knew that Lance would not allow himself to be used as bait in the flak trap that the senior officers of the 366th Fighter Wing had described in their letters.

From where he sat, Syl could look up at the family picture gallery which filled the entire stairwell to the second floor. There was Lance at Bay View High in his gaudy silk costume as the King of Siam, the lead role in the school's spring operetta *The King and I*. As a sophomore with no stage experience, he had decided one day that he would win the lead in the operetta, that he would work hard and beat all the considerable competition from the seasoned upperclassmen. Lance had set his course, and he had held it. That May, the school's production of *The King and I* was acclaimed all over town as a truly professional effort, and a good deal of the acclaim went to Lance.

Higher up the wall was a picture of Lance in his football uniform, tight end, Number 23, all-city captain of the city championship team, 1959. Below this was another theatrical picture, the school production of *Around the World in Eighty Days;* Lance was Phileas Fogg, again the male lead.

Syl's eye moved across the familiar gallery. Lance shaking hands with Senator Wiley before the senator presided at Lance's inauguration as president of Bay View's student government. Lance as commencement speaker, Lance at the Academy in dress uniform. And all the others.

In each framed photograph a handsome, self-possessed young man with dark, sensitive eyes stared out into the living room. It was impossible for Syl to reconcile these pictures of Lance—literally the athletic, artistic, and social epitome of his generation—with the image of Lance as a brutalized, half-starved prisoner. But, for Lance's sake, Syl hoped that he had found some way to surrender, that he was now in enemy custody so that his wounds could be treated. He knew his son's physical strength and incredible determination from long experience. Unless Lance was already now a prisoner, he might drive himself to death in those mountains, evading capture.

And if Lance met enemy soldiers in the jungle, he might well put up such a fight that they would never capture him alive. Syl had not known Lance to be a fighter as a boy, a rough, competitive athlete, sure, but never a guy who liked to use his fists. But two years earlier he had seen Lance the adult in a fight, and Syl had been shocked at his son's savage competence.

The Sijan family ran a tavern, a well-known neighborhood landmark called the Log Cabin on Milwaukee's South Side, across the street from the Allen Bradley factory. Every New Year's Eve, it was an Allen Bradley tradition for hundreds of employees to fill the tavern at quitting time and line the long oak bar for a few holiday drinks. New Year's 1965 Lance was home from his last year at the Academy and, as always, helped out at the bar.

That afternoon three drunken young strangers decided to wreck the fun of the Allen Bradley regulars by attacking a customer with a broken beer bottle and provoking a free-for-all brawl. No sooner had the tallest most foulmouthed of the outsiders broken his bottle of Schlitz than Lance had vaulted the bar. In a blur of smashing violence, Lance pummeled the man with karate chops until he dropped the bottle and fell to the floor. Then Lance immobilized the second man with a finger lock while Syl Sijan throttled the third hapless troublemaker with a viselike forearm across the throat. Less than two minutes after the abortive brawl had been provoked, Lance threw his two victims out onto the icy sidewalk.

What most impressed Syl that afternoon was not his son's strength or even his courage but rather the cool, detached, and professional manner with which he dispatched the armed thugs. Lance, he saw, had become a soldier. And Lance did not do things halfway. He never had, and he sure as hell would not start now, in the middle of a war.

Syl began to write, a steady flow of even block letters, the straightforward hand of a man who knew who he was and had decided what he had to say.

"The Livingroom, at Home, 4 Dec., 1967," he began.

"Dear Son,

"No need to say that this is the most difficult letter to write. We know to some extent what has happened to you, approximately where and when. . . ."

Syl wrote another line, then paused. It was important to let Lance know that the family's prayers were directly focused on him.

"May the Good Lord keep you and watch over you," Lance's father wrote. "Win, lose, or draw, we are with you all the way. . . ."

Syl Sijan leaned forward in the warm firelight. The letter, which had been so difficult to begin, was moving now. He felt back in contact with Lance. But he had only one page. That was the arbitrary limit imposed by the North Vietnamese. One page with so little space to try to say so much.

Chapter Nine

★

The Mountains of Laos

Winter 1967

The stream bed split and twisted on the valley floor. Water-smoothed stones gave way to rough shelves of rock half-covered with moss. Mudbanks blocked the channel. Above the cut of the stream bed, the second-growth scrub jungle arched into a dense tunnel. Two feet back from the muddy bank, the solid tangle of vines and undergrowth prevented any possible escape from the stream.

Sijan dragged his body across the wet rock ledges and through the cloying, deadwood tangles of the mudbanks. The fabric of his flight suit had torn away from his shoulders, hips, and the right leg. Although some of the stone of the stream bed was smoother than the dry rock of the karst, the rocky shelves were still abrasive limestone. The flesh on the exposed parts of his body had now been scraped down to a red pulp that oozed clear liquid. Both his hands were raw and swollen now. His good left arm was gouged open from the elbow to the wrist.

He had tried to keep track of time, to count the days and nights since he had found water and begun crawling down the stream. But time had stopped moving as it did in the normal world. Some warm days seemed to last impossibly long. Biting flies and leeches. Some nights roared by in a fast agony of lurching backward, his chest filling and collapsing, his raw flesh on fire. Sometimes he moved only through space. Distance, not time.

But still he moved east, toward the northern loop of the orange laterite roadway he had seen while he was hanging shocked and battered in his parachute harness. Sijan had finally accepted the fact that he had no way to gauge how many days he had been dragging his crippled body east. But he could feel that his beard and hair had grown long. And he could also sense the low rain clouds above the tangled jungle tunnel closing the stream bed from the sky. If he could find a break in the trees, on a clear night, he might be able to tell from the phase of the moon how long this . . . struggle . . . had been going on.

He was sure it had been at least a month since the plane had exploded on bomb release, more than a month since that terrible afternoon when the Jollys had come so close. When he bothered to look at his arms or the exposed flesh of his right leg, he was repeatedly surprised at how much weight he had lost. He did not *feel* that skinny. Maybe his eyes were getting weak from this constant moldy green gloom.

Sometime in the past few days, the hunger had left him. It had just gone away while he was sleeping, propped against the mudbank. Now, with his hunger gone, he felt lighter, stronger, less distracted. He drank as much water as he could whenever he stopped, but now he did not bother to drag down handfuls of grass or the tendrils of overhanging vines. He did not need anything to chew anymore. Water was enough. The hunger had left him. It was waiting . . . until he reached open ground and called the Jollys in. Then his body would switch back to a more normal operating mode and accept food. For now water was all he needed.

Morning. The stream widened to three channels, separated by open mud and gravel banks. Overhead the branches of the brush became naked gray, spindly. Hot sunlight blinded him. Cold rain hurt his face. The sky was so wide. Sunshine. Polychrome butterflies danced above the drying mud. Night. Truck engines. Branches like splintered bones against the pale sky. Day again.

Night, cold rain. Time. Flies and leeches. Daylight again. Sun.

With the weak morning light he saw that the stream was cutting through a flatland of red mud and gray leafless brush. This area was close to the road. The Ranchhand planes had sprayed defoliant; the Phantoms had hit the area with 750s and cluster bombs. There were scattered rocky humps that blocked his view to the road. The sunlight was brutal. It brought flies. He found a shady undercut in the bank and slept.

Night. Wind and chill rain. Now scudding cloud and cold stars. A left-handed sliver of waning moon. He lay with his bleeding shoulders against the bank, gazing at the moon. Below him the weight of his splinted leg floated in the shallow stream. His brain was trying to reason . . . twenty-eight days in a lunar cycle. New moon the night they went down, now old dying crescent. New moon to full, to no moon, to new moon . . . to full . . . to last quarter, *again*? How many days? More than thirty . . . more than forty. Clouds. Darkness.

Trucks passing close by in the night. He could see the yellow glow of their headlights. The enemy. He slid lower down the mudbank. Escape. Evasion and escape.

He had come so far, so long. All that pain. The hunger before it had left him in the night. No surrender now. Open ground. Call the Jollys. Now it was almost over.

Morning. Gray mist. He filled his water bag and heaved his body over the crusty lip of the stream bed, into the fetid mud of the defoliated scrub jungle. Puddles gleamed with greasy rainbows. There were no butterflies. He pulled his shrunken frame through the mud, around the wide bomb craters. The dead roots of the trees snagged his splint. His raw hips scraped the dry mud and the splintered wood. He moved. He did not think.

Day. Then rainy night. Mosquitos spilled up in clouds from the flooded craters. Sunshine. Heat. He tried to think. There had been a plan. But now his brain would not tell him. Mirror. Radio . . . strobe light?

His vest hung loose, a mass of caked mud, dried blood, and slime. His holster was empty. The strobe light was gone. Its pocket in the vest was also gone. Night, truck lights close by. They could not see him, lying against the heaped mud side of this bomb crater.

His mind came back. Find the road. Use your mirror. Call the Jollys. Find the road. Rain and dark wind in the bony trees. He dragged himself to the edge of the road and lay hidden by a jumble of mud and smashed branches thrown up in a low wall by a bulldozer. He could think again. In the morning he would crawl out onto that open roadway and call in the Jollys. The NVA did not travel during daylight. In the morning he would have the road all to himself.

Night and cold rain. He did not sleep. Green mist and wet daylight. He clawed over the mud wall and slid down the bank toward the rutted laterite road. His body would not move through the jumbled branches. He thrashed and squirmed. His heart thudded in his chest, in his throat and ears. The branches held him fast. He kicked and grabbed at splinters with the bloody hooks of his fingers. The branches broke, and he tumbled to the road. Darkness.

Daylight rose misty green along the ridges. Lance Sijan lay unconscious on a truck track three miles northeast of the Ban Loboy Ford. It was dawn on Monday, December 25, 1967. Christmas morning. Sijan had been on the ground, evading capture by the enemy, for forty-six days.

The first group of trucks to leave the hidden rest area halfway down the pass reached the valley just after dawn. This was a convoy of camouflaged Soviet military trucks carrying NVA infantry replacements for the pending victory offensive in the South. The big trucks traveled fast, jolting across the deep ruts, careening around the turns and abrupt detours that skirted bombed-out sections of the road. The Christmas cease-fire and bombing halt would last only twenty-four hours, and transportation battalions had priority orders to move as many troops and as much materiel as far south as possible during the lull in bombing.

The lead driver saw the body sprawled across the road and braked hard. Behind him the trucks of the convoy also braked, some almost hitting the trucks ahead.

A soldier jumped from the muddy cab and approached the strange shape on the muddy ruts. It was some kind of a . . . *man*, a long skeleton in muddy rags, bound together with twisted straps and metal buckles. White skin near the head and raw, bleeding expanses of flesh showed everywhere.

Chapter Ten

Ban Kari Pass, North Vietnam

Winter 1967

No aspect of Lance Sijan's struggle has received as much attention as the events that took place at the NVA road camp near the Ban Kari Pass. It was in the camp's primitive dispensary that Sijan displayed his truly indomitable spirit, his unquenchable determination to escape captivity, to somehow return to his family in America. His actions at this camp played a large part in securing him the impressive honors later bestowed on him. Therefore it is important to note that it was not Sijan himself who first described these events to other American prisoners of war but rather the North Vietnamese officer known as the Rodent who provided the incredible details to Guy Gruters and Bob Craner at the Bamboo Prison near Vinh.

Once Gruters learned of Sijan's actions at the camp, he closely questioned Lance about what happened there. Subsequently Gruters and Craner both repeatedly verified Lance's story with him to be sure his memory—recounted between bouts of delirium—remained consistent. The dramatic re-creation that follows is based on their accounts, delivered in their official POW debriefings and in subsequent lengthy interviews.

Rain fell steadily on the thatch roof of the dispensary hut. The unchinked walls of vertical bamboo allowed the chill wind to swirl through the narrow room. Puddles lay on the beaten earth floor.

Sijan was sprawled on a wet pallet of split bamboo. The North Vietnamese road security troops who had received him at this transportation battalion camp had stripped away the shredded remnants of his flight suit and parachute harness and sluiced him with water while he was still unconscious. Then they had clipped off most of his impossibly tangled hair and matted beard and left him in the care of a young People's Army medical orderly.

Probably the medic had never seen a living person in such horrible condition. It was obvious that the American would die soon, so it was just as well that the medic had not received authorization to use any of his precious reserve of antibiotics, iodine, and sterile dressings to treat the prisoner's wounds.

Sijan's head rested on a block of hardwood. His bony torso was covered by a black cotton peasant's shirt. The orderly had managed to slip his lower body into a pair of black cotton trousers, the left leg cut open to accommodate the grossly swollen mass of his fractured limb.

Twice the next day, in midmorning and late afternoon, the orderly tried to feed the prisoner rice and boiled greens from the camp kitchen. But the American managed to swallow only a few strangled mouthfuls before his jaws clamped shut.

On the third morning Sijan awoke and rose on his least-injured elbow. He looked directly at the startled orderly and called out in a surprisingly loud voice, "Water . . . can you give me some water?"

Sijan awoke in daylight. The small Vietnamese who wore the green shirt that stank of woodsmoke was leaning over him with food, gesturing with the greasy tin spoon for him to open his mouth. In the hollow of the spoon Sijan saw a clot of rice laced with green shreds and flecks of gray fish. Food. He turned his head away and tried to think of sleep. The medic brusquely flipped his chin back and gestured once more with the spoon and food bowl.

Sijan opened his lips. The tepid ball of rice and greens lay in his mouth. He closed his lips and let the saliva pool. Gingerly he moved his jaw from the right to the left and back again. The lump of rice moved in his mouth, hard, cold, like a chunk of wood. He did not immediately understand what he was to do with this object in his mouth. Food . . . He was supposed to swallow this. Swallow food like you swallow water. But . . . there was no place for the food to go . . . Before . . . before all that time in the mountains, there had been a place for food to move inside his body. A stomach, liver, intestines . . . a *system* for food to be converted into energy through the complexities of metabolism. He understood the process. But now, all that had changed. He was no longer part of the old way, that original system.

Still . . . it was better to play this one along for a while, to swallow the lump of rice and greens, even if it would just stick down there below his ribs undigested. Sijan knew that this man brought him water, and water was important if he were going to keep up his strength for his escape. He let the food jerk slowly down his tight throat. Obediently he opened his mouth again for the next spoonful. As the man leaned forward, Sijan looked past his shoulder at the gray sky, visible through the gaping doorway of the hut. The heavy green forest began only a few yards from the doorway.

It was important now to gain their confidence, to let them think he was a docile, badly wounded enemy prisoner who depended on them for everything. Soon, when he had more water, he would be strong enough to escape from here. Now, he had to pretend to need their food.

Hard, slashing rain. Rats squeaking overhead in the mildewed thatch. Sijan lay on his back staring out at the rain bouncing off the beaten mud. The young medic dozed on his mat with his back to the large supply chest. Sijan tried to guess the time of day and the number of days he had lain here on this bamboo mat. It was late afternoon, probably around five. Sometime earlier, the medic had brought him food again and had spoken in that grunting, flip-flop language that seemed so completely different than the Vietnamese he had studied with tapes and phrase book in his spare time back at Da Nang.

Maybe North Vietnamese *was* a different dialect. No. There was a better explanation. Fever. Lingering fever . . . wound shock. His mind was affected. Just now, he could think pretty well. But, he knew, there were long periods, hours, even days at a time, when his brain shut down, when his thoughts weren't anywhere near straight. Then perceptions got weird. The rats up in the roof *said* things. The medic's words sounded like a tape recorder playing backward . . . underwater. There hadn't been too much of that crazy stuff out in the jungle. Why now?

It didn't matter. What was important was to use the times of straight thinking the best way he could. He was in a bad situation here, but it sure as hell wasn't as bad as it could be. They had not shot him. They hadn't even tried to interrogate him. The food they kept forcing him to eat was much better than he had expected from the descriptions of prison camp food he'd gotten at survival school. As far as he could tell, he was being fed the same rations as the medic and the two little helpers who came in here sometimes to eat. Rice with some kind of bitter spinach in it and little pieces of fish. If he was getting the same food as the medic and the soldiers, it probably meant that this was not a real prison camp. More likely this setup was one of their camouflaged R and R bases in the jungle alongside the Trail. The hut itself looked like one of those Montagnard buildings he'd flown over near the Special Forces camps down in II Corps when they'd do the regular flybys to keep the Green Berets happy and the NVA on their toes.

In fact, at some point that morning, Sijan had seen what looked like a Montagnard worker or coolie right outside the door of this hut . . . a tiny, shrunken guy with brass loops in his ears in a kind of loincloth and blanket cape lugging something heavy on his back in a big old woven basket. An NVA soldier in green fatigues had screamed at the guy when he stared in through the door to see the prisoner. The little fellow had double-timed out of there, obviously scared of the soldier.

Interesting. According to Intel, the Montagnards hated the VC and NVA. They hated the ARVN, too, but they tended to get along with the Special Forces teams who ran the Salem House deep recon missions up here and with the various other assorted American spooks who flew in and out of these mountains in their souped-up black H-34s.

The Montagnards liked money . . . *gold*. And the Americans had *beaucoup*. If a guy could get back up in these hills and find a friendly clan or tribe or whatever they called themselves, he could make a deal. The Green Beret recon teams were coming in and out of here all the time. Almost every mission Intel briefing had a different restricted zone to plot on the charts where you couldn't dump ordnance either safe or armed because there were spooky groups crawling around down there. They had people all the way up north past the Mu Gia and all the way down into Cambodia. And most of the teams worked with the Meo and the Mungs and the other tribes of hill people who hated the lowland Vietnamese, North or South.

So the situation was not as bad as it might have been. If a guy could get out of this hut, the forest started thirty feet away. There had to be trails, so the going would be fast. That little guy with the cape was barefoot, wide old stubby feet with thick toes. The NVA soldiers wore these canvas, rubber-soled Bata boots. They left a pretty clear footprint in the mud. All he had to do was find a path without those boot prints and head on up. Sooner or later he'd come on some Montagnards, and he could make his deal. The word from Snake School was that these guys spoke French more than they did Vietnamese. Their own language first, naturally, but after that, French, from colonial days . . . scouts for the French Army.

That made things easier. He had no idea what the word in Vietnamese was for gold. But he remembered it in French . . . Or . . . *Vous aurez beaucoup d'or, si vous m'aidez.* . . .

Sijan rested his head on the smooth block of hardwood and began to focus his mind on the French phrases he would use when he found the friendly Montagnards. . . . *Je suis un pilot Américain. Si . . . vous m'aidez . . . vous aurez beaucoup d'or. Contactez les soldats Américains. . . . Je suis un pilot Américain.* . . .

The monsoon rain slashed into the verminous thatch of the hut roof. A kilometer away, heavily laden Soviet trucks rumbled up the steep, muddy roadway in low gear. The rutted lanes separating the hut and *marao* longhouses of the village were deserted. Sijan lay in painful silence, his mind focused once more on escape, on the hope of continuing his life in freedom.

Another morning of pounding rain. Sijan ate most of the rice bowl the medic forced on him and drank three cups of water. The medic lit a kerosene lamp as much for warmth as light and huddled near it, wrapped in a blanket. Sometime later a soldier burst through the doorway, wrapped in a clumsy rubber poncho. He and the medic jabbered at each other for a while and the medic seemed to be arguing. After a long discussion, the medic pulled on his own poncho, picked up a canvas kit bag, and disappeared out into the downpour.

The soldier folded his poncho into a cushion and sat on it, his back to the medical chest, watching Sijan. The only sound in the narrow hut was the drumming rain and the occasional jibber of a rat or lizard in the roof thatch. Sijan closed his eyes as if he were sleeping. He forced slow, loud breaths through his dry mouth. Soon he heard the guard settle lower on his improvised pallet. Sijan waited inside his injured body, his mind straight and cool, in absolute control . . . like during a tricky crosswind landing on a wet strip, his hands on stick and throttles, his feet even on the rudder pedals. Every element of the problem under control, mind and body in tune . . . a perfect reverse pattern that caught the secondary, flat-assed faked, twenty yards away. Timing . . . the stage floodlights dimming and the hot blue spots blinking on from above the balcony. Move right, with mind and body exactly in synch . . . karate. Unarmed combat. The focusing of body and mind. Some of the guys called it Zen. When you hit, strike *through* the opponent. The target is the other *side*. . . .

Sijan slowly opened one eye, then the other. The skinny soldier in wet green fatigues was sleeping in his place. A stumpy carbine with pale wooden stock rested next to him. So did his webbed ammunition pouch and steel water bottle. A carbine. Too bad it wasn't an AK-47. With a fast-firing gun like an AK and enough ammo, a guy could defend himself. But . . . a carbine was better than nothing. At least he could trade it to the Montagnards. Time . . . somewhere around noon. But dark. Heavy cloud deck, hard rain. Nobody's moving around out there today unless they have to. Rain like that will cover tracks. It had to be now.

Sijan watched the dozing guard. His mind was cool and straight, just like on ground-controlled approach final to a dicey, crosswind flare-out. But part of his unconscious went back home. Dad, in the park. In the living room, at night in the winter, talking to him and Marc about the family. Sijan was a proud Serbian name. Serbia had been a great country, a tough mountain country, fought over, crushed, but *never* defeated. The Serbs were known all over the world as savage, courageous soldiers, especially when outnumbered. They would struggle against any odds. In a close-quarters fight, there were none better. The Austrians had learned that; so had the damn Nazis. The Serbs were a peaceful people, until they were invaded. Then they fought back like lions. . . .

Mom always smiled. *Irish*-Serbian, she'd say softly but with a firm tone, not Serbian-Irish. It was an old family joke, a warm, ongoing rivalry. The Attridge side of the family was just as tough as the Sijans, she'd add. The Irish were no sissies. *They* had been crushed but never defeated. They . . .

Child memories. Two strong, resilient, and deeply loving parents. Winter evenings after dinner, the homework on the dining room table. Family stories of Serbia and Ireland. Outside, the long Wisconsin winter moaned against the storm windows. How could he have ever known as he spread open his World Geography book on the tablecloth that fifteen years later he would be required to test the ultimate fabric of his inherited mental and physical toughness?

Now. Sijan drew his maimed right hand across his face and produced a strangled, sputtering cough. He moaned loudly, then called out. "Hey . . . Guard. I need help. Come here. . . . come on over here, man." Beckoning with the bloody hook of his right hand, he willed the muscles of his left forearm and hand into metallic rigidity.

The guard stumbled to his knees and grunted. Staring sharply at Sijan, he shook his head, then looked to the open doorway and the gray wall of rain. Sijan moaned again and beckoned the guard. Slowly, with an obvious mixture of disgust and apprehension, the guard moved nearer Sijan's pallet. Sijan opened his mouth and whispered some faint gibberish. The guard spoke, an angry query. Again Sijan whispered, beckoning with his right hand.

Rocking on his muddy boots, the young guard did not seem eager to bend low over the bleeding skeleton. Sijan produced a choking, garbled whisper. At last the soldier leaned close over Sijan's face.

The karate chop fell like a slaughterhouse hammer, striking the soldier at the base of his skull where the cervical vertebrae are most vulnerable. His head jerked back at an impossible angle. His eyes sparked and extinguished, and his arms flew out in reflex. A harsh sigh was the only sound from his gaping mouth.

Sijan heaved the unconscious body aside and ripped away the soldier's fatigue shirt. He threw himself off the pallet and tied the shirt as best he could around his swollen leg. Then he scurried backward to the medical chest and retrieved the soldier's web gear and carbine. Using the butt of the weapon as a support, Sijan thrust himself backward, out the door of the hut, into the stinging downpour.

His chest was burning with excitement and the stress of savage effort. His injured limbs blazed pain. He rowed himself backward on the fleshless bones of his skeleton, up the muddy lane to the green edge of the jungle. His lungs filled with the rotting scent of the monsoon forest. His head jerked from side to side in the hard rain, searching for any sign of the enemy. The gray, thatched huts were dark, silent.

A trail opened, spliced in three directions. Rock. More bare limestone, bordered here by rutted mud. Vines. Arching green jungle overhead. Again the path branched, and he took the narrower, upper branch, away from the downslope of the pass, away from the main axis of the Trail, away from the enemy. Up the narrow track through snagging vines, over sharp limestone. His lungs and heart were going to crash through his fragile ribs. Breath would not come. He forced himself further. Overhead the jungle darkened, the cooling rain pulled back into the sky. Only fire now. Flame in his body, shiny flecks of fire pulsing before his eyes. He sagged into the mud, the sparks weaving through his vision. Too weak, too much pain.

Again he threw himself backward, up the narrow path. The pain and pulsing embers washed around him. In the center of his bony shell was his brain, still cool, still straight. But his body was going away, cut and slashed by these pulsing chunks of fire. Shiny fire. Little dancing bulbs of red-and-yellow flame, weaving, touching . . . Christmas bulbs of dazzling pain. But so sharp, so deep they cut.

Far away his left hand gripped the wet metal and wood of the enemy weapon. The butt dug into the mud and his bare right heel thrust down. The sodden, half-naked skeleton jerked a few feet further up the Trail, deeper into the dripping jungle.

A thousand meters below, in the rain-battered road camp, a People's Army officer stood in the downpour blowing his whistle. Shrill, mournful blasts. Soldiers tumbled out of the dripping huts pulling ponchos over their heads. The officer screamed angry orders and pointed his long Nagant pistol up the jungle trail. Rain beat harder on the frightened faces of the soldiers and the half-naked Montagnards. High overhead, above the gray roof of the monsoon, jet engines growled and rumbled.

Chapter
Eleven

Rao
Nay
Valley,
North
Vietnam

December 1967

Years after the gloomy monsoon afternoon of December 21, 1967, Bob Craner and Guy Gruters retained clear memories of the last moments of their final combat mission.

Misty 3 flew four-hundred-knot S-turns beneath the low stratus deck, fifteen hundred feet above the Rao Nay River Valley of North Vietnam. In the frontseat of this F-100-F fast FAC Major Bob Craner gazed with mounting alarm at the cherry-red tracers looping up at them. His backseater, Captain Guy Gruters, had the detailed chart folded neatly on his map case and was plotting the exact position of the sixth 57mm flak site that the NVA had recently moved into the valley. The guns were dug into camouflaged positions to protect the valley roads, major LOC tributaries feeding up to the Mu Gia Pass and the Trail inside Laos. With the Christmas bombing halt coming, the enemy would be sending truck convoys up this valley nonstop. And under the holiday cease-fire rules, the Americans could do nothing to stop the convoys. But there were still seventy-two hours until the truce, plenty of time to get some F-4 and F-105 flights fragged in here to take out these new 57mm sites.

The smoking cannon tracers arced up from the green ridges, bright in the dull afternoon under the clouds. Trolling like this, Craner could not jink. Violent evasive maneuvers would have thrown off Guy's position plotting. But, even at four hundred knots, S-turns at low, level flight were not going to fake out those veteran NVA gunners much longer. Already the gray tube of daylight bounded by the overcast, the jungle ridges, and the flat green farm valley was laced with the bands of tracers that now began to cross and converge ahead and behind the banking jet.

From the cockpit, the tracers seemed to sail far out ahead of the plane, then fall slowly, almost lazily back, gaining speed as they approached. In the last seconds of their visible flight, they tore past the thin Plexiglas cockpit at supersonic speed, some missing the plane's thin metal skin by inches. Only a cool, experienced pilot like Craner could continue to fly his slow turns up this narrowing valley as the enemy battery commander found the range. Craner was the epitome of the professional Air Force officer in combat. He had the uncanny ability to focus his intellect and squelch fear, even facing this display of lethal flak. Craner's disciplined comportment under fire was not simply bravado. There was no senior American officer observing his performance that afternoon in Rao Nay Valley. If he had been an F-105 pilot, he would have shown equivalent discipline as he dove through the flak above Thud Ridge, north of Hanoi. Craner was a self-directed man in his mid-thirties, a smalltown boy who had joined the Air Force in his late teens, had risen inevitably through Air Cadets to become an officer and a fighter pilot, and, in the process, matured into a sophisticated adult who embraced a wide range of humanistic interests beyond military aviation. But Renaissance history and Slavic languages were not Bob Craner's immediate priority as he gripped the control stick of his Super Sabre and gave the fuel-flow gauge and exhaust temperature dial a quick glance. Another neon hardball sailed past, just above his helmet.

Finally Craner broke silence and spoke into his mask. "Guy, you got that one yet?"

In the backseat, Guy Gruters bent over his detailed one-to-fifty thousand chart, his sharp pencil-tip just above the point in the middle of the valley where he was sure the final camouflaged 57mm gun was dug in. He needed only one more burst of tracers out of those trees to be certain.

"Bob," he said, his voice filled with the strain of his demanding task, "just give me a few more seconds, okay?"

At that moment they both saw the glowing cannon round stop out there at seven o'clock. Gruters opened his mouth to yell "Break right!" But before he could form the words, the heavy shell slammed into the saddleback section of the top fuselage, just behind the backseat cockpit, destroying both the plane's hydraulic pumps in the sharp explosion. The impact of the shell threw the large fighter-bomber onto its starboard wing. Craner struggled for control, but there was none possible without hydraulics. The jet continued to roll, now onto its back, and sank at five hundred knots, only fifteen hundred feet above the green-and-orange mud paddies.

Gruters hung in his seat harness, gazing down through the gray twilight at the thatch roofs and bamboo sheds of the farming villages. This was no place to punch out. "Bob," Gruters said, as calmly as he could, "the mountains. Head for the mountains."

Craner did not answer for several seconds as he desperately tried each backup system and emergency procedure to regain flight control.

"Negative," Craner ordered. "Get out!" Their plane lost forward speed and careened vertically toward the valley.

The two pilots fired their rocket ejection seats with the aircraft inverted. They shot downward from the falling airplane on cones of flaming white smoke. First one, then the second orange-and-white parachute canopy deployed at less than twelve hundred feet above the ground.

In the violent ejection, Gruters became separated from Craner. Gruters found himself hanging beneath his chute directly above a thatch-roofed hamlet, about one thousand meters from an oval stand of trees and scrub jungle. He was an experienced parachutist, a member of the Skydiving Club with Lance Sijan at the Academy, and he had gone through army jump school before taking up his first Vietnam assignment, an o-1 Bird-dog FAC with the 173d Airborne in the central highlands. Only two missions before, Gruters had been shot down and had ejected over the Tonkin Gulf.

As he pendulumed beneath his canopy, he saw at once what he had to do. If he could slip fast to the right, he just might be able to make that patch of jungle. It would be dark in thirty minutes. In the jungle he could hide from the enemy patrols, then make a break for the forest ridges that paralleled the flat valley. Without further hesitation, he took his new Randall survival knife and slashed through the center four suspension lines on each of the two rear risers of his parachute. With these lines cut, he fell much faster but had gained considerable lateral velocity: sideslip.

This maneuver, from canopy opening to cutting his shroud lines, had taken only seconds. For a few moments more he hung in silence, hearing only his own thudding heart and hoarse breath. Then he heard the gongs and whistles of the enemy troops and farmers below, alerting each other to the direction he was moving. He dragged down harder on the front risers and slipped faster toward the patch of trees. People in black were streaming out of the small village houses, trotting on beaten mud paths that led them inexorably toward the oval stand of trees.

In each group of farmers there were one or two men armed with rifles; the rest brandished machetes or hoes. A small squad of green-uniformed soldiers ran down a paddy dike from the north. Among the armed villagers, people were now stopping to kneel and fire their rifles at Gruters. Small-caliber green tracer bullets cut past him in the gloomy twilight. Several ripped through his canopy, but none came near his body. He hung on his risers, dragging the maximum speed out of the slip.

In the last two hundred feet, he saw that he was going to make the trees, so he released the front risers. The canopy popped back with a metallic twang, and Gruters bent in his harness to hit the deployment lanyard of his rubber dinghy and survival seat pack. Landing in trees with a seat pack under your ass, he knew, was a sure way to break your leg.

Just before the forest swept up to hit him, he twisted in his harness and saw a stocky farmer kneeling on a paddy dike less than a hundred feet away, firing his automatic carbine. The shots were wide to the right, too low. *Are you shittin' me?* Gruters thought, the omnibus irony of the 173d Airborne. *Get it over with, you clown. How can you miss?*

Suddenly Gruters was seized by a rush of excited confidence. These people weren't *soldiers*. It was Amateur Hour down there. Once in those trees, he could hide or outrun them. He sure could outshoot them. Up at Dak To with the 173d, Gruters had practiced firing his .38 revolver for months, using up thousands of rounds on the improvised firing range the FACs and chopper pilots had set up to amuse themselves. He knew that he could hit an enemy soldier with a killing shot, every time, at seventy-five yards. And it was clear that these clowns firing at him down there had not spent much range time.

Just below him the green treetops rocked and swooped. Enemy tracer rounds whined through the dull sky, wildly off mark. Gruters gripped his knees and ankles together, then relaxed; his elbows came close to protect his throat and face.

In a slashing blur, he cut through the edge of a fifty-foot tree and spilled into a small round clearing in the jungle. When he hit the grassy ground, he unconsciously executed a smooth parachute landing fall that would have warmed the heart of the crustiest old master sergeant at Fort Bragg. He popped his riser quick releases and sprinted for the cover of the low brush thirty yards away. All around him in the shadowy forest he could hear whistles and shrill cries of the pursuing Vietnamese.

Under a tangle of brush and vines, he dug down to retrieve his pistol from the leather holster attached to his survival vest. The holster was empty. Frantically he scratched around the leaves and rotting jungle muck. Nothing. The gun was gone.

From the clearing he heard the shouts of the enemy, who had just found his chute and survival pack. As quietly as he could, he rolled onto his side and crawled away into the green shadows. Behind him the enemy sounded closer, louder, but not as loud as the crashing heart within his chest.

They began Guy Gruters' interrogation the next day. It was late morning. The clouds were low again, and no American planes had yet flown over the valley hamlet where they had taken Gruters at dawn.

The night before, after the soldiers had finally captured him in the small stand of jungle, they had stripped him of his flight suit and boots and lashed his hands behind his back.

Marching him to the road, the squad of soldiers had been forced to level their fixed bayonets at the furious crowd of farmers that had boiled out of the nearby villages with the intention of hacking him to pieces. That night his captors actually fed him a passable meal of rice, boiled greens, and dried fish. He realized then, while he squatted on the mud of the nearby village eating rice with his fingers, that they probably were not going to execute him. The NVA did not waste food on condemned men, he reasoned.

Around nine o'clock the next morning, a North Vietnamese government official and two silent, glowering NVA officers arrived at the hut in which he was being held under armed guard. The guards gestured for Gruters to sit on a low stool, facing the panel of interrogators. It was the civilian, dressed in a drab, unadorned military tunic, who questioned him. The other two officers apparently spoke no English, and the cadre's command of the language was, at best, rudimentary.

The civilian official flourished Gruters' Air Force identity card. "You Gruters. You *lieutenant.*" He pronounced the rank lieute*nant*, with French inflection.

Gruters had recently been promoted to captain, a proud achievement for so young an officer, a recognition of his work as a FAC in II Corps and now as a volunteer with the Misty FAC, the outfit that flew much of the low-level armed recon missions in Package I and Steel Tiger. Gruters had an urge to correct the interrogator as to his rank, but he remained silent. In survival school they had taught him never to volunteer anything. When asked direct questions, give some kind of answer, even if the response was that you were forbidden to answer. So far the official had asked no question.

Now the interrogator opened a neat cardboard ledger to a blank page and made a show of preparing a clumsy Russian fountain pen, as if he fully expected Gruters to spontaneously volunteer important information.

"Gruters," he said after a suitable pause, squinting down at the white page. "Gruters . . . what base fly from . . . Da Nang, Udorn? You tell me what base fly from."

Gruters remained silent, crouched on his low stool, his hands tied behind him with sharply knotted hemp rope. He had been expecting this question, but he still felt a warm pulse of dread as he heard the actual phrases of direct military interrogation. The Misty FAC organization—the 416th Tactical Fighter Squadron—was not just another F-100 outfit assigned to interdiction strikes against enemy LOCs. The Misty Forward Air Controllers were secretly known as Superfacs. They flew armed reconnaissance in fast, maneuverable jets all up and down the enemy's infiltration routes. Their assignment was to keep very close tabs on flak and SAM missile sites, as well as to identify and pinpoint important enemy troop concentrations and obviously special—heavily defended—supply convoys. Misty FAC crews were all experienced fighter pilots who also had considerable combat expertise as forward air controllers. Their modified Super Sabres carried heavy loads of electronic sensors, and the Misty pilots were skilled at locating and pinpointing hidden enemy positions. The NVA did not realize it yet, but wherever the stubby, camouflaged Misty jets loitered very long, banking low overhead, a devastating American airstrike was sure to follow.

Now Gruters was undergoing his initial interrogation, and he was determined not to betray his outfit's identity or its role in the bombing war.

He stared silently at the official.

"You must answer me," the civilian officer said. "What airplane you fly? One zero five? F-four? We know all airplanes. What plane you fly?"

Again Gruters sat in rigid silence.

"What name your commander?" The man's voice was edged now with real or well-feigned anger, verging on righteous outrage. "What base you fly from? What airplane you fly? You *must* answer all questions."

Another lesson of survival school was the preparation of a cover story. Air force policy was that the downed airman was to resist answering all military questions, that he should stick to name, rank, service number, and date of birth, as delineated in the Code of Conduct—until he was tortured. Then, after an undefined period of torture, he was to start giving the enemy false information *slowly,* as if the pain and shock had broken his will. Gruters was well versed in this policy. He also knew that he would be responsible for any cover story he developed. If the fabrication resulted in the injury, capture, or death of another American, he could face court-martial. This was not a pleasant or easy prospect for a young man of twenty-four, a husband of a young wife and father of two small children, to accept.

But Guy Gruters knew that he was tough enough to take *some* slapping around, some working over with those stout bamboo clubs the guards had stacked in the corner. Up at the 173d Airborne's base camp airstrip near Dak To, Gruters had tested his own toughness several times by going off on deep penetration patrols with LRRPs, dropping into known NVA staging areas near the Laos border from a blacked-out Huey late on moonless nights and living on his wits and two canteens of water for a day while the LRRPs scouted out enemy concentrations. At the time, he had convinced his superiors that such volunteer ground patrolling would increase his understanding of enemy formations, as well as firm up the rapport between a FAC and his clients, the LRRPs. But, beyond the official rationale, Gruters knew he had actually been testing his own guts and toughness.

Now, bound up like a pig at the market, half-naked before his interrogators, he had the chance to test himself even further.

The interrogator leaned closer. "You will be punished if you will not answer questions. You *must* give answer. We can *not* let you not talk to us. Talk or be punished."

Gruters tried to square his head in a self-possessed but not overly defiant manner. "I am a soldier," he said in slow, neutral tones, appealing as much to the silent NVA officers as to the civilian. "All I can tell you is my name, rank, service number, and date of birth. I *will* tell you this. Gruters, Guy David . . . Captain, United States Air Force. Service number FR 3 . . ."

"You will be *punished!*" the official screamed.

Behind Gruters, two guards jumped forward to seize his neck and shoulders. They dragged him off the stool, backward, out the doorway of the bamboo house, across a muddy yard to an even smaller outbuilding, a mildewed, thatch-roofed shed that had been cleared of tools and rice baskets. Two more guards burst into the crowded little room and unleashed a cascade of kicks and clubbing, striking Gruters about the chest, belly, and arms. Then all four guards forced the tall American to his knees. Behind him, three of the soldiers got to work with a length of rough hemp rope. They tied a series of shockingly tight hitches around his naked right bicep, then dragged the coiled line under his left armpit and yanked, *hard.*

Gruters felt muddy, cleated boot soles on the back of his neck where the soldiers were getting leverage. *What the hell are they* DOING, he thought, *trying to rip my* ARM *off?*

The answer came quickly. With the taut line, the soldiers jerked up three more biting hitches on his left bicep, then bound the two upper arms so close together that his elbows touched behind his back. He felt himself begin to howl but bit his lips to squash the outburst. The pain was horrible, shooting through his arms, chest, and shoulders, down his back. Within a minute his lower arms were cold, completely numb, but the pain pulses increased in his chest. It felt as if his sternum had ruptured. Incredibly, as he swayed on his knees, the soldiers found some way to bind the ropes even tighter. The pain swooped up a quantum leap. These bastards knew what they were doing; they'd pulled this stunt before.

As he rocked on his knees, the short, grim-faced civilian in the drab green tunic ducked under the thatch roof and faced him. "Gruters . . . you will not come back until you say you will talk to us."

The official jerked back out of the shed. One soldier remained behind, out of sight. The other three took up their posts outside.

Swaying now with the agony of the rope torture, Gruters had a strange flash of insight. *Writhing,* he thought. *So this is what they mean when they say "writhing in pain."*

He had expected fists, clubs, maybe even whips and red-hot branding irons, all the old war-movie, Gestapo stuff. But nobody at survival school had ever said anything about the simple, devastating rope torture. Now there was no feeling in his arms from the shoulders down. His chest, neck, and back were blazing, solid, uncompromising pain. Again he found himself moaning aloud, so he forced his mind to concentrate on something else . . . he would count silently. One thousand, two thousand . . . *impossible.* He decided to pray. That helped. But the agony would not go very far away.

Thought intruded on his silent prayer. *My arms are gone.* The medics always said never keep a tourniquet on longer than twenty minutes. Gangrene. Then they have to cut off your arms. These bastards are not kidding around here. They mean to have me lose my arms. Here go my stinking arms.

He swayed on his knees, stunned by the sudden knowledge that unless he gave in and talked, the enemy had every intention of letting his arms atrophy from blood loss and become dead, gangrenous flesh.

Still, Gruters' training, his years of academy discipline, prevented him from giving in so soon. When the pain and fear mounted to an unendurable level, after he'd spent perhaps two-and-a-half hours on the mud floor of the shed, the guards came back in and pushed him face down to untie the ropes. The pain of the blood returning to nerves and muscles was shocking. They sat him up against the bamboo wall and brought him a tin cup of rice and boiled greens. Like a grateful unquestioning animal, he choked down his afternoon meal. Then, abruptly, the rest period was over, and the guards fell on him again with their length of coarse hemp rope.

After another three hours of torture that afternoon, the guards dragged him before the interrogators once again. He hobbled with pain back into the bamboo farmhouse.

As he slumped to his stool, he realized that the interrogation team had lost all patience, that they were probably here only for the day and that day was almost over. He had to give them something now or they would leave him in the ropes all night. He planned to make a break from the shed hut after dark, and he couldn't do that trussed up like a pig. So he opted for a cover story. He was, he lied, the pilot of an F-4 from Takli Air Base in Thailand. His squadron was the 227th TFS, and his commanding officer was Colonel Johnny L. Jones. His mission had been to bomb the northern roadways in the valley. It was a radar-vector sweep from offshore. He was not careful with his cover story because he was optimistic he could escape into the mountains once he broke away from this hamlet.

As he spoke, he waited for the officer to order the hovering soldiers to begin clubbing him. Instead the civilian scratched in his clean blue ledger and offered a running translation to the two NVA officers who sat beside him on the edge of the hardwood plank bed, smiling now that the prisoner had agreed to cooperate. They actually seemed happy with this bullshit.

Gruters waited in dread that the interrogator would begin the next phase of the questioning, demanding technical information about the F-4. Phantom pilots, he knew, were especially apprehensive about interrogation because the F-4 was nuclear-capable with its low-altitude bombing system. Also, the Israeli Air Force had made such spectacular, successful use of the Phantom that summer during the Six Day War that rumor had it the Russians were sending their own professional interrogators to North Vietnam to question captured F-4 pilots. Despite these risks, Gruters knew that his cover story would keep the line of questioning away from the Misty FACs, and that was as far as he could think under the present conditions.

Instead of more questioning, however, the official launched into an obviously rehearsed diatribe about the "criminal" conduct of the United States and the just revolutionary struggle of Socialist Vietnam. After a while the three enemy officials left, and Gruters was given yet another cup of garnished rice. Later a soldier brought a new set of black cotton shirt and trousers that had been hastily sewn together to fit Gruters' tall frame.

Night was sudden under the low monsoon overcast. He lay on the plank bed of this alien little house, watching the ghostly flash and shadows of the flares that the American planes were dropping further down the valley. Exhausted by the torture and the protracted fear of the long day, he still found it impossible to sleep. Now that they had broken his initial resistance, he knew that there would be more interrogation, probably somewhere else, with a more highly skilled and fluent questioner. He had to use this quiet time alone to plan his story.

Outside the doorway of the hut, flare light washed across the mud parapet of a slit trench leading to a crude bomb shelter. Gruters wondered if any of those American planes were from the Misty FACs. He tried to imagine what was happening at home with Sandy and the kids. That line of thought led only to despair. Instead he lay in the flare-sparkled darkness and began to plan his escape. But it was hard to concentrate when he heard the wheezing breath of the armed enemy guard, awake and alert, only a few feet away in the dark hut.

They brought Guy Gruters and Bob Craner into the Bamboo Prison just north of Vinh at dawn on the day after Christmas. All night the jolting truck had carried them north on bomb-cratered roads and narrow paddy-dike detours. The traffic coming the opposite direction was almost continuous—Soviet trucks, some pulling mobile flak guns, and a score of flatbed semitrailers carrying squat, camouflaged Soviet tanks. When Gruters managed to push aside a corner of his blindfold, he was shocked to see the enemy tanks and the diverse complexity and sheer volume of the materiel the NVA was moving south under the cover of the Christmas bombing halt.

Once more he vowed somehow to escape while they remained down here on the southern coast. Still thinking like a FAC, not a prisoner, he felt he had to get back to South Vietnam and warn MACV about the incredible scope of the NVA supply buildup for the offensive everybody expected.

But when they were shoved off the back of the truck and pushed into the stinking confines of the bamboo jail, he began to understand that escape was not going to be at all easy.

The holding jail and interrogation center—known as Duc's Camp to some American POWs or the Bamboo Prison to others—was located in coastal paddy fields, four kilometers north of Vinh. Inevitably, the buildings of the jail complex were constructed of rough, unsplit vertical bamboo with sloppy rice-straw thatched roofs. The American bombing along Route 1, the main north-south supply line inside North Vietnam, had been so devastating that the enemy had given up trying to build any more concrete or masonry structures. Almost all civilian and military building in the panhandle was now uniform, monotonous one-storey bamboo and straw thatch. The jail faced a rectangular mosquito-ridden paddy pond, connected to a primitive latrine trench. About fifty feet long and twenty wide, the jail hooch was divided inside by walls of lashed bamboo into six narrow cells, a central walkway, and a guard room. The floor was beaten laterite mud. On the cell floors, there was straw. There were no windows, but insects, leeches, and other vermin entered freely through the unchinked walls. Forty feet to the right of the jail hooch was a smaller interrogation hooch with a lower straw roof and one window facing the paddy pond.

When Bob Craner and Gruters were led into the dark central walkway of the jail, they both immediately noted that this was no farmhouse that had been pressed into service as a temporary lockup for American airmen en route north. The bamboo of the walls was thicker than a man's arm; each vertical section had been anchored deeply in the hard-packed clay, and the cell doors were locked with chains. All the guards were armed with AKs, and they weren't underage, green militia, either, but hardened NVA troopers who seemed to know their way around Americans. Probably, Gruters guessed, these guys had a pretty good detail going here, guarding POWs. They weren't about to blow it and get their asses shipped south by letting anybody escape.

Gruters' guess was confirmed almost at once. A guard threw back the door of the unoccupied cell facing the doorway and ordered the two pilots to halt. Inside this narrow chamber, Gruters saw a pile of rusty handcuffs, ankle irons, and what appeared to be gruesome medieval torture implements: limb-stretching racks with metal cuffs, spiked boards, wire whips, ominous ropes with pulleys. . . . He looked away, a queasy clot forming below his throat. Now the NVA was going to have a chance to truly test the fabric of their cover story.

The guard came out with a jangling load of cuffs and ankle irons, and the two Americans were ordered to bind each other's limbs with these chains. As they bent to the unfamiliar task, Gruters and Craner were able to whisper a few phrases of mutual encouragement. On the truck ride out of the valley, Craner had secretly provided Gruters with a detailed account of his own interrogation and cover story. Because Craner had been led stripped and barefoot to the wreckage of their plane—already identified by the NVA battery commander as an F-100—and then on a brief propaganda-rally circuit of the six gun sites in the valley, he had not tried to disguise the type of airplane or its home base in the cover story he provided after his initial bout of rope torture. Instead, he had freely admitted that he and Gruters were flying an F-100 from Phu Cat. But, he claimed, they were simply part of a normal fighter-bomber outfit on a flak-suppression mission, supporting an F-4 flight from Thailand. Gruters was now hopeful that he could adjust his original cover story accordingly by pleading that the interrogator had misunderstood his English during the initial questioning.

Once they were shackled, the guards shoved them down the narrow corridor and into their cells. Gruters was pushed into the first small cubicle on the left, and Craner was given the end cell on the right. Thus they were separated from each other by several empty cells and multiple bamboo walls. To further discourage any attempt at communication, a scowling guard took up his post on a stool directly outside Craner's cell. An hour later, when they heard the guard leave the corridor, they began whispering. Their breach of orders was immediately rewarded with the appearance of *two* guards, armed with thick bamboo clubs. They screamed at Gruters and pummeled him with their clubs, then slammed shut his cell door and gave Craner the same treatment. Obviously any kind of voice communication between their cells was going to be impossible.

Their second interrogation began around midday. It was carried out by the same civilian who had questioned them in the Rao Nay Valley, but now he had been joined by another NVA officer, a silent, pinched-faced man of about forty-five. The prisoners christened this new interrogator the Rodent, a reference to his face and cruel manner.

Craner, the senior of the two pilots, was the first to be questioned. The civilian and the Rodent made a serious blunder by speaking loudly to Craner in the nearby interrogation hooch. Gruters, sitting with his back to the wall, jammed his head against the bamboo and could hear all the questions and answers.

"Wing commander?" the civilian demanded.

"Colonel Robert E. Lee," Craner answered.

Gruters was too intent on memorizing the sequence of the questions and Craner's answers to be alarmed at his audacity. But then he realized Craner's defiant lies were more than dangerous bravado. If the civilian swallowed a name like Robert E. Lee, he was obviously open to further deception.

"Commander of squadron?"

"Lieutenant Colonel Stoney Jackson."

"Stoney? What name is Stoney? Spell name."

Obligingly, Craner spelled it.

When the questioning turned to other key personnel, Craner provided the names of several well-known football players. Thirty feet away, Gruters sat with his eyes closed in concentration, memorizing Craner's answers.

After two hours of questioning, the interrogation team returned Craner to his cell. They marched Gruters across the muddy yard to the interrogation hooch. As he stumbled along in his ankle irons, prodded by the impatient guards, his mind was alive with lurid images of the torture racks and wire whips he had seen at dawn. He had lied to the civilian officer up in the valley, and now Gruters was convinced that he would be tortured.

Indeed, the official's first line of questioning concerned the lies Gruters had told about being an F-4 pilot. Spitting and fuming for the benefit of the Rodent and the other silent NVA officer seated beside him at the rough wooden table, the civilian threatened Gruters with "hard" punishment for his criminal conduct.

Using all his energy to seem earnest, Gruters leaned forward and feigned surprise. The official, he said, had unfortuantely misunderstood his statements. "I said that I was *supporting* F-4s, not flying them. I thought you knew I was flying an F-100 because it crashed right there in the valley."

"You say Takli base, Thailand. Craner say Phu Cat. You tell us many lies."

Gruters tried to smile in a manner indicative of a friendly misunderstanding. "Our base *is* Phu Cat, but we were *staging* out of Takli . . . you understand? Staging is temporary duty."

Clearly, the terms were unfamiliar to the civilian; his comprehension vocabulary was even more limited than the few rote expressions he employed during direct questioning and political diatribes.

"Good," he grunted. "Now you say truth." He made notes in his ledger and spoke to his two colleagues.

Gruters was overcome with relief. He would not be tortured for his original deception. With his renewed optimism came a sudden insight that the interrogators here at the provincial level were minor bureaucrats, absorbed with the *form,* not the true content of these interrogations. What was important to them was not so much the actual information the American pilots provided but rather the fact that they could be persuaded to provide some answer to the unimaginative list of stock military questions . . . aircraft flown, operating base, names of commanders.

Now, as if on cue, the civilian snapped out his next question.

"Wing commanding officer. What name?"

"Colonel Robert Lee," Gruters said eagerly. "Colonel Robert Edward Lee."

"Squadron commander? Give us name. No lie."

"Lieutenant Colonel Jackson," Gruters answered respectfully. "His first name is Stoney. . . ."

The official thrust out his ledger and ordered Gruters to take the thick fountain pen and spell out the names of his apocryphal unit's commanders.

When he had completed his list, the civilian, the Rodent, and the other brooding NVA officer leaned over the ledger. Gruters realized how lucky he and Craner were. Phu Cat was a new base, and the NVA intelligence network in the South had not yet produced a detailed command structure for the 12th Tactical Fighter Wing. As long as he and Craner kept their stories consistent, they might be able to continue the decpetion and avoid further torture. By answering the questions, Gruters saw, he was giving the civilian a needed boost in status before the two military officers. It really didn't matter what answer he gave, as long as he gave one. Conversely, he realized, outright refusal to answer or answering with a blatant lie would cause the civilian to lose face badly. Gruters had already experienced the painful retribution the official delivered when threatened with loss of face. Now that Gruters and Craner had launched into their joint deception, they had to find some way of communicating with each other to refine their story, to hone the details for future interrogation.

As the civilian fell into the singsong tones of another political harangue, Gruters forced himself to think about contacting Craner to let him know that their cover story was still holding water. But it was hard to concentrate. With his wrists bound tightly in the rusty cuffs, he could not fan away the swarming flies. The stench of his own unwashed body and the nearby paddy bothered him more than he thought they would. Even with the monsoon overcast, the heat of midday was heavy, enervating.

He felt himself begin to yawn but ground his teeth shut and tried to form an expression of concerned interest as the official continued his incomprehensible nasal diatribe.

From the detours a kilometer away, the incessant rumbling of trucks competed with the man's voice, the flies, and the stinking heat to produce a deepening anguish in Gruters. For the first time since being shot down, he squarely faced the reality that he would not escape, that he was a helpless prisoner in an alien land, facing perhaps years in the custody of a cruel and inflexible enemy.

It was late night, at least an hour before dawn: American flares were falling inland. Flak batteries crumped and echoed to the north. Gruters awoke with spiders biting his swollen ankles. Just outside the bamboo walls he heard the rhythmic pulse of an idling truck engine. Vietnamese voices, shrill, then guttural, soldiers answering

Rao Nay Valley, North Vietnam   173

commands. The metal screech of a tailgate. Finally, another obviously different voice, deeper. Unclear.

In the corridor the guard trotted past Gruters' cell toward the main door.

"*Bob,*" Gruters said, trying to pitch his whisper toward Craner's cell. "You awake? I think they're bringing in another prisoner."

"I'm awake," Craner answer. "Try to get a look at him. See if he's got an Air Force or a Navy flight suit on."

"Roger," Gruters answered, inordinately happy to hear another American voice after two days. "You hanging in there?"

"Damn right," Craner called. "Room service is lousy, but I can't complain about the price."

Gruters was about to offer a witty rejoinder when the hot beams of the guards' flashlights cut down the corridor. He thrust his face against the bamboo doorframe at an angle, so that he could gaze out a two-inch gap. He was not sure exactly what he saw in the shadow and glare of the two flashlights, but he was deeply troubled by the glimpse of the dark figure the soldiers dragged between them.

The prisoner they threw into the end cell opposite Craner seemed to be very tall but impossibly thin. The only mass to the shape the guards pulled along came from the huge, crudely fashioned cast of dirty plaster that dragged from the figure's lower body where his left leg should have been.

There was a clanking of chains, some muttered comment among the guards; then the flashlights went out. Gruters crawled to the far side of his cell and listened, trying to hear the sniffling breath of the guard at the end of the corridor. Instead, he heard Craner whispering to the new prisoner.

Craner was asking him his name. But the only reply Gruters heard before the corridor guard returned to his post was the muffled moaning of the new prisoner.

Mosquitos whined in Gruters' ears. Somewhere in the night a flock of chickens began their random, predawn cackling. He settled back in his verminous straw, trying to sleep again, despite the hungry twisting in his belly. But it was more than hunger that kept him awake. The image of the grotesque skeleton in muddy black pajamas, dragging that crude plaster cast behind him, flooded his consciousness. What in God's name did they do to *that* poor guy?

The next morning the guards let the new man sleep until amost noon. Then the Rodent, accompanied by the more sadistic of the three day-shift guards, slammed open the door of the end cell and began screaming questions at the prisoner. Gruters could see nothing but a narrow slice of empty walkway directly before his cell, but he could hear the entire interrogation process in the end cell. The angry questions of the Rodent were followed by silence from the prisoner. More questions. Silence. The interrogator was yelling now. Gruters heard thuds, harsh cracks, the sound of a bamboo club striking bone, the awful crunch of a boot striking the man's body.

The prisoner shrieked in agony. More garbled questions followed. Again silence from the new guy. Gruters could hear more blows. He threw himself to the far side of his cell and began to pray for the injured skeleton thirty feet away. His consciousness filled with the reassuring verses of Paternosters and Hail Marys. If he concentrated hard enough, he could almost block out the man's screams.

Bob Craner crouched in his cell, his fists clenched in outrage as he heard every detail of the brutal interrogation. For maybe the fourth time, the Rodent was repeating his stock litany of questions. Unlike the civilian interrogator's, the Rodent's English was reasonably clear when he raised his voice to shout his questions.

"What airplane you fly? What base you fly from? Name of wing, name squadron. You must answer every question. You are criminal prisoner in Democratic Republic of Vietnam. *All* questions to be answered."

The new guy's voice was weak, and Craner had to press against his cell door to hear the man's words. "I'm not going to tell you people anything," the new guy wheezed. Craner heard the hoarse breathing between each defiant word, as if the guy were rationing his dwindling strength to the end.

"Name of base commander!" The Rodent was yelling as loudly as he could.

"I'm not . . . going to tell you anything. . . ." The guy's voice would phase in and out like a badly tuned radio receiver. "I can't talk to you. It's . . . against the code. Can't you understand?"

"Your arm," the Rodent shouted, "very bad, very bad. Your leg, bad. We hurt your arm, your leg, if you do not answer all questions."

Craner heard no answer from the prisoner. Then came the crack of club blows striking bone, and the new guy's screaming filled the entire bamboo jail hooch.

"Criminal to answer *all* questions," the Rodent bellowed.

"You bastard!" the man shouted, his voice clear and precise now for the first time. "When I'm better, I'm going to break your neck."

Craner literally blinked in disbelief. How could anybody with such obviously terrible wounds and injuries continue with this defiance?

There was a brief spell of quiet, when only the prisoner's harsh breathing was audible. Then Craner heard the shuffling grunts of the Rodent and the guard, as if they were heaving a dead-weight load or wrestling with the lever of a balky machine.

"Name of base! Commander name!"

The new guy actually *roared* with pain now, as loud as any tormented animal. "I'll get you, you fucker!" he screamed. "I'll kick your ass."

"Airplane you fly. Name of base!"

Again Craner heard the two NVA interrogators grunt and heave. Again the new guy's screams of absolute agony dominated the jail hooch. After an indefinite period of anguished screams, the man's voice broke through in words, hoarse and rasping. "Sijan! My name is Lance Peter Sijan . . . first lieutenant, United States Air Force. Service number . . ."

Craner pressed the heels of his hands against his ears. Whoever Lieutenant Sijan was, Craner realized, he was too damn brave for his own good. If he kept up this amazing defiance very long, these people would kill him. Craner stared down at the smelly straw, at the beaten mud of his cell floor. God help that poor bastard if they didn't let up on him.

Carner thrashed about the narrow cell. If he yelled at the guards, if he screamed at the sadist in the opposite cell to stop, there was no guarantee that the Vietnamese soldiers would understand. Threatened by loss of face, they might react in an unpredictably violent manner; the poor young man on the floor, nine feet away, might be the loser in any macho exchange with the NVA interrogator. Now was the time to use his unusual and imaginative intelligence. In his next interrogation session, he would try to convince the Rodent to ease up on Sijan.

It was dusk, and Gruters was swarmed by mosquitos. But he was hardly aware of the discomfort as he listened to the screams and shouting of the new guy's second interrogation session. Now the Rodent was trying a new approach, the brute application of torture not having gotten him very far.

"Listen to me!" the Rodent shouted. "This leg . . . very bad. *Bad.* We cut your leg off if you don't talk to us."

Gruters could not hear the guy's answer, but the Rodent screamed at him in Vietnamese, and the guy howled in pain.

"If we do not give medicine," the Rodent said, speaking lower now, "you will not have leg. This is *gangrene . . .* you see, from here, from there? You *smell?* Talk to us. Name of base commander. What plane you fly to Democratic Republic of Vietnam?"

The guy did not answer.

"You are criminal to be punished," the Rodent said.

Gruters heard the crack of the clubs and the guy howled again. As he had that noon, Gruters threw himself to the far side of his narrow cell and went to his knees in prayer, imploring God to spare that poor young man from further suffering.

The humid monsoon twilight fell. Jets snarled in the distance. From the end of the corridor, the sounds of torture and unshakable defiance continued in the alien darkness.

They left the prisoner alone the next morning. About four hours after daybreak, the guy called weakly out to the corridor guard.

"Come *on* . . . somebody, let me out of here. Take me to the latrine. I got to take care of myself. *Some*body. Hey . . . the latrine."

In the narrow walkway between the cells, the day-shift guard laughed, then bellowed at the prisoner to be quiet.

After half an hour of cries from the prisoner, the Rodent dragged open Gruters' cell door. Craner stood, unbound, between the Rodent and a guard. Working with practiced speed, the guard unlocked Gruters' leg irons and cuffs. The Rodent stepped back, beckoning to Gruters but obviously wary of letting himself be hemmed in between the two muscular pilots, each of whom towered above him by almost a foot.

"You will take criminal prisoner for toilet and washing. Go now." He gestured in distaste toward the end cell.

When the guard unlocked the chain on the cell and flung back the lopsided bamboo door, Gruters saw Craner flinch back at the sight of the prisoner. A moment later he himself went through the identical involuntary reflex of shocked anguish when he saw the guy lying on the fouled straw of the cell.

The man's face was a battered skull. His three exposed limbs were bony sticks. But it was not the skeletal limbs that most shocked Gruters. It was the *sores*, the terrible expanse of raw flesh that covered most of his body. Gruters' initial reaction was that this poor bastard had been the victim of some grotesquely savage and maiming torture, that the NVA interrogators had literally tried to scrape the man's flesh from his body using wood planes or rasps . . . or some kind of horrible tool.

When Gruters had overcome his first immobilizing shock, he forced himself to look more closely at the figure on the straw. The man's hip bones, his entire pelvic structure, protruded in clear, anatomical detail. The scraped flesh was stretched so tightly across the bone and cartilage that the guy had developed the obscenely exaggerated waist of a Playboy bunny. Normal musculature was just *gone.* What little flesh he still retained was tautly stretched across his skeleton, conforming to the harsh geometry of his bones.

Flies crawled and spun around the edges of the long leg cast. There were dribbles of pus running from both ends of this cast, and Gruters realized with a sickening slump that the NVA medics had actually placed a closed cast around a compound fracture and that this pitiful wounded limb was the leg that the Rodent and his helper had twisted and clubbed during their torture session.

Up in the highlands, Gruters had observed his share of badly wounded G.I.s and the mangled corpses of Americans and Vietnamese when the dust-off slicks came clattering into the fire bases and forward airstrips. He had seen men blasted into pieces by mines and artillery. But he had never been near a *living* person in such horrible condition.

Gruters broke free of his stunned immobility when Craner spoke. "Okay, buddy," Craner said softly. "We're here to help you out.

We're going to take care of you now. Don't worry. Everything's okay now. We're going to take you out and clean you up."

The dark eyes moved deep inside bony sockets. The man's hot gaze swept across them, then turned to the guard. Gruters felt that the guy had been driven delirious by his wounds and the agony of the torture.

Craner and Gruters stooped to hold the man under his shoulders and lifted him to a vertical position. Drawing him up, Gruters was overcome with the incongruity between the man's weight and his height. Both Gruters and Craner were over six feet, and this breathing skeleton was taller than them. But lifting him was like raising a child. He seemed to weigh less than a hundred pounds. The only *weight* came from the cast. The man's head sagged onto his chest, and Gruters thought he was unconscious.

"Boy," Gruters muttered to Craner, "this guy's one big troop, isn't he?"

The battered skull turned on the neck. His mouth opened, and soft, almost normally inflected words were formed. "Aren't you Guy Gruters?"

Gruters stopped in midstride. *"Yeah,* I am." He swallowed with apprehension. "Who are *you?"*

"Lance." The voice was friendly, relaxed.

Gruters was churning with anguish and excitement. Who was *Lance* supposed to be? "Lance? Lance who?"

"Sijan," the skull answered. "Lance Sijan."

Gruters shook his head violently in autonomous reaction. "Lance *Sijan* . . . No, oh no."

His eyes clouded with stinging tears. My God, this mangled, dying scarecrow was Lance Sijan. Lance had been one of the biggest, strongest, and certainly the best-looking cadet in the 21st Squadron, probably in the whole damn academy. But more than his appearance, he had always projected a warm, guileless vitality, a kind of physical optimism, an unspoken assertion that his strength and beauty were invulnerable, that he was, indeed, one of those knights of the New Frontier who had been well prepared to fight any battle in the defense of liberty. Now that handsome, thoughtful athlete had been transformed into this travesty.

As they carried him between them down the walkway and out into the weak sunlight, Sijan uttered sharp, involuntary gasps of pain.

Gruters realized that *any* motion produced agony in Lance's injured and infected limbs. Looking down, Gruters was again shocked; the upper edges of Lance's hip bones actually protruded through the tight, dry flesh. Filmy white bone was exposed to the air and swirling flies. The fingers of his right hand were bent back and twisted. Each of his knuckles was worn down to raw, bleeding white bone. The right arm was deeply gouged and puffy with old infection.

Any normal person would be howling with agony from these multiple wounds. Sijan managed to suppress his cries and to speak in weak but clear and rational phrases. "Listen, Guy," he whispered, "how secure *is* this place? What are the chances of us getting out of here?"

Gruters and Craner stared at each other behind Sijan's bobbing skull. He was talking about *escape.* Incredible, absolutely unbelievable.

"Yeah . . . well," Craner stammered. "We're doing a recce, Lance. We'll keep you posted, buddy, don't worry."

Sijan actually smiled, a sad parody of his old face. "Outstanding," he whispered. "Count me in, okay? I can handle my end of it."

"Right," Gruters mumbled. "We're all in this together."

Sijan swung his head to face Gruters. "We're going to get out of here, aren't we?"

"Damn right, Lance," Gruters managed.

They lay Lance down as gently as they could near the stinking latrine trench at the edge of the paddy pond. After helping him with his fouled cotton trousers and shirt, they held him while he was seized by spasms of diarrhea. Finally Craner fetched some reasonably clean water in a leaking bamboo pail and they washed him as best they could. As they bent close over him, Craner whispered.

"Listen, Lance. When they interrogate you again, give them *some*thing . . . a cover story. Answer their questions. Tell them you're a one-oh-five driver from Udorn. . . ." Craner's voice trailed off when he saw the defiant scowl form on Sijan's face.

"Yeah, Lance," Gruters added. "Just feed them some bullshit and they'll leave you alone. You're in bad shape, man. Don't let them keep hammering on you . . . *please.*"

Sijan shook his head. "I'm all right. Don't worry about me. They're not really hurting me that bad. You guys just figure out some way that we can get *out* of here."

The guard, who had squeamishly turned away while Gruters and Craner washed Sijan, now saw them whispering. He bellowed an order and gestured with his rifle barrel for them to carry Sijan back into the jail hooch.

As they stooped to pick him up, Lance smiled again. "We're going to get out of this place, aren't we?"

The two Misty FAC pilots exchanged anguished glances. Clearly the only force that was keeping Sijan's ruined body alive was his indomitable spirit. And that tough, driving spirit was irreversibly bonded to his will to defy and resist the enemy interrogators and ultimately to escape from captivity, to regain his precious freedom. Both Gruters and Craner now realized they could not discourage Sijan. His heroic resistance had become meshed with his sustaining life force.

Gruters leaned close to Sijan's ear. "Yeah, Lance, we will. . . . don't worry. Just eat your food and get strong again."

They raised him to an upright position. Again he smiled. "I'm all right. Don't worry. I can take care of myself."

As they carried him back to the bamboo jail, the clumsy, wet edge of his cast bumped across the mud, sending spasms of pain through Sijan's body, tremors that both Gruters and Craner could feel as they gripped his bony frame.

The next day and the day after that, the Rodent returned to interrogate Sijan. Probably aware that intense physical torture would kill the prisoner, the Rodent concentrated instead on psychological torment. From his cell, Gruters again could hear everything that went on.

"You criminal. No medicine for criminal until you answer all questions. Name of base commander?"

"I can't answer. . . ." Lance's voice was markedly weaker. ". . . the Code. You don't understand. I can't. . . ."

The Rodent was screaming in Vietnamese. He now spoke more softly in English. "Sijan, you die with no medicine. You bad criminal. You *must* answer questions."

Lance mumbled something, then spoke up. "Sijan, Lance Peter, first lieutenant, U.S. Air Force . . ."

The Rodent slammed the cell door so hard that Gruters felt the jolt through the bamboo, thirty feet away.

Once more, Sijan had defied his interrogator. Again Gruters went to his knees and prayed for him.

The next morning they took Gruters to the interrogation hooch. At the rough plank table, another officer was seated with the Rodent. The two guards tried to reach up and force down Gruters' head in a bow of respect, but he easily resisted them, a small act of defiance in sympathy with Lance's unbelievable, stubborn resistance.

Gruters crouched on his stool and waited for the questions. Instead he was treated to a long, monotonous, and obviously rote political lecture delivered by the Rodent, probably for the benefit of the visiting officer. Gruters had to struggle to control the hatred he felt swelling inside him for this pompous sadist. Finally, after an elaborate, redundant explanation of the rules of captivity for American "air criminals," the Rodent asked Gruters if he had any questions.

Guy Gruters did not hesitate. "My friend, Lieutenant Sijan, is sick in his head, you understand?" Gruters was trying to keep his voice calm, persuasive. "It's no good asking him questions now. Wait until he's better. Give him medical treatment, and he'll get well. Then he'll answer your questions."

The Rodent scowled and shook his head. Now the other officer spoke at animated length in Vietnamese. The Rodent translated.

"Sijan criminal. Sijan *only* trouble. Nothing but trouble. We take Sijan from jungle Christmas day, almost dead. We give him food, water, put on medical bed. What Sijan do? Criminal hit officer's soldier. Man hurt very bad, very bad. Sijan run away to jungle again. Officer have many men, many. . . . half day all village hunt for Sijan." The Rodent again shook his head in disgust. "They put plaster on leg so he will not run away. He only trouble. We should kill him, lei him die. So much trouble."

Gruters sat staring at the Rodent's eyes. This was an astonishing story. He knew that Lance had gone down on a night strike early in November. Sijan must have crawled around that stinking jungle up in Laos until *Christmas.* And then, when they finally captured him, he decked his guard and escaped again. What kind of person was capable of such an effort?

Regaining his composure, Gruters now dipped his head in a gesture of mock respect. "Sir," he began, almost choking on the word, "sir . . . Lieutenant Sijan is very sick. His head is not good . . . too long in the jungle. Give him medicine and good food. Let him rest. Then he'll cooperate with you. He . . ."

The Rodent shouted an angry order and jumped to his feet. Two guards dragged Gruters back to his cell. As he stumbled along, he began to memorize the Rodent's exact words. Sijan might well die before he could tell his own story, and Gruters realized that he had just heard an account of resistance and heroism of historic proportions.

For the next seven days, the Rodent let Sijan languish without medical treatment of any kind. The only care he received was from Gruters and Craner, who were allowed to carry him to the latrine trench once a day and wash his bleeding body as best they could with muddy well water. When he was rational, Lance gave them a detailed account of his six weeks in the mountains. But talking exhausted him. Without question, Lance was deteriorating both physically and mentally. It was a real effort to get him to swallow a few spoonfuls of rice each day. His voice was now not much more than a rasping whisper. And there were increasingly long periods when he didn't seem to know who they were.

Then he would rally and regain his spirit and cunning. When he did speak to them, he whispered of escape. On the fourth day he began digging with his food cup at the underpinning of his cell wall, then scratched and shoved at the bamboo with his bare hands. The guard burst in and beat him savagely on his injured arm and leg. Both Gruters and Craner screamed their outrage, but the guards only yelled at them to be silent.

On the fifth, sixth, and seventh days, Sijan again lapsed into delirium and tried to scratch and push his way out of his cell. On each occasion the guard beat him horribly with a stout bamboo club. Now Sijan's periods of lucidity were occasional. Most of each day and night, he drifted in a stupor of mumbling pain. Gruters and Craner had to feed him very slowly so that he would not choke on the rice.

The monsoon overcast dropped even lower, and fine, soaking rain fell continually. Chill flooded the primitive jail. Sijan began to cough.

On the afternoon of the ninth day, the Rodent brought both Craner and Gruters to the interrogation hooch and told them that they would be leaving for Hanoi by truck that night. They would be responsible, he added, for the care of the criminal Sijan. All three prisoners would wear leg irons and handcuffs for the journey.

Craner protested immediately. Sijan was too weak to attempt escape. Chaining a man in his condition would probably kill him; he had to be protected from the pain.

The Rodent pondered this outburst a moment, then, surprisingly, agreed with Craner. The prisoners would each be tied loosely with rope. In that way they could feed and wash Sijan.

It almost seemed to Gruters that the Rodent was so eager to see the last of Lance that he was willing to bend his normally inflexible authoritarian stance and agree to Craner's brazen request. More likely, Gruters thought later that afternoon when they were washing Lance and trying to feed him in preparation for the truck ride, the Rodent realized how near death Sijan had slipped because of the complete lack of medical care and from the brutal treatment he had received in this camp. The Rodent probably did not want him to die en route to Hanoi because he had orders to deliver three live prisoners.

After nightfall they carried Lance from his cell and placed him on a pile of straw spread on the steel bed of a battered old Soviet deuce-and-a-half truck. Two rusty fifty-five gallon fuel drums stood in greasy puddles on either side of the truck bed, near the dented cab. Craner and Gruters sat down with their backs to the splintery wooden slats, and Lance lay between them on the straw. Each man was loosely bound about the wrists. Four armed soldiers threw their rain-soaked rucksacks up into the truck and took their guard positions on the short benches near the tailgate.

With a violent lurch, the truck sped off into the wet darkness, jolting wildly across ruts and potholes. Almost immediately, the terrible nature of the ordeal they were facing in this truck became clear. The fuel drum on the left side of the truck bed banged up into the air and careened past Gruters' shoulder, falling right at Lance's unprotected head. Craner sprang across Lance's body to intercept the barrel, but as he moved, the other fuel drum wobbled and rolled out to strike Sijan's injured right arm.

Lance screamed, then caught himself and clamped shut his jaws, swallowing his agony. Gruters thrust himself up now to his knees and grabbed the second fuel barrel with both arms to wrestle it away from Lance. As he did so, Craner cried out that the first barrel was loose again. For a moment they both hugged the fuel drums, but then they saw Lance's entire body bounce clear of the steel planking and rise over a foot, only to slam back down when the truck wheels cleared the rut in the washboard road.

Shouting over the jolts and banging cacophony, Gruters volunteered to hold Lance's head and torso if Craner could jam the two fuel drums into the far corner and hold them there.

Once they had the situation under better control, they both yelled at the guards and the driver to slow down. In the misty darkness the guards only laughed. The truck careened through the night on the terrible road, slamming across potholes and banging around curves. Gruters tried to hold Lance's skull tight against his belly, but the motion of the truck bed was too violent. With every slamming jolt, Lance's head snapped up, then down, painfully, into Gruters' abdomen, like the blow of a stone ball.

Again Craner cried out to the guards. Again they only laughed. The truck banged and rattled north on the dark, bombed-out detour. On the rain-slick steel truck bed, the two pilots fought desperately to protect Sijan from further injury.

Inland, to the north, there were chalk-white flares falling through the monsoon overcast.

The next day they did not leave the sanctuary of a small rice-farming village where they had stopped at dawn. Despite North Vietnamese propaganda that America was conducting a genocidal bombing war and randomly bombing villages, the driver obviously had orders to seek out the protection of a civilian settlement in which to wait out the dangerous hours of daylight when the American planes were most effective.

The guards spread a tarp across the back of the truck to cover the three Americans. They also removed the half-full fuel drum and did not replace it. That meant that Craner and Gruters would have only one savagely dangerous steel barrel to worry about for the remainder of the trip north.

Around midday the guards pulled back the tarp and ordered forward the assembled villagers who had been drawn up in a ragged formation to view the three captured pilots. A grim-faced NCO led the guards and villagers in several choruses of propaganda chants. The black-clad peasants dutifully shook their fists in unison, stamped their muddy feet on cue, and offered theatrically plausible scowls and frowns. It was vintage agiprop, loud and frenetic but lacking spontaneous emotion. When the group chants were over, several peasants crept nearer to the tailgate to get a better look at the Americans. Now the farmers wore expressions of guileless curiosity, not ritualized outrage.

That afternoon the rain fell harder. Sijan managed to sleep for two hours after Craner patiently spoon-fed him several mouthfuls of cold rice and greens. When he awoke, Lance spoke with unusual lucidness for almost an hour, carefully answering Gruters' whispered questions about the long ordeal on the karsts and ridges above the Ban Loboy Ford. He forced himself to be precise when he spoke of the bomb-fuse defect that had destroyed his plane. Craner and Gruters alternated their questions with encouragement, aware that Lance needed to tell his incredible story, but also aware that he was now so weak that conversation left him utterly exhausted.

Finally, after perhaps fifty minutes, his words were hardly audible. Gruters leaned close to hear. "Listen . . ." Lance managed. "I got . . . *away* from them up in the . . . hills. We'll escape again. . . ."

Gruters shook away the warm tears on his face so that Lance wouldn't see. "Right, Lance. Don't worry. We're working on it."

The injured skull composed itself in a smile. "Great! You count me in, Guy. I can . . . handle . . ."

He was gone again, adrift on his private sea of fever and pain.

Late afternoon. The brief tropical dusk thickened. Wind pressed down the wet thatch of the village roofs. Now the rain drops were heavy, stinging. Cold rose from the orange mud below the truck. A guard sneezed, another hacked and spat. Bob Craner huddled in the pounding rain, now shivering himself, his bare feet inordinately cold on the chill, rusty steel of the truckbed.

Gruters slept, somehow, crumpled in his loose ropes, in the face of the chill rain. Sijan lay on his horribly wounded back, his eyes hard, unblinking, open. The rain slashed down, bouncing with terrible velocity off his bare chest and face. Without fully realizing what he was doing, Craner dragged his way out of his own soaked black pyjama jacket. He wrung out the garment and spread it across

Lance's exposed chest and throat. Sijan seemed to recognize the gesture of protection. His eyes closed, and he slipped away into brief sleep.

At the side of the truckbed, Major Robert Craner crouched beneath the surprising force of the monsoon downpour, as chilled and desolate as he had ever been in any northern winter.

That long night, the battering ride was even worse than the night before. But now there was only one barrel to wrestle, and they had learned how to better protect Lance from the bouncing torture. Craner and Gruters took turns holding him between their legs, with Lance's upper body and head cushioned by their belly and chest. Gripping him firmly across the chest with one arm and clinging to the slats, Craner and Gruters gave him the maximum protection they could, absorbing the worst of the shocks with their own bodies. But even this protection was not enough to prevent further injury. By dawn, when they entered another coastal farming community, it was clear that Sijan was slipping into an apparently terminal coma.

For two hours under the tarp, with the rain popping on the mildewed canvas, Gruters worked on Lance, massaging his face and neck, wiping the clammy flesh of his chest with a wet cloth, and speaking clear, optimistic words of encouragement directly into his least-injured ear. Around eleven, the guards brought a chipped blue enamel bowl of garnished rice and one dirty spoon. The scent of warm food filled the back of the truck. Bending over Lance again, Gruters tried to bring him back to consciousness so that he could take a little nourishment. Slowly Lance seemed to regain a semiconscious state. Gruters eased a tiny spoonful of rice between Lance's lips, hoping that the taste of warm food would help restore consciousness.

For a cruel, indefinite period, Lance lay there with his eyes halfopen, waxy and glazed, his mouth agape, the beige clump of rice on his tongue. Gruters held his shoulders upright so that he did not choke. But Lance showed no sign of breathing. His flesh grew cool.

With tears welling up, Craner looked across the wet straw to Gruters. "He's dead, Guy."

Gruters, his own muddy face streaked with tears, violently shook his head. "No," he said flatly, "not Sijan."

Craner scooted across the truck bed and took Lance's face in his hands. For a long time he gently kneaded and massaged the flesh. Sijan lay in his arms, the uneaten morsel of rice still in his open mouth. Gruters sat beside Lance now, sobbing audibly, the tears streaming down his cheeks and off the tip of his nose.

With no warning, the guards threw back the tarp. A crowd of villagers in ragged black cotton had been gathered behind the soldiers for the inevitable agiprop chanting. But there were no shouts and gestures of ritual outrage. Instead, a truly spontaneous moaning sigh of shock and compassion swept across the assembled peasants. The tableau of the bruised, filthy, but powerful American pilots crying with uncontrollable grief as they cradled their dying comrade was so emotionally awesome that the sight transcended the cultural and political barriers separating the Asians and Americans. The contrite young soldiers dropped the tarp back across the stakes and dispersed the now-silent peasants.

Rain fell. Craner held Lance in his arms. A long time later, Lance mumbled, raised his face, and finally swallowed the bit of rice. He spoke again, an incoherent rambling about escape, then settled lower on the straw, his breathing shallow but regular . . . a semblance of normal sleep.

Craner leaned down to peer into Lance's face. It was amazing that he had brought himself back once more from the edge. "Okay, buddy," Bob Craner whispered, "my hat's off to you."

Gruters rubbed the tears away from his eyes. "He's going to make it, Bob," he said, his voice warm with feeling. "He's really going to make it."

Rain hissed and rattled on the canvas. They waited for the night and the next stage of their terrible journey.

Chapter
Twelve

Hoa
Lo
Prison,
Hanoi

January 1968

The truck reached the southern
fringes of Hanoi in the middle of the third night. When they
bounced off the rutted surface of the detour road and onto the
unbombed asphalt of Route 6 at Ha Dong, Gruters realized that
their protracted ordeal was almost over. The driver now switched
his headlights to high beam and sped down the potholed but otherwise undamaged highway. Ahead of them, through rips in the flap-
ping tarp, Gruters could see the scattered lights of the city.

After a few minutes on this narrow colonial highway, they reached
a roadblock, and new guards clambered up to join those at the rear.
The tarp was lashed down more securely; Craner and Gruters had
to kneel to be roughly blindfolded with moldy strips of the ubiquitous black cotton. The guards did not bother Sijan, who lay in

mumbling delirium on the scattered straw.

They were in the city itself. Around them they heard other vehicles, rumbling truck convoys, jeeps with squealing tires, an occasional backfiring motorcycle. This was not the traffic of a peacetime city late on a Saturday night, but rather the movement of men and materiel in the capital of a country at war, a country that was about to unleash an audacious offensive six hundred miles to the south. But Tet and its brutal fighting were still two weeks off. Now the complex logistical buildup was still in high gear within the unbombed sanctuary of Hanoi.

The truck skirted several restricted military districts and drove north toward the embankment of the Red River. After passing cursory examination at one more roadblock, they turned right, bounced down a lane, and stopped under dripping trees. Guards threw open the screeching tailgate. Gruters and Craner knelt again to have their blindfolds removed. As they blinked in the glare of the flashlights, they got their first look at the thick concrete walls of Hoa Lo Prison.

To Gruters the nineteenth-century prison looked like something out of a grade B Korean War movie. The high walls were topped with shards of broken glass and a triple strand of barbed wire; one strand, he noted, was beaded with white enamel insulators which indicated electrified wire. The only window facing the street was about ten feet up in the gray concrete blockhouse guarding the main gate, and even this window was barricaded by a double grid of thick iron bars. The walls stretched away left and right, encompassing an entire city block.

Bob Craner stood at the rear of the truck swaying with exhaustion from the battering, sleepless ride. The combination of diarrhea from the foul food and water he had consumed since the shootdown, the physical ordeal of the truck ride, and the protracted mental anguish that had gripped him as he held Sijan in his arms had debilitated Craner to the edge of despondency. He looked up at the somber concrete walls, the glass shards, and the wire and realized that he had come to a truly evil place. But he really did not care what went on inside those walls. He had been in captivity for twenty-three days, and his reserves of strength and optimism had reached the first low ebb of his long imprisonment.

With a grating rumble the double main gates of Hoa Lo Prison swung open, and the two pilots stood facing a small Vietnamese officer in a drab green uniform. He squared the peaked cap on his head, then turned and spoke in a high-pitched voice to the two stocky, club-wielding guards who stood behind him at a respectful distance. When he turned back, Craner got his first good look at the officer's moon face and dark eyes.

This diminutive officer with the seemingly inoffensive face was a senior captain in the People's Army of Vietnam, the commanding officer of the Hoa Lo Prison. He was an educated man in his early forties, a longtime party member with a reputation for tough competence and utter loyalty to the revolutionary struggle. In his dedicated obedience to the just orders of the politburo and to his command section, the senior captain left no ostensibly unimportant detail or duty to the care of his subordinates. Thus he was there in person at two on this rainy Sunday morning to meet the latest group of American prisoners arriving from the Vinh holding camp.

The captain's duties also included the interrogation of American prisoners. He supervised the long and brutal process of persuading them about the rightness of the party, that they should cooperate with the party and people of Democratic Vietnam by voluntarily making public statements and by writing confessions about their notorious war crimes. It was this senior captain who had worked so diligently and with such impressive results on Lieutenant Commander Richard Stratton, who had arrived at these same gates almost exactly one year earlier.

The American prisoners were never told the names of their guards and interrogators. Instead, the POWs supplied appropriate and pejorative English nicknames to the captors. The captain was called the Bug.

But Craner and Gruters were now the newest of the new guys; they understood nothing about the Bug or about the long days of interrogation that awaited them inside the damp concrete walls. In their despondent and exhausted condition, they could only obey orders with clumsy stiffness.

Languidly waving a flashlight, the Bug ordered Craner and Gruters back into the truck to lower Sijan to the board pallet the guards had produced from the dark entrance tunnel of the main gatehouse. The Bug smiled benignly down at Sijan's mangled body and fouled black clothing. Again he gestured with his flashlight, now into the grim tunnel of the main gate.

"Wash him," he said to Gruters and Craner.

They grasped the wet boards at either end and hefted the pallet between them. A silent guard wearing an incongruous pith helmet on the chill, dripping night led them through the tunnel and a narrow side door beside the barred inner set of double gates. They found themselves in a bare courtyard paved with worn cement. On both sides of the long courtyard were the whitewashed walls of parallel, two-storey cellblocks with peaked roofs of stained, orange tiles. Every twenty feet or so there was an arched, glassless window, barred with a double steel grating and further barricaded by five strands of barbed wire strung from rusty stanchions set at angles along the walls. There were naked light bulbs burning inside those open cellblock windows, even at this lonely hour of the night. A piercing, chill dankness exuded from the walls and the open cellblock windows, as if this jail never saw the sunlight, as if a permanent wet despair clung to these mildewed walls.

To Gruters it felt as if the temperature had dropped to about forty degrees when they entered the courtyard. He began shivering now, as much from the somber recognition that he had entered the harsh world of a professionally run military prison in the capital of a communist enemy as from the physical chill. Within these walls there would be no possibility of escape. In those stark cellblocks, he could expect no compassion. There were no friends here.

They lay Sijan down beside the waist-high cistern and gently removed his shirt and trousers. In several places the black cotton had adhered to the open sores, and they had to wet the material to free it from the oozing scabs. A guard brought a bucket and tossed them a block of strong-smelling, yellow laundry soap. After lathering their hands as best they could, they soaped down Sijan's wounded body and rinsed him. The rain fell harder, and Sijan stared in delirium straight up into the cold, stinging drops.

Once they had Lance dressed again in his wet clothing, the guards prodded them along as they lugged the clumsy pallet down the courtyard to a locked gate at the end of the right cellblock. The gate clanked and squeaked, then swung open onto a dimly lit corridor of peeling walls and anonymous steel doors. Following the guard, they were led to a cell about seven feet long and wide. A crumbling cement bed platform stood at the end beneath the barred window. Rain blew in between the bars and dripped down the walls to stand in muddy puddles on the floor.

When they had placed the pallet onto the bed platform, Gruters expected the guard to cover Lance with a blanket. Instead the soldier gazed down at Sijan's dripping flesh, then up at the open window. He grunted some incomprehensible comment and ordered Gruters and Craner out of the cell.

Sijan lay on his back, as he had at the cistern, his eyes half-open, his jaws jammed shut against the pain.

At the far end of the courtyard, near the main gate, Craner and Gruters were handed off to another set of guards who led them down a dark alleyway, through two steel doors, and into another dank, double-storey cellblock with flaking whitewashed walls. Issuing curt commands, the guards separated the pilots, shoving them each into a solitary cell.

Gruters's cell was smaller than the one where they had taken Lance, and there was no window. Nevertheless, puddles had collected on the concrete floor from the dripping walls and leaks in the ceiling. The cell was even chillier than the courtyard, and he felt himself beginning to shiver with alarming violence, as if he had lost control of his limbs. The battering exhaustion of the previous three days and the bone-piercing cold of the cell were wearing him down. He needed sleep. But when he crouched against the driest wall, his knees clutched to his chest for warmth, the guard screamed through the inspection grate in his door for him to stand up.

He had no choice but to obey. Through his exhaustion and uncontrollable shivering, he found it baffling that the goddamn guard objected so violently to his crouching down to try to get a little sleep. It was three in the morning, and obviously he wasn't going anywhere.

But sleep was not part of the agenda for the inmates of this particular cellblock that stood in isolation to the right of Hoa Lo's main gate. Neither Guy Gruters nor Bob Craner then had any way of knowing they were in New Guy Village, the central interrogation center for newly arrived prisoners of war. Here, the guards and interrogators, under the dedicated and energetic leadership of the Bug, had one assignment: break the prisoner's will to resist. Through sadistic torture, combined with constant harassment and sleep deprivation, they were to force the Americans to go beyond the five authorized answers delineated in the Code of Conduct.

Ostensibly this brutal treatment was necessitated by the need for military information. But in reality the interrogators were not competent to conduct detailed technical questioning with any true military value. Here, in the four "quiz rooms" facing the New Guy Village courtyard, the prisoners were beaten and strung up in variations of the rope torture for purposes other than obtaining straightforward military information. Here their *will* was broken; they were made to experience utter despair. Here they were taught that their captors were all-powerful, that any resistance to future demands for propaganda statements and war crimes confessions before visiting American peace delegations would be futile.

For the hardcase prisoners who defied the Bug's initial punishment, there were special torture centers—"knobby rooms"—such as Room 18, just down the narrow passageway from the cells where Bob Craner and Guy Gruters spent their first night in Hanoi. Room 18 was not just a spare cell that the Bug chose to conduct interrogations; the room had been renovated specifically for use as a torture chamber. The walls had been replastered with fist-sized knobs of stucco protruding at regular intervals on each wall: soundproofing to muffle the screams of the men undergoing heavy torture. Room 18 was rectangular, about twenty feet by twelve. The green stucco walls were stained with ochre smears, the spattered blood of men who had been beaten for hours with rubber-strip whips and bamboo clubs. On the high ceiling and on two walls there were rusty steel hooks that were used in various combinations when prisoners were strung up by their leg irons to be beaten or when their limbs were twisted in the rope torture. The Bug or his assistant interrogators, the Cat, the Rabbit, and Pig Eye, usually sat at a small wooden table near the end wall—well clear of spattering blood—smoking Marlboro cigarettes that had been taken from captured Americans.

Unlike the disorganized interrogation sessions conducted by the Rodent and his colleagues in the South, however, the Bug's team had amassed a considerable body of military background information against which they could verify the answers they extracted from their prisoners. Thus, if a Navy pilot finally admitted he was flying from the carrier *Enterprise* and, eventually, after hours or days of uninterrupted torture, revealed that his squadron was VF 96, the Bug would then realize that the pilot's original statement that he flew an A-4 Skyhawk had been a lie, part of a cover story. The North Vietnamese knew from *Stars and Stripes* and other unclassified

American service newspapers that VF 96 flew F-4B Phantoms. The man would then be put back under torture to show him the error of his ways in resisting the just demands of the People's Army.

The Bug's interrogators also kept the recent arrivals isolated from their fellow prisoners so that the new guy could not benefit from advice and encouragement; nor could frontseat and backseat pilots of crewed aircraft consult with each other over a cover story. After initially breaking a pilot through torture and demolishing as much as they could of his cover story, the interrogators were usually content, and the man was transferred from Heartbreak Hotel or New Guy Village to the three- and four-man rooms in the cellblock to the left of the main gate that the prisoners had named Little Vegas.

Those pilots who continually resisted the interrogators' efforts to demolish their cover stories, however, were held in the solitary cubicles of the reception cellblocks. Such men—often senior officers with command positions—took terrible torture for impressive periods. The normal treatment for these determined resisters was to deprive them of rest, sleep, and the oblivion of unconsciousness produced by physical battering. The rope torture and "light" club beatings on the shins, elbows, and knees were the standard procedure. They were tortured around the clock on one-hour cycles, strung up from the ceiling hooks of Room 18 and the other knobby rooms that the Bug renovated and pressed into service as Hoa Lo became crowded in the autumn of 1967. At the end of three or four days of this treatment, deprived of sleep or rest of any kind, with no respite from the pain, almost every pilot broke and offered to supply straight answers.

The Bug and his assistants, especially the Rabbit and Pig Eye, then had one more surprise for their pain-crazed victims. When the man broke and finally said he would talk, the interrogator often left him hanging in his agonizing ropes for as long as eight more hours: "punishment" for having resisted the just demands of the party and its army and a warning that further resistance would be futile.

After their debilitating truck ride north, both Guy Gruters and Bob Craner were prime candidates for heavy torture and eventual breaking. Their audacious but flimsy cover story would certainly not stand up to the scrutiny of the Bug's experienced interrogators.

Once the secrets of the Misty FACs began to spill out, they would be subjected to more protracted torture that would leave them vulnerable to fruitful propaganda manipulation. However, they were not subjected to heavy torture in New Guy Village: Their cover story held water after four days of intensive interrogation. Ironically, they owed their good fortune to Lance Sijan, the prototypical defiant, unbroken American resister.

The first morning in Hoa Lo—when the ubiquitous corridor loud-speaker began blaring its daily twelve hours of propaganda—Bob Craner was taken from his solitary cell to one of the quiz rooms across New Guy Village courtyard. His interrogator was the Bug in person. Craner had gotten control of himself during the night in the chill, drafty cell and now produced a believable impression of a man in a near stupor, a man whose will to resist had been completely eroded by exhaustion, fear, and despair. Obediently he repeated a refined, detailed version of the cover story he had first told three weeks earlier in the Rao Nay Valley. Craner delineated the command structure and mission of the bogus F-100 fighter-bomber squadron stationed at the new American air base, Phu Cat. As he spun out his cover story, he silently prayed that Guy Gruters could produce a semblance of this deception during his own interrogation.

Then, incredibly, at midday he was not returned to his solitary cell but instead joined up with Gruters himself and marched down the Heartbreak Hotel courtyard to the cell where Lance lay on his wooden pallet. There they were given their chipped bowls of watery pumpkin soup and their morning bread ration. The guard ordered them to feed Sijan and to clean his wounds with water from a pail. Slamming shut the steel cell door, the guard angrily yelled at them to get to work, to obey all orders.

As they bent over Lance, Craner spoke in a steady whisper, reiterating all the questions and answers of the morning interrogation. Concentrating with visible intensity, Gruters strained through his fatigue to memorize the answers. After a tense quarter hour, Craner repeated the questions and Gruters supplied the memorized answers. They were both still exhausted, cold and hungry. But for the first time since arriving in Hanoi, they began to feel their confidence return.

Their reborn optimism, however, did not extend to Lance. Lying on the damp pallet in this drafty cell, he appeared even weaker than he had the night before. Clearly, the jolting truck ride north and the lack of medical treatment had left him near death. After they had washed his open wounds as best they could, they propped him up and slowly, patiently fed him. Wetting pinches of bread in their own soup, they carefully placed them between his lips. When Lance had forced himself to eat as much as he could, they eased him back down onto the cold boards of the pallet, gently molding his limbs and torso until they found the least painful position.

Sijan had followed the entire question-and-answer memorizing process; he understood the importance of this exercise and had remained alertly silent while Craner and Guy concentrated. Now he spoke up, his voice hardly more than a strangled whisper.

"Listen," he said, painfully forming each word. ". . . I'll get . . . these guards . . . to have you come back . . . care of me . . . you can talk . . . *here* . . ."

His voice dropped to an inaudible wheeze. As Gruters leaned close to Sijan's face, he could hear a wet crackling down inside his lungs. With great effort, Sijan spoke again.

"When you . . . back here . . . check . . . how secure that gate . . ."

Incredibly, his will to escape had not abated.

At the end of the third day of intensively questioning Gruters and Craner in the quiz rooms of the NGV, the Bug and his staff were apparently convinced that the two pilots were telling them the truth. On the fourth morning, guards escorted them to a three-man cell in the wing of the Little Vegas cellblock known as Thunderbird. When they arrived at the cell, they found Lance Sijan lying on a wet canvas cot against the dripping wall of the cell.

The first thing Craner did when the guard unlocked the door was to turn to the man and say, "*Bao Cao.*"

In three days at Hoa Lo, he had learned this pidgin Vietnamese phrase meant "call the officer." Amazingly, a fairly senior officer dutifully appeared only minutes later.

Craner made a point of bowing respectfully, then pointed to Sijan's cot. "Our friend is very sick," he said, speaking with low, clear enunciation so the officer could understand. "He needs a doctor. He needs blankets, dry clothes."

The officer scowled and nodded, impatiently. "Doctor come. You wait."

Hoa Lo Prison, Hanoi

The cell door slammed shut, and they went to Lance's cot.

He seemed to be sleeping, but the hoarse sounds that came from his open mouth were not snores. He was having trouble breathing. The wet, the chill, the dank air had definitely gotten to him. Snot and stringy phlegm streamed from his nostrils and mouth. Working carefully, Bob Craner and Gruters propped Lance up so that he could breathe more easily. They held him to warm his body. After a while, he came around and smiled at them.

"On the way . . . here," he whispered, ". . . a look at . . . setup. It's . . ."

Again the subject of his half-lucid conversation was escape.

Early that afternoon the camp doctor arrived at the cell. He was a little old fellow in patched civilian clothes sporting a dirty Red Cross arm band on his left sleeve.

Smiling with incongruous warmth, the old man shuffled into the cell muttering, *"Bonsoir, bonsoir."*

He went straight to Lance's cot and took his pulse. Next he held an antique glass-bulb thermometer under Lance's armpit. When he read the temperature, he clucked loudly and shook his head. With a dim flashlight, he scanned the putrid edges of the leg cast and again clucked his tongue.

He opened his canvas medical kit and removed a primitive chrome-and-glass hypodermic syringe assembly. Working patiently, he sawed off the tips of several glass vials containing a yellow fluid and gave Lance a massive, subcutaneous injection.

Sijan exhibited no visible reaction to the probing of the thick steel needle.

When the doctor examined Lance's mangled hand and the bone-deep abrasions on all his knuckles, he shook his head, mumbling in singsong French, *"Ça, alors . . . il a passé trop longtemps dans la brousse . . . dans le bled, vous savez?"*

Bob Craner was an intelligent, self-educated officer who had worked his way up through the aviation cadet program. He had mastered reasonably fluent night-school French, enough to realize that this old doctor spoke in the ungrammatical argot of the French Army. Craner was shrewd, a survivor. He understood that the old man was undoubtedly a former colonial army medic, upgraded to the status of medical practitioner after the revolution. His sympathies were probably as much with the Americans as with his new masters. Craner guessed that they could secure adequate medical treatment for Lance from this medic, as well as permission for Guy and him to stay together with Lance in this cell.

"*Oui, docteur,*" Craner began, again bowing with respect. "*Notre ami a passé longtemps dans la forêt. . . .*"

After a few minutes of quiet conversation, the doctor said he understood the seriousness of Lance's condition. He made notes in a battered schoolboy's *cahier* and called for the guard to unlock the cell door.

Following the midday siesta, the guards came and took both Craner and Gruters to separate, follow-up interrogation sessions in the quiz rooms on the other side of the bathhouse in the Little Vegas courtyard. This session went well for each of them. In Guy Gruters' case, he was able to plead ignorance of the recent bombing war with a certain sincerity. He had been shot down on December 20, he insisted, on only his second mission after a three-week convalescent leave following his first shoot-down and rescue in early November.

His interrogator, the arrogant Pig Eye, seemed inordinately proud that he had before him an American air pirate who had once been shot down and rescued but had been captured after his second shoot-down. When Pig asked what type of antiaircraft weapon had downed Gruters' two planes, Guy simply muttered, "a cannon, I think."

Pig Eye laughed. "American plane too slow for People's Army air defense."

Gruters nodded earnestly. "The F-100 is a very *old* airplane."

"F-100!" Pig Eye could not contain his scornful laughter. "Old, very old aircraft from Korea aggression. The F-100 has no secrets for us. We know *everything* about famous F-100 Sabre Jet."

Gruters nodded in sad agreement. The idiot seemed to be confusing the F-86 Sabre of Korean War fame with the F-100 Super Sabre that had first flown three years after the 1953 armistice in Korea. With the arrogant assertion that the modified F-100 held "no secrets" for the North Vietnamese, Pig Eye was passing up his best chance to unlock the secrets of the Misty FACs. Intel reported that the NVA were baffled by the accuracy and speed with which American fighter-bombers struck flak and SAM sites and any sizable concentration of trucks in Route Package I and Steel Tiger. They did not realize that the constant low-level visual and electronic recon sweeps of the Misty FACs' "obsolete" F-100s played a big part in the mounting success of the interdiction campaign in North Vietnam's southern panhandle and Laos.

Gruters, of course, knew that one of the founding leaders of the Misty FACs, Major Bud Day, had been shot down striking a SAM site in Pack I in late August. Word was that he was now a POW; if that were true, then Bud Day had obviously kept the secret of the Misty FACs and their old airplanes from his interrogators.

Swaying on his tired legs in the smelly, airless quiz room while Pig Eye went into one of his rambling diatribes about the technical prowess of the People's Army and the People's Air Force, Gruters began to realize that he was, indeed, still a soldier, that he was still at war, even though he now wore the striped cotton pajamas of a prisoner instead of a jungle-green flight suit. He was a professional officer, just like Bud Day, Bob Craner, and Lance Sijan. And he was performing his duty as best he could, carrying the fight to the enemy, resisting.

When Guy Gruters had come back to Phu Cat from his brief convalescent leave and resumed his tour of combat missions with the Misty FACs, he assumed he would complete that tour in late May 1968. Now, he knew, he would be in a different kind of combat much longer. In this extended campaign, his skills as a pilot meant nothing. Here in the prison system of the NVA, he must learn to practice cunning; he must learn to take pain; and he must deepen his resolve to resist, to keep the faith with his fellow prisoners, as they said in the Code, and to never for one moment doubt that this ordeal would end one day and that he would then be accountable for his conduct while a prisoner.

As he swayed on the wet concrete, half-listening to Pig Eye's diatribe, Gruters realized that he was very fortunate to have been with Lance Sijan these past two weeks. If there was any single person who epitomized the qualities a prisoner needed to survive and return with his honor intact, that model now lay in the three-man cell across the courtyard.

When they returned to the cell that night, they found that the doctor had removed the grotesque plaster cast from Lance's leg and covered the wound with a clean dressing. They had also shifted Lance to a board pallet. Beside this pallet, a pitted chrome intravenous feeding stand held a bottle of what they guessed was a saline-dextrose drip. Lance lay under a stained but reasonably dry blanket, wheezing in troubled sleep.

An hour later the guard brought their soup bowls and a separate, covered mess tin with special food for Lance. His ration consisted of a meaty broth, bread smeared with colorless margarine, and several cut pieces of banana. Their own food was the usual thin pumpkin soup and a half-pound loaf of stale bread.

Before they woke Lance to feed him while his broth was still warm, they cleaned his face as best they could of accumulated phlegm and mucus. Then they went through the ritual of propping him up and slowly spoon-feeding him the soup.

Gruters was cheerful this evening, heartened by the medical treatment and special food Lance was now receiving. "Hey," he said, smiling, "look at this . . . there's real damn *meat* in this soup, man. Eat all of it, Lance. It'll make you strong."

Sijan's eyes rolled from left to right, then down to take in the spoonful of grayish broth. Obediently he opened his mouth and swallowed. But it was obvious to Gruters that Lance was weakening steadily, despite the antibiotic injections, the intravenous drip, and the blanket. Suddenly a terrible image flooded Gruters's mind.

"Lance," he whispered, "did those bastards hammer on you over in that other cell?"

"A . . . *little* . . ." Lance croaked. "I was trying . . . off the bed . . . they . . ."

"It's okay," Bob Craner interrupted. "We're with you now, and we're going to take care of you. The doctor's on our side, Lance. He's a good guy."

Sijan nodded, his eyes focusing with lucidness for a moment. "I gotta eat . . . soup . . . get strong." He turned his terrible face toward the door. ". . . Outta this place . . ."

After an hour of patient feeding, Sijan had been able to consume half a cup of broth and one small piece of banana. Despite their own gnawing hunger, Craner and Gruters carefully covered Lance's leftovers with a scrap of towel so that they could feed him later.

Cell doors clanged. Footsteps echoed in the corridor. They heard no voices above the monotonous din of the propaganda speaker. There had to be other Americans in this wing, but the cells had been constructed without abutting walls, and their steel doors opened in alternating patterns, either into dead-end walkways between cells or facing the blank whitewashed wall of the opposite cell. There was no way the prisoners could communicate other than by shouting, and it was impossible to be sure a guard wasn't waiting in the silent corridor to pounce on any hapless prisoner who attempted such an audacious breach of discipline.

Bob Craner and Guy Gruters weren't yet aware of the cruel punishment that awaited men caught trying to organize communication networks. A day or more in a knobby room was usually enough to dissuade the residents of Little Vegas that communication among cells was not worth the terrible punishment.

But Gruters and Craner soon discovered a very important piece of prison intelligence. The guards were so repulsed by Sijan's appearance, and by his frightening spells of delirium when he would glare and mumble, that they avoided entering the cell if they weren't ordered in by an officer. Therefore, when Gruters would call, "*Bao Cao,*" periodically to ask the duty officer when the doctor was coming to tend to Lance, the guard in the corridor would not slam open the peephole grate and bellow at him to be quiet. Instead, the guard would leave his post, go all the way down the corridor past the two foul latrines to the officer's post at the other end of the next wing. This process left their corridor unguarded for up to five minutes, during which they could call to the men in the other cells.

The response they received was not overly encouraging. Don't try to communicate by voice, they were admonished. Don't keep yelling *Bao Cao.* There were men in this wing who had suffered severe torture for attempting to communicate, and *they* would be the ones who got into deep shit again if the new guys were caught tricking the guards. Hang in there and *wait,* they were told. They would be contacted about communication by other means than shouting.

The "go to sleep" gong rang at nine each night in the various cellblocks of Hoa Lo Prison. But the dim light bulbs in the cells were never extinguished. At midnight the men in Little Vegas and New Guy Village could hear the chiming bells of a Catholic church several blocks away. The bells were a reassuring sound, a reminder that despite the barbaric cruelty of the interrogation center, the North Vietnamese shared *some* cultural traits with the West, that maybe, eventually, they were people a man could reason with.

But the church bells also had a darker significance. Men selected for special treatment in the knobby rooms were usually taken from their cells between midnight and two in the morning when, as Scott Fitzgerald once put it, it was "the dark night of the soul."

Bob Craner awoke shivering just as the church bells fell silent outside their barred window. It was raining, and water streamed down the walls. Automatically, he rose from his bare wooden bunk boards to check on Lance. What he saw shocked him fully awake.

Sijan was hunched over on his side, staring with delirious fascination as the fingers of his left hand stroked and plucked the syringe tip of the intravenous drip. Before Craner could act, Lance tore the needle from his arm and dragged his right leg off the edge of the low pallet. He was trying to leave his bed, another impossible escape attempt.

"Lance," Craner yelled, "no."

Bob Craner swung off his bunk and splashed across the puddles to grab Lance just as he rolled from his pallet. In a moment, Gruters was beside him. But they were too late to prevent Lance dragging his one thin blanket in the standing water.

They lay him back down, and Gruters covered him with his own blanket. But the thin Russian *drap* was soaked from leaks in the roof. Lance continued to wheeze and shiver. His eyes were frightening in the glare of the overhead bulb. Mumbling and shaking his head, he tried repeatedly to rise from the pallet. Patiently Guy and Bob Craner restrained him.

The syringe tip of the IV setup dangled down into a brown puddle, and they knew they could not reinsert it in Lance's vein.

For the rest of that night, they took two-hour shifts, crouching beside Lance's pallet to prevent him from dragging himself off.

The next day, Craner was led to morning interrogation, and Gruters was allowed to remain with Lance. That afternoon, the pattern was reversed. After the second daily feeding, the doctor arrived and gave Lance another large injection of antibiotics. The old man clucked and pursed his lips as Craner explained how Lance had torn out the syringe. Instead of setting up the IV drip with a clean needle, however, the doctor called a guard, who lugged the jangling assembly away. Next, the old man changed the pus-soaked dressing on Lance's leg, again clucking and shaking his head at the condition of the wound.

Craner begged the doctor for some dry blankets, but the old man only opened his hands in a pantomime of Gallic resignation. There were, he said, no blankets to spare.

Out in the corridor the loudspeaker scratched and echoed, a Radio Hanoi propaganda broadside condemning America's assertion that the People's Army intended to violate the upcoming Tet cease-fire.

That night they split the watch in two. Guy stayed awake until the midnight church bell, and Bob Craner took the second shift. About three he dozed off, then awoke a few minutes later when a gust of rainy wind shook the ragged bamboo screen that covered half their window.

Lance had managed to raise his shoulders and lift his head above his wooden block pillow. He was staring intently at the cell door. When Craner turned to face the door, he saw the inspection grate open and the head of a guard silhouetted against the brighter lights of the corridor. Sijan beckoned the guard to enter the cell, gesturing with his twisted right hand. Beside his hip he kept his left hand hidden, cocked into a bony karate fist.

Craner literally shook himself to be sure he was not hallucinating this bizarre scene. Here was Sijan, a dying cripple, luring in a cruel, disciplined enemy guard so that he could attack him. Recovering his composure, Craner reached out and made a show of stroking Lance's forehead. Then Craner waved to the guard and smiled. "All okay here," he said, "okay."

Sijan sank back to his boards, muttering and growling.

For the next several days there were no interrogation sessions for either Gruters or Craner. They spent their daylight hours trying to feed Lance his special food. In the evening they talked to him about his time alone in the mountains, hoping to keep him rational until he slipped into sleep, to distract him from his pain so that he would not drift into delirium.

Lance was lucid during the daylight. After dark he appeared to lose his rational reference points; his mind floated on pain. Sometimes he would whimper when the agony was at its worst. But never once in the time Craner and Guy Gruters had been with him did he make an explicit complaint about his terrible suffering. Never once did he say, "It hurts. I'm in pain." Instead, he would often apologize to them for the trouble they went to washing and feeding him. "When I'm better," he'd say, "I'll make it up to you."

But it was becoming increasingly clear to Bob Craner that Lance was not going to recover, that he was fighting his last battle here in this cell. His breathing now was strained; he hacked and wheezed, often coughing up thick, choking strings of phlegm. More and more he drifted, his mind far away from Hanoi. It was now almost impossible to feed him. After a few spoonfuls of broth, he would turn his head away and slip into an exhausted, wheezing sleep. The doctor came one morning and drew a small syringe of blood for a laboratory analysis. Early that afternoon he returned, muttering sadly to Craner about Sijan's *"sang blanc."* After a brief conversation, Craner realized that Lance had a runaway white–blood-cell count and that the doctor found this alarming.

That night Gruters dozed off during his early watch shift and awoke to hear Lance growling again at the guard who peeked in through the inspection grate. Amazed at the sight, Gruters did not immediately try to silence Lance. Sijan lay there on his back, too weak to raise his head, but he was now lucid, and he obviously realized that his terrible appearance frightened the squeamish guards in the corridor. He bared his teeth, flashed his feverish eyes, and growled savagely. The guard slammed down the inspection plate and strode away with loud footsteps. Lance sagged back lower on his pallet, chuckling warmly.

The next morning Craner suggested to Gruters that they start doing calisthenics in their cell to keep their muscle tone so they wouldn't get hurt too badly if they underwent more rope torture but also just to stay warm. They began doing push-ups, and Gruters amused them by trying to demonstrate the famous one-armed push-up of the Airborne. After a few minutes of exercise, Lance called weakly from his pallet and they went to him.

They had to lean close to his face to catch his words. "Come on . . . pull me . . . up. . . . I want . . . some exercise for my . . . arms. . . ."

As they often did, Craner and Gruters exchanged glances of utter amazement above Sijan's head. Rather than discourage him, however, they folded a blanket for a backrest and propped him up. Sijan set his face in grim determination and began to stiffly flex his skeletal arms. Back and forth. Again. His eyes clenched against the pain, his forehead slick with sweat. After a few spastic cycles of arm flexing, he paused, his breath rattling in his throat.

"When you get ready to go," he blurted in a choking whisper, "I want to be . . . in . . . shape. . . ." The effort had exhausted him, and he swooped away into shallow sleep.

Craner sighed, then shook his head. "Maybe you're right, Guy," he said quietly. "Maybe this son of a gun *is* going to make it."

Gruters stared at Sijan's face. "He *will* make it, Bob. I know he will."

Two days later the rain was relentless, driving and cold. That afternoon they huddled near Lance to protect him from the leaks and chilling draft. Now, for the first time, he was floating utterly adrift with delirium in the daylight. But Bob Craner was determined to keep Lance connected to some kind of rational mooring. Craner chatted slowly about football, about the way the game had changed over the years he had followed it and about the fine Falcon teams that the Academy had fielded when Lance was a cadet athlete there.

Briefly Lance seemed to respond to this conversation. But then he floated away again. After several minutes, he opened his eyes and spoke. "Do you . . . know . . . Bart Holaday?"

"I remember the name," Craner answered, trying to keep Lance lucid. "Wasn't he a football player?"

For several moments Sijan's expression was blank, unfocused. Then Lance turned with a sudden flash of emotion in his eyes and shocked Craner by speaking in soft but otherwise normal tones. "I just was talking to Bart," Lance said. His head fell and he was unconscious.

The next afternoon, Lance awoke and smiled at Guy and Bob Craner. "Hey . . ." he said, visibly struggling to speak in a bubbling whisper. "How about going out . . . get me a burger . . . and french fries. . . ." His smile twisted into a spasm of violent coughing. But the warmth of his joke flashed in his eyes as he hacked and gasped for breath.

The following morning, however, there were no more jokes. Lance's face, already pale, took on a flushed, translucent waxiness. His skin was hot and dry to the touch. His eyes shone with soaring fever. When he tried to speak, the words would not come; his lips clicked open and shut, but no coherent sound escaped, only the choking bubbles.

Bob and Guy propped Lance up so that he could breathe and helped him spit up several cupfuls of strangling phlegm. But Sijan had still not given up. He formed single letters with his lips, his eyes gazing fiercely into their faces.

"*I . . . M O . . . K. . . .*"

By night his breathing became even more labored. Now he could no longer form even single letters with his lips. As Craner and Gruters struggled to adjust Lance's sitting position so that he could breathe, they asked him to indicate by blinking—one blink yes, two blinks no—if they were helping him. Repeatedly they screamed, "*Bao Cao,*" and repeatedly the alarmed duty officer assured them in an almost conciliatory manner that the doctor was on his way from another camp and would be there soon.

Guards had brought the afternoon meal hours earlier, but Guy and Bob didn't touch their soup. They were struggling to help Lance breathe. Every few minutes they would bend him painfully forward so that he could hack up mouthfuls of the mucus that was literally drowning him. As they tended Lance, Guy Gruters kept up a steady encouraging monologue.

"Lance, you're going to be okay. The doctor's coming, and he's going to take you to the hospital. That's *good*, Lance. They'll have a real bed for you and dry blankets. . . ."

Lance's eyes lost their hot shimmer. He was lucid but too weak to answer. Carefully, he blinked in single sequence to indicate that he understood.

But when the doctor finally arrived, Lance's eyes became wild again, feral. Clearly he understood what was going to happen. Gruters struggled to buoy up Sijan's spirits.

"It's *good,* Lance," Guy insisted. "You're going to get some real medical treatment now . . . in the hospital. . . ."

The doctor came back with a dry blanket and covered Lance's lower body. Three guards with muddy canvas boots entered the cell, and the doctor ordered two of them to lift the pallet while the third guard was detailed to prop up Lance's shoulders so that he could breathe.

As the soldiers hefted up the pallet, Lance's face flashed with savage intensity. He *knew* they were taking him away to die.

Suddenly his loud, clear voice filled the cramped cell with a force that shocked them all. "Oh, my *God,*" he called. "It's over . . . it's *over.*" His face rippled and clenched with terminal emotion. "Dad . . ." he cried in the same powerful, commanding voice. *"Dad . . .* help me. Dad, I *need* you. . . ."

The cell door clanged back and the guards shoved their burden out into the corridor. Behind them the old doctor clucked and mumbled sad phrases in singsong French.

The steel door banged shut. Bob Craner and Guy Gruters sat slumped on the splintery edge of the low bunk, utterly spent with despair, their faces sticky with tears.

Out in the corridor the loudspeaker box squawked a long propaganda speech about the inevitable victory of the People's just struggle. Rain fell more softly now. Sometime later, perhaps one hour, perhaps two, the air-raid siren went off and they heard the distant scratching of Navy A-6 Intruders, snaking down through the dark overcast to hit the railway bridges west of the city.

Sijan was gone and the war went on as it always had.

Syl Sijan drove alone through the night, east along the expressway that paralleled Milwaukee's industrial heart, the Menominee River Valley. In happier times he enjoyed these solitary drives back from the Hillcrest Dining Room, his new restaurant in the western suburbs. But, since Lance had been shot down, two-and-a-half months earlier, the ritual of the late-night drive home to Bay View after a busy, satisfying day no longer offered pleasure.

On this chill Tuesday night in late January, he was so burdened with anguished worry about Lance that he couldn't even abide the soft classical music on the car radio. A few weeks after Lance went down, Syl had written to Da Nang requesting any additional information on rescue attempts. The void of uncertainty about Lance's status was agonizing. "We live day to day," he wrote, "in a vacuum of despair."

Now, two months later, that despair had literally seized hold of Syl Sijan. Suddenly his fist pounded the cold plastic of the steering wheel.

"Lance!" he screamed. "Lance . . . where *are* you?"

Shocked by his outburst, he felt a weird certainty that Lance was trying to reach him, that Lance was calling for his father.

"Lance . . . *Lance,*" Syl Sijan moaned as his eyes washed with tears and he struggled to control the car.

Two days later Guy Gruters and Bob Craner were transferred from Hoa Lo to the prison camp on Hanoi's northeast outskirts that the POWs called the Plantation. This complex had originally been the summer residence of the French colonial mayor of Hanoi. The crumbling two-storey villa was used by NVA staff, and the outbuildings, kitchen garden patch, and former servants' quarters were fenced in to form the lockup for prisoners. Several large rooms behind the "Big House" villa were used for propaganda cells where prisoners who had been tortured into submission met with visiting American peace delegations. Here David Dellinger, the antiwar activist, was shown the clean, comfortable quarters ostensibly assigned to Navy Commander Richard Stratton, the "zombie" POW whose plight had so fired Sijan's will to evade capture.

About five days after they arrived at the Plantation, Bob Craner was taken from his narrow, vermin-infested cell in the real lockup and allowed to scrub himself down at a cistern.

It was a misty day of weak, occasional sunshine. As he rubbed his body with a block of laundry soap, he again marveled at how luxurious a crude bath in cold water had become. He also pondered the luck he and Guy had had, being given the chance to collaborate on their cover stories while they cared for Lance Sijan, both at the Bamboo Prison in Vinh and in Hanoi.

Here at the Plantation, they had been able to plug into the "Comm Net," the prisoners' communication system that employed a tap code between cells and clandestine notes left at prearranged drops in the latrine and bath area. Craner was now learning the full extent of his captors' brutal torture policy, the treatment they gave uncooperative prisoners.

He dried himself on the scrap of towel he had been issued with his toothbrush, second set of striped pajamas, and his tin cup. As the guard led him back to his cell, Craner saw the Bug with another officer, strolling in quiet conversation toward the Big House. On an impulse, he caught the Bug's attention by bowing in his direction, then calling out.

Puzzled by Craner's audacity, the Bug actually crossed the muddy yard separating the villa from the cellblock called the Warehouse.

Craner bowed as the Bug approached. "Captain," he said, "can you tell me the condition of my friend Lieutenant Sijan?"

The Bug turned his smooth face toward Craner and smiled sweetly. "Sijan die," he said.

Bob Craner felt the words hit him like the blow of a club. "When?" he asked coldly, abandoning pretense of respect.

Again the Bug smiled, speaking in his high-pitched, emotionless voice. "Five days . . . Sijan spend too long in jungle. Sijan die."

The Bug nodded vaguely, dismissing Craner, then strode off toward the villa. Craner felt the thrust of his escort guard's club. He trudged along the cellblock, past the blank wooden doors. He knew men were watching him through cracks and gaps in the chipped concrete doorframes. Sijan was dead. But Bob Craner resolved, as he stumbled along before the prodding enemy, that he would do his best to commit to memory and spread the incredible story of Lance Sijan's heroic resistance—his protracted struggle against pain and overpowering adversity—among his fellow prisoners and, eventually, to the nation Sijan had served with such distinction.

Five monsoons after that harsh morning in the muddy courtyard of the Plantation, Bob Craner was back in Hoa Lo Prison. In the long group cellblocks on the prison's western wing, he met Colonel John Flynn, the senior American officer. Repatriation was near, and the record of the Americans' captivity was incomplete. After they had shaken hands and engaged in that smiling, but guarded initial small talk common to American POWs in Hanoi during this period of tense boredom, Bob Craner began to brief his superior officer on the incredible story of Lieutenant Lance Peter Sijan. The performance of that young officer, he said, was worthy of the Medal of Honor.

"All right, Major," Colonel Flynn said. *"If that's true, give me something in writing."*

Bob Craner took his recently issued, lined note pad and leaky Polish ball-point pen, sat down on a cool concrete bench in the noisy cellblock, and began to compose Lance Sijan's Medal of Honor recommendation.

Part III

Honors

Chapter
Thirteen

The
White
House

March 4, 1976

It was a bright Thursday in early spring. President Gerald Ford had campaigned earlier in the Florida presidential primary, and he still faced a weekend schedule of appearances in Illinois. Sandwiched between these political duties, the President had his normal hectic schedule of appointments and meetings.

But on this crisp afternoon Gerald Ford undertook a matter of state which he considered more important than any other pressing business. Ford was the first President since John Kennedy to have served both as a combat officer and as Commander-in-Chief during time of armed conflict. The President was familiar with bravery in battle.

For this reason he had insisted on officiating at the ceremony scheduled to take place at three in the East Room. There he was to award the nation's highest decoration for valor, the Medal of Honor, to a Rear Admiral in the Navy, an Air Force Colonel, a lieutenant in the Navy reserve, and to the parents of a young Air Force captain named Lance Sijan. All four men had served in Vietnam. Three had been taken prisoner by the North Vietnamese. They had displayed incredible bravery before and during their brutal captivity. Three of the recipients had returned home alive.

But Captain Lance P. Sijan had died of pneumonia, untreated wounds, and malnutrition in Hanoi's Hoa Lo Prison on January 22, 1968. His Medal of Honor would be presented posthumously to Jane and Sylvester Sijan, his mother and father.

As the President took his place near the Chiefs of Staff and the Secretary of Defense, the band played "Hail to the Chief." The television camera lights were hot, glaring, but the spring sun pouring through the tall windows of the East Room was brighter. The sun highlighted the colors of the service flags and the vases of spring flowers on the nearby tables.

Jane Sijan stood with quietly erect dignity beside her husband, just to the President's right. She wore a red jacket, a white silk blouse, and a tailored skirt of rich blue. Mrs. Sijan was a thoughtful woman who combined a strong and forthright character with artistic sensibility. She realized when she chose the clothes she would wear to the ceremony that, literally, she and her husband would be representing their son on his final military assignment. She therefore chose the colors that she knew would demonstrate the devotion to duty Lance had shown up to the moment of his death.

President Ford stepped forward to the rostrum. The first medal awarded that afternoon would be to Lance Sijan. Following Air Force tradition, the President would present the medal to the dead airman's father. Syl Sijan had hoped that tradition could be altered slightly so that Jane would be the one to receive the medal from the President. "There is only one mother to a son," he had said earlier that day. But, he added, a young man like Lance had been formed by modeling himself on several men, not just his father. The Air Force, however, prevailed.

With obvious emotion, the President drew himself up beside Air Force Secretary Thomas Reed.

"The President of the United States of America," the Secretary read, speaking clearly into the sunny room, "authorized by Act of

Congress, March 3, 1863, has awarded in the name of The Congress the Medal of Honor posthumously to Captain Lance P. Sijan, United States Air Force."

President Ford looked directly at the Sijan family.

"While on a flight over North Vietnam on 9 November 1967, Captain Sijan ejected from his disabled aircraft and successfully evaded capture for more than six weeks. During this time, he was seriously injured and suffered from shock and extreme weight loss due to lack of food. After being captured by North Vietnamese soldiers, Captain Sijan was taken to a holding point for subsequent transfer to a prisoner-of-war camp. In his emaciated and crippled condition, he overpowered one of his guards and crawled into the jungle, only to be recaptured after several hours. He was then transferred to another prisoner camp where he was kept in solitary confinement and interrogated at length. During the interrogation, he was severely tortured; however, he did not divulge any information to his captors. Captain Sijan lapsed into delirium and was placed in the care of another prisoner. During his intermittent periods of consciousness until his death, he never complained of his physical condition and, on several occasions, spoke of future escape attempts. Captain Sijan's extraordinary heroism and interpidity above and beyond the call of duty at the cost of his life are in keeping with the highest traditions of the United States Air Force and reflect great credit upon himself and the Armed Forces of the United States."

The Secretary lowered the citation. In the large room, men in impressive uniforms and costly vested suits and women in cheerful spring pastels stood motionless and silent, somber in their contemplation of the words. The stark text of the citation contained a wealth of evocative imagery, some of it savage, some tender to the point of heartbreak.

President Ford left the rostrum; a group of senior officers drew up beside him to hand forward the glass-covered walnut case containing the medal. There was a certain liturgical quality to this part of the ceremony, the passing of a sanctified object among a circle of anointed leaders. The President approached Jane and Sylvester Sijan. The gold star and its pale blue, star-flecked ribbon shone in the sunlight. The two men, the President and the father, both handsome in vigorous middle age, gripped each other by their strong hands. Sylvester Sijan took the case, thanked the President, and passed the medal immediately to Jane.

When Gerald Ford addressed them, his voice was soft but even. He deeply regretted, he said, having the duty of awarding this medal posthumously. Lance Sijan was a man of "uncommon courage who gave the country a cherished memory and a clear vision of a better world."

The President returned to the rostrum and the ceremonial speaker from the Defense Department read the three other citations.

Rear Admiral James B. Stockdale had been a prisoner of war in North Vietnam for almost eight years. The North Vietnamese had singled him out, as a senior officer, for especially savage interrogation and "attendant torture"; by so doing they hoped to cow younger and more junior prisoners into submission and cooperation on propagandistic war crimes confessions. During years of repeated torture, Admiral Stockdale had resisted; when driven to the point of utter despair by the brutality, he disfigured himself so as to deny the enemy useful propaganda film of a "repentant" senior officer. His lonely, protracted struggle against his tormentors became a "symbol of resistance" to his fellow POWs. By his example, they, too, learned to resist, and the planned propaganda campaign failed.

Colonel George "Bud" Day was an F-100 pilot with the Misty Forward Air Controllers who spent six years as a POW. Like Lance Sijan, he was shot down deep in enemy territory, and although badly injured, he escaped from his initial captors and worked his way south on foot through the jungle. Despite savage torture, he resisted interrogation once he had been recaptured.

Lieutenant Thomas Norris was a SEAL special warfare officer in Quang Tri Province during the North Vietnamese spring invasion of 1972. He twice led small ARVN commando patrols into the middle of the concentrated NVA forces to rescue downed American pilots whose hiding places were too exposed to enemy fire for helicopter rescue to be possible.

Clearly Lance Sijan was in good company during his final military assignment.

When the President had presented the medals to Stockdale, Day, and Norris, and the assembled dignitaries had congratulated the officers and the Sijan family, Gerald Ford did something that was fully in keeping with his compassionate nature. He moved away from the hovering circle of senior officers and cabinet officials and took Jane Sijan's arm to escort her from the East Room to the reception in the State Dining Room.

The White House ceremonies on March 4, 1976, honored four men of uncommon courage and indomitable spirit, even by the impressive standards of other Medal of Honor winners. Unlike many soldiers and marines who had won the medals for incredible bravery during the horrible excitement, noise, and collective madness of battle, the men whom President Ford honored had struggled alone, without the bolstering presence of fellow Americans. These four men had displayed remarkable self-knowledge and unshakable dedication to duty as well as transcendent physical bravery.

Without question, their stories would provide inspirational models for the nation, especially the country's young people.

But this was the spring of 1976; the shameful fall of Saigon had occurred less than a year before. The leaders of American news media were in no mood to celebrate the heroes of Vietnam.

This was also the spring of our Bicentennial Year; school children all across the country were learning a great deal about Nathan Hale, the Minutemen, and the Continental soldiers who wintered at Valley Forge.

But it is unlikely that kids in school that spring learned much about the steep jungle karsts above the Ban Loboy Ford, about the rivers of Quang Tri Province, or about the torture cells of Hoa Lo.

Part IV

★

Requiem

Chapter
Fourteen

★

United
States
Air
Force
Academy,
Colorado

May 1983

I stood in the mountain sunshine watching the cadet formations jog across the Terrazzo, under the soaring aluminum wings of the chapel, and up the Trail toward the forested slopes of the Rampart Range. Every first-year cadet in the Academy's forty squadrons was running this morning, escorted by his cadet officers. It was Recognition Day, the final event of the spring semester. The freshmen—Doolies—had to pass one last test before being "recognized" as colleagues by the upperclass cadets of their squadrons.

By Academy tradition, their test was to run two-and-a-half miles up those narrow trails to retrieve the heavy lump of their squadron rock, place the rock in a blanket, then run all the way back to the dormitories, sharing the ungainly burden among them. A five-mile run at over seven-thousand-feet elevation, half of it up steep trails, and half back down with the wobbly rock clutched in a blanket, represented both a physical challenge and a test of teamwork.

My visit to the Academy was the second-last stop on a long interview trip—from Washington to Florida, across the South and Southwest, to California—during which I had spoken with friends and former squadronmates of Lance Sijan and with surviving prisoners of war. Two days earlier I had been in Sacramento, meeting Lenora Monaco. In three days I would fly to Milwaukee to interview the Sijan family. I had been on the road for a month and was emotionally wrung out. Reliving Lance's ordeal with those who had known him in Vietnam was not pleasant.

The story did not have a happy ending. Lance Sijan was dead. He died alone, probably in a solitary cell in Hoa Lo Prison, the morning after he was taken from Craner and Gruters. The seemingly endless military struggle in which he had displayed such heroic determination was over. North Vietnam had finally overrun the South and had made virtual colonies of Cambodia and Laos. Russian reconnaissance bombers now used the long concrete runways at Da Nang. For a few of the former POWs I had spoken to, the ultimate debacle in Southeast Asia was a bitter and demoralizing tragedy, almost a personal betrayal. It was as if their years of stoic resistance and suffering in North Vietnam's prisons had been in vain. Others, though, seemed to have already put their Vietnam experiences behind them and were fully absorbed with their families and careers, thinking optimistically of the future, not obsessed with the brutal past.

But everyone I had spoken to agreed on one thing: Lance Sijan had been a hero, a man of astonishing courage and determination. It had not been necessary for me, however, to travel across the country to discover that Lance Sijan was a hero. Simply reading the text of his Medal of Honor citation was sufficient evidence of his uncommon bravery. What I wanted to learn from those people who had flown with him and who had suffered and struggled with him as prisoners was more difficult to ascertain than the incredible but well-documented facts of his heroism in Laos and North Vietnam. I wanted to discover if they now felt that his lonely, protracted struggle to evade capture, his resistance to interrogation, and his unquenchable drive to escape once he was in enemy custody had been a futile effort, a one-man Charge of the Light Brigade, tragically flamboyant but ultimately meaningless.

I was also curious about the people and institutions that had forged his character. And everyone I spoke to urged me to visit the Air Force Academy. "Go to the Academy," they told me. "You'll see where Lance learned his sense of duty."

So now I stood here this bright May morning in the Rockies, on the terrazzo courtyard of the Air Force Academy, the school Sijan had loved so much and that had over the past few years elevated him to near mythical status. Was this indeed still the same institution, I wondered, where Sijan had acquired his unshakable sense of duty? As the trotting ranks of Doolies and their upperclassmen escorts passed me, I was immediately struck by the obvious differences between this morning's run and the days when Lance Sijan and Mike Smith were Doolies, harassed and goaded up those same rugged trails. Now the upperclass cadets and the Doolies all wore the same uniform, combat boots, fatigue trousers, and T-shirts. The days when upperclassmen in gym shorts and sneakers viciously hazed the staggering, overburdened ranks of Doolies had ended. As the cadets ran by, they clapped in unison and chanted hearty, encouraging cadence songs, extolling their squadron's virtues. Clearly this run was a group effort meant to enhance unit esprit rather than the final chance for the senior cadets to inflict mass humiliation on the Doolies.

The human composition of the squadrons struck me more dramatically than the unexpected camaraderie among the classes of cadets. When Sijan attended the Academy, the entire cadet wing was male and almost exclusively white male. But the ranks of young people jogging up the Trail this morning were composed of both men and women, white, black, Oriental, and Hispanic. Twenty-eight years ago, when the Academy was founded, such a sight would probably have been considered a utopian pipe dream. Here was yet one more example of the profound social changes that had swept the country in the recent past.

Crossing the sunny flagstones toward Sijan Hall, I realized that instilling a sense of tradition—through rituals, rites of passage like Recognition Day, and group reverence toward heroes like Lance—was especially important at an institution less than thirty years old. I also had to bear in mind that the short duration of the Academy's history coincided with one of this country's most socially and politically chaotic periods. Establishing worthwhile traditions would not have been easy in the past three decades of fluid, confusing uncertainty.

Everywhere I went at the Academy, I encountered organized programs designed to foster a sense of tradition, to promote exemplary military models. In the main classroom building, Fairchild Hall, the corridors had recently been named for and decorated with memorabilia of famous aerial engagements: the Battle of Britain, Doolittle's Raid on Tokyo, the Berlin Airlift, Korea's MiG Alley, and the 1972 Linebacker II "Christmas Bombing" of Hanoi that finally forced the North Vietnamese to sign a cease-fire. The campaigns and battles celebrated on the walls of Fairchild Hall served the same purpose as Valley Forge and Cemetery Ridge among West Point cadets or John Paul Jones and Admiral Farragut in the hearts of Annapolis midshipmen.

And here at the Air Force Academy, Lance Sijan, the first graduate to win the Medal of Honor, had been molded into an inspirational model of monumental proportions. On Memorial Day 1976, as the keystone of the Academy's Bicentennial celebrations, the new aluminum-and-glass dormitory on the southern edge of the Terrazzo was dedicated Sijan Hall in Lance's memory. In *Contrails,* the pocket-size cadet handbook all Doolies are obliged to carry, Sijan was given the most prominent place in the "Outstanding Graduates" section. Any Doolie worth his (or her) salt had to be able to recite the pertinent details of Lance Sijan's gallant struggle.

It was safe to say that Sijan had become the best known and most revered of the seventeen thousand young people who had marched off the Academy's parade ground as second lieutenants on graduation day.

Before entering Sijan Hall, I paused at the southeastern corner of the Air Gardens. There were aircraft standing on mounts at the four corners of this wide courtyard; on the southern side of the square were the two mainstays of the air war against North Vietnam, the F-105 Thunderchief and the F-4C Phantom, both in the mottled beige-and-green camouflage of the Southeast Asia theater. I reached up to pat the cool flanks of the long, hulking Phantom, once again impressed by the graceful composite produced from the bulges and incongruous angles of the airplane's separate parts.

This particular aircraft had flown scores of missions over Indochina. Probably it had dodged flak and been hit by some as well on strikes in Route Package I and Steel Tiger. Now its aluminum skin was whole again, its bomb racks empty, its engines silent. The machine had been relegated to a respectable retirement, analogous to an antique howitzer on the courthouse lawn. Undoubtedly, twenty or thirty years from now the Phantom will appear to future generations of cadets just as quaint as the muzzle-loading cannon do today on the ramparts of West Point and parade grounds of Annapolis.

I stroked the gritty texture of the camouflage paint. How long would it actually be, I wondered, before the memory of our long military endeavor in Vietnam slipped into neutral historical perspective, before the mere mention of places like Khe Sahn, Da Nang, and the Ho Chi Minh Trail lost their power to incite controversy and inflame rankling memories, both among those Americans who fought there so gallantly but lived to see the enemy win their victory and those Americans who opposed the war with such bitter vehemence?

Today student groups from Alabama and Wisconsin tour the Gettysburg battlefield side by side, laughing as they trade school sweatshirts. German veterans of the Afrika Korps drink beer with their Eighth Army counterparts at El Alamein, and Japanese visitors bow respectfully toward the sunken mausoleum of the battleship Arizona, resting in the mud of Pearl Harbor. How many years before a visiting Vietnamese delegation strolls across this impressive campus square and stands to ponder the interesting aesthetics of the old warplane's camouflaged tail seen against the gleaming roof wings of the chapel? Will Guy Gruters, Tom Moe, or Lee Ellis take their children to Da Nang, to the Rao Nay Valley, or through the dank corridors of Hoa Lo Prison?

And when that time comes, I wondered, as it surely must—a day when middle-aged veterans with thick waists and graying hair return to the A Shau Valley and Con Thien, and to the misty ridges above Dak To—how will Americans then consider the sacrifice of young men like Lance Sijan who will have been dead for thirty years? Will Sijan be seen as a quaint historical oddity, like the Confederate cannon on its spoky-wheeled carriage and this silent, chunky aircraft? These were questions that had begun to coalesce as I conducted my interviews and that were now haunting me. Had Lance Sijan, the boy I knew at Bay View High School as the very best my generation had to offer, been, after all, a meaningless anachronism, a man whose stubborn sense of duty was stronger than his survival

United States Air Force Academy, Colorado

instinct, who loved country more than life itself? Was Sijan truly the proper inspirational model for today's cadets who would serve the bulk of their careers in the twenty-first century?

I continued to ponder these matters as I crossed the southern margin of the Terrazzo toward the entrance of Sijan Hall. Under the eastern eaves of the dormitory, I stopped before the polished stone façade to read the inscription. Off to one side, through a wide lobby window, I saw the tall, imposing oil portrait of Lance painted by Maxine McCaffrey. A cadet in blue classroom uniform, carrying a bundle of books, trotted up the staircase from a lower floor and paused under Sijan's portrait. With an obvious lack of embarrassment, he snapped off a smart salute and continued on his way, probably, I guessed, to a makeup exam or an academic conference. My academy escort officer mentioned that some cadets in Sijan Hall considered the portrait a talisman and saluted the canvas for good luck before examinations or important athletic events.

I leaned closer to the glass to study the dramatic painting. Lance stood in his combat flight suit, facing full front, his right fist clenched on the hip of his G-suit just above the pistol holster, his left arm cradling helmet and oxygen mask. He wore his survival vest and parachute harness open at the chest, as if in deference to the humid heat of Da Nang. His hair was short and dark, his eyes slightly hooded in thoughtful contemplation of the mission he had just flown or, perhaps, the one he was about to fly. At the lower right of the rectangular canvas the artist had rendered a larger-than-life Medal of Honor.

When I entered the lobby of Sijan Hall and studied the portrait more closely, I was able to better appreciate the artist's skill. She had clearly captured the essence of Lance Sijan, the determined and dedicated warrior. His stance and carriage exuded strength, the set of his chin and the flash of his eyes epitomized courage and stubborn resolve. Without question, McCaffrey had ably fulfilled her commission. She had captured Lance on the eve of his long ordeal. If the cadets wanted a talisman, I realized, this portrait was a pretty good choice.

Then, as I was about to leave the lobby, I realized that something was missing from the painting. Turning back, I saw at once that Lance wore no mustache. When I mentioned this to my escort officer, he replied that the artist had given Lance's family final approval over the details of the canvas. Maybe, he said, his mother or father had preferred to see Lance as he was before he went to war.

As we crossed the Terrazzo again on our way to interview the Academy's senior officers in Harmon Hall, I couldn't help thinking that the portrait's missing mustache was emblematic of a wider issue. Lance and a number of other young backseaters at Da Nang had, indeed, grown mustaches that summer to protest the "war" in America, the increasingly vociferous antiwar demonstrations that had swept the college campuses and onto the country's streets. These young pilots were being asked to fight a difficult and dangerous war against a well-armed and aggressive enemy while their contemporaries on the other side of the planet reviled them as baby killers. And this unprecedented circumstance had angered them.

But now the wounds in American society no longer bled so readily. Perhaps, I saw, it was better for Lance to be portrayed as a strong and courageous, but not angry, fighting man.

I also realized that the official descriptions of Lance's heroic struggle—from the Medal of Honor citation and the *Contrails* text to the Academy press releases—all avoided the issue of where Sijan had been shot down and where he had waged his lonely struggle on the ground. In those official documents, Lance's plane was disabled "while on a flight over North Vietnam." This tone was not only misleading, it was unworthy of the actual event. By these words, it almost seemed as if Lance's last dangerous mission to the karsts and ridges of Laos was a milk run, a flight *over*, safely above, enemy territory. Also, this language made it appear that Lance had perhaps come down in the low eastern foothills, not in the merciless karst formations above the Trail on the Laotian side of the long ridge. Perhaps, I saw, the myth that America was not bombing enemy invasion routes in "neutral" Laos was still being fostered, even after all these years.

An hour later I talked about bombing the Trail in Laos with Colonel Joseph Koz, the deputy commandant of cadets. Colonel Koz was known as Lieutenant Joe Kosciusko when he was Lance's roommate in the BOQ at Da Nang in 1967. Like Sijan, Joe Koz had been selected for upgrade in theater to aircraft commander. He completed his tour of over a hundred missions against North Vietnam, flying frontseater in an F-4C. Four years later he flew another combat tour out of Udorn during which his wing helped smash the NVA Easter invasion of 1972. Before coming to the Academy, he had commanded a Phantom squadron in Spain.

Joe Koz displayed the same lean and angular features that he had in 1967, but his hair was prematurely gray. He spoke with the direct, open frankness of a person who had gained considerable self-knowledge under rigorous conditions. Yet there was a balanced introspection to his remarks, and I wasn't surprised later in our conversation to learn he was writing a graduate dissertation for an advanced degree in social psychology. So much, I mused, for cliches about the narrow "military mind."

The aerial interdiction war, he said, the bombing of the Trail and North Vietnam, had been a frustrating business for thoughtful young pilots like Lance and him. There wasn't much glory or satisfaction sitting in the backseat, checking off map features while the aircraft commander flew the plane. Also, there had not been, in Joe's opinion, that many targets in the whole theater that were worth the lives of an aircrew. Given the terrain, the jungle, and the weather patterns, crews were often ordered to face inordinate risk while hitting a few thatch-roofed hooches along some well-defended river in Pack I that Intel had proclaimed a "suspected storage area." Choke point targets such as the Ban Loboy Ford and the Mu Gia Pass were equally frustrating. Scheduled fragged missions that arrived on target each night at the same time with the same call sign were symptomatic of poor tactics.

Lance and he had often talked about these tactical shortcomings that had been necessitated by the wider policy considerations of a limited war of attrition. But, Colonel Koz said, he still wore his uniform with pride every day, and he did not want to appear a bitter malcontent, "bad-mouthing policy." From a historical perspective, though, it was now clear that the war's ill-defined strategic goals had produced equally muddled tactics. However, he continued, those young officers who thought about the constraints and clumsy tactics under which they had to work soon learned some very valuable lessons. In this kind of combat, you had to use your imagination and be unpredictable if you were going to survive.

Lance, he said, learned those lessons early in his tour, but he never had the chance to employ that knowledge as an aircraft commander.　　　　　　　　　　　　　　　　　　　　　　　•

Joe rocked back in his chair and looked out the window to the impressive campus below. It was ironic, he said with a poignant smile, that in the process of disseminating the story of Sijan's heroism, Lance has come to be remembered almost exclusively as a physically tough, indomitable brute of a warrior, the undefeated cripple who disabled an enemy guard with a karate chop and crawled away into the jungle, the epitome of the Code of Conduct's American fighting man who defied his torturers to the end of his life. Joe said that he worried that cadets at the Academy got the idea that Lance Sijan had been mindless in his dedication to duty. And the Academy was not in the business of producing mindless officers, robots who blindly followed orders, sometimes wrongheaded orders, with disastrous results. The cadets had to learn to question authority as well as to respect it. They had to learn to think independently. In that regard, Lance had been a good model.

Sijan, Joe Koz said firmly, was a thoughtful, serious guy. He was, indeed, dedicated to his duty as a disciplined, professional officer. But he had considerable imagination and always displayed insight into what he was doing. The real Sijan was far from the stereotypical military automaton; he knew exactly what he was doing and why. Lance Sijan should also be remembered, Joe added slowly, for his incredible self-discipline not only for his physical courage.

"Here at the Academy," he continued, "we don't talk about self-discipline enough. But one of the basic tasks of this school is to teach the cadet that kind of discipline. I like to consider it mind over matter."

He frowned as he searched for the best example. "When you have a job to do that requires real concentration—and so much of professional military life, especially aviation, requires this—it takes some people forever to get in the mood to concentrate. But to be a good professional officer, you have to have the self-discipline to say, 'This is what I'm going to do because it's *right.*' Even though your body tells you to call it quits . . . to go to the club and have a drink, to give up until tomorrow. You can't afford that attitude as a professional officer."

Joe leaned across his desk and stared at me with his pale, appraising eyes. "Lance Sijan had that kind of self-discipline." He nodded sharply. "Without a doubt Lance had that quality, and it's that as well as his courage that the cadets need as a role model."

"And," I added, "he had the self-discipline to recognize the hard duty he had as a downed pilot . . . to escape and evade."

"You've got it," Joe said somberly. "Self-discipline, even though he had the same reservations about the political conduct of the war we've just been talking about."

"Let me ask you the same question I've been asking the others who knew Lance," I said. "You're a full colonel now. You were a 1965 service academy graduate, just like Lance. You're now deputy commandant of cadets here. Had Lance Sijan survived captivity, he might be sitting right where you are now. Is it better for the Air Force, is it better for the United States as a country, to have Lance Sijan as a dead hero, a Medal of Honor role model, or would it be better for America if he were now a young colonel like you, giving living inspiration to cadets?"

Joe again nodded decisively. "I have no question what my answer is, but I'd like to preface it. In some cases . . . with some people, the really aggressive, gung ho fighter pilots who were too caught up in the thrill of combat to recognize the very real danger around them . . . they're better off as dead heroes. They do not have the right qualities we need in future officers. Many of them had such good pilot skills that they survived a hundred missions, but some of them were just going to buy the farm; you could tell that ahead of time."

Joe's cool blue eyes again went hard. "Lance Sijan was another kind of guy. I really feel that the country and the Air Force would be better off with Lance alive today. There's no question at all in my mind about that." Joe opened his long fingers. "I only knew him over there for three or four months, but I learned what kind of a person he was, how dedicated he was to being a good pilot. . . . he used to spend a lot of time down at Intel, researching each mission. He was a true professional. So, based on what I saw of Lance in combat, there's no question in my mind that he'd be much more valuable alive, because the qualities that he showed me were exactly the kind of qualities that we want every one of these cadets to have."

I jotted down my notes quickly, then looked up. "Colonel," I asked, "is the story of Lance's heroic resistance fifteen years ago, his physical endurance and his raw courage, a good model for these cadets, who are going to serve most of their careers in the twenty-first century?"

"Sure." Joe Koz did not hesitate. "I think that it is. I can easily see in the Space Shuttle Program, for example, where that kind of courage and also that kind of self-discipline is going to be needed one day. Think about it. You'll see what I mean."

I sat in the warm May sunshine, in Joe Koz's handsomely appointed office, staring into his unblinking eyes. I did, indeed, see what he meant. The possibilities for disaster, for lonely decision making and protracted, dangerous struggle, would abound as the shuttle program expanded. It was not at all absurd to think that ten or fifteen years from now one of those young cadets who considered Lance's portrait a good luck charm would be called on to perform some terrible duty in which he or she would face self-extinction to save the crew of a shuttle or an orbiting space station. And when it came time to make those harsh decisions, they might well remember the pages on Lance Sijan they had memorized in their *Contrails*.

When I left Harmon Hall to have lunch with a group of graduating seniors, I realized that Joe Koz's answers to my questions had coincided very closely with the answers to the same questions I had received from Glenn Nordin, Guy Gruters, Mike Smith, Tom Moe, and the others. They all still mourned the loss of Lance as a friend, and they all felt his living example as a senior officer, alive today, would be very valuable to the service and country he loved with unselfconscious intensity. They also felt that there was great value in Lance Sijan as an inspirational model who now stood in America's military pantheon alongside Nathan Hale, Sergeant Alvin York, and Audie Murphy.

Glenn Nordin had been adamant about the selection of Lance as a role model for future Air Force leaders. Glenn, on his last tour of duty before retirement, had been director of the Air Force Manpower and Personnel Center. In 1980, when the Air Force decided to create a new decoration to be awarded to enlisted personnel and officers at the wing level and below who had shown "the highest qualities of leadership in the performance of their duties and the conduct of their lives," Glenn Nordin was one of the officers named to the committee that would select the Air Force figure in whose name this award would be given.

From the beginning of the process, however, he encountered resistance to his candidate, Captain Lance P. Sijan. Some members believed that the selection of a Vietnam pilot, and a prisoner of war at that, would only open old wounds, inflame almost-forgotten controversies. Most of Sijan's heroic actions, they said, had taken place in Laos, following a bombing mission that at the time had not even officially occurred. Other senior officers on the committee held that the award should be named in honor of a general whose entire career, from a junior officer in the heat of combat to a senior manager and strategist, would provide a better-balanced model than Sijan's courageous but isolated sacrifice.

But Glenn Nordin had never forgotten that terrible afternoon thirteen years before when Lance's voice, sharp with pain but precise, came up on Guard Channel from that jungle karst below. Lance had refused to allow the commander of the hovering Jolly Green Giant to send down a parajumper rescue man. *"The enemy is too close,"* he said. *"Stay where you are. I'll crawl to the penetrator."* Nor had Glenn Nordin forgotten his reaction six years later when the POWs returned to be debriefed and the details of Sijan's incredible struggle and heroism on the ground became widely known for the first time. Nordin decided then that he would do his best to assure that the name of Lance Sijan achieved an honored place, at least within the Air Force if not before the entire country.

Colonel Nordin got to work "writing up a goddamn *blizzard*" of justifications for his candidate. He countered potential arguments that Sijan's heroism had not been properly documented by producing the detailed debriefing reports of Bob Craner and Guy Gruters, which proved that it was the North Vietnamese, not Lance, who had first revealed that he was captured on the roadway of the Trail on Christmas Day and that he later overpowered a guard in the mountain dispensary and escaped. The stark facts of that enemy's own report, Nordin insisted, bespoke volumes about Lance's determination and dedication to duty. He went down on November 9, at least three miles—three terrible miles of jagged karst and tangled jungle—from that roadway. During forty-five days without food, he struggled to reach open ground so that he could signal American planes again.

Sijan was in *control* of himself, Nordin argued, under the worst possible conditions. He had not only been courageous during his long struggle, he had been imaginative, cunning. Sijan had known very well that surrender to the NVA road-security troops that hunted him on that karst would have been tantamount to suicide. During the SAR effort, those enemy soldiers had been ruthlessly battered by the Sandys and the F-4 ResCap flights. If they had found Sijan, they would have no doubt extracted a small measure of revenge for their dead and maimed comrades. Sijan had read all the Intel reports about the nature of the enemy along the Trail; his impossible odyssey across the slopes of the jungle mountains was not a flamboyant, suicidal gesture. Equally, Sijan knew that the SAR forces would be forced to enter a well-deployed flak trap if he had stayed up on that karst top and called them in for a second or third effort. As a professional officer, he had been obliged to accept the hard truth that his own life was not worth again risking the crews of the Sandys and vulnerable Jolly Greens that would answer his renewed Mayday calls. So he made his cruel decision, then got on with implementing it.

The ability to make hard but necessary decisions under difficult conditions, Colonel Nordin insisted, then to show the strength of character to implement those decisions, despite hardship, despite resistance, both in combat and in times of peace, was quintessential to military leadership. And, Glenn Nordin argued passionately, he could not think of another man who had better shown these qualities of leadership than Lance Sijan.

So, at the end of the day, Colonel Nordin prevailed. The first annual Lance P. Sijan Leadership Awards were presented at the Pentagon by Air Force chief of staff General Lew Allen, Jr., on November 10, 1981, exactly fourteen years after the morning that Lance Sijan regained consciousness on the top of that limestone karst above the Ban Loboy Ford. The awards were granted to a senior and a junior commissioned officer and to a senior and a junior NCO.

Among the first recipients, the senior officer, Lieutenant Colonel Frederick F. Haddad, Jr., and the senior NCO, Chief Master Sergeant Charles H. Pettit, had worked tirelessly to inspire and motivate their men and to overcome problems of poor morale caused by bad housing and harsh working conditions at the isolated bases on which they served.

The junior officer and NCO recipients, Major Gerald J. Uttaro and Technical Sergeant Donald V. Green, had displayed uncommon bravery when faced with great personal danger. Major Uttaro had been a pilot during the ill-fated attempt to rescue the American hostages in Iran in the spring of 1980. After the C-130 transport and the Navy CH-53 helicopter had collided on the dark desert airstrip, he repeatedly risked his life to pull survivors from the flaming aircraft, which were loaded with ammunition, explosives, and fuel. Sergeant Green was on security police duty at Little Rock Air Force Base, Arkansas, on the September night in 1980 when the Titan intercontinental missile launcher caught fire and exploded in its silo, throwing its nuclear warhead out into the darkness. Despite the flames and blasts of toxic gasses from the burning launcher's fuel tanks, Sergeant Green led his rescue team into the launch site and searched the underground firing facilities for forty-five minutes to rescue injured airmen. Only when they had located and evacuated the last survivor, did Sergeant Green lead his team to safety.

The award that General Allen presented these men consisted of a citation and a bronze plaque. Glenn Nordin had collaborated with the artist to create that plaque, which was to highlight the key events in Sijan's struggle. The plaque's bas-relief showed the karst in Laos, the towering hardwood forest, and the hovering rescue helicopter. Sijan was rendered as the wounded survivor, dwarfed by the trees, speaking into his radio to guide in the aircraft overhead.

Fourteen years after that long, terrible day in Laos, the splintered, often disorganized, and sometimes panicked moments of combat had coalesced into monumental bronze.

When the four airmen had received their awards, General Allen asked Lance's father to read the comments he had prepared to mark this first presentation ceremony:

"General Allen and all contributing staff members, please accept my humble thanks for your part in honoring our son, Captain Lance Sijan, in such a memorable and significant way.

"I would like at this time to tell you about Lance as we, his family, knew him—our love for him, his love for us.

"I think I can summarize the primary motivating factors of Lance in terms of understanding what went on in his heart and mind whenever he was faced with a situation of great danger or risk. His first thought was to get the job done—get it over with, and prepare to return home at the next available opportunity. He wanted always to come home. Home and family was the place he loved so very much. So much that he was willing to die for it.

"The Vietnam conflict has never been resolved within the minds of many Americans. To this day, our country seeks and has needed a symbol for the true meaning of our involvement. Captain Lance Sijan is eminently qualified. For this to become a reality, his character and his valor must be common knowledge to all America. *What* he did has been well documented and duly recognized by our military, and by our government. *Why* he reacted as he did is the key to understanding the future and direction this country will take in choosing people for its roles of leadership.

"What we are dealing with is not an idea, but rather an ideal.

"When you love something as much as Lance loved his home, it is worth fighting for. When you love something as much as Lance loved his country, it is worth fighting for. This story has to be told. When the nation knows the story, the ideal will take care of itself."

I met the three cadets outside Arnold Hall and we went to the snack bar for lunch. Carl Nordin was short and wiry, like his father, Glenn, but he had his mother's blond hair. Jim Post looked like a model for a recruiting poster, tall, muscular, deeply tanned. Wynn Botts was an attractive brunette with warm, fluid eyes and a precise but soft-spoken manner. The two young men wore the shoulder-board insignia of senior cadet officers and the arched wings of free-fall parachutists. Carl Nordin displayed the silver laurel and star of the Superintendent's List that identified him as one of the Academy's elite in terms of academic and military performance.

In a few days, all three would be sworn in as Air Force second lieutenants: All three had been selected for pilot training, the most coveted postgraduate assignment.

We sat over sandwiches and coffee, talking about Lance Sijan as a role model for young officers who would spend their careers in a military environment that would be dominated by the incongruities of bushfire wars in the primitive backwaters of the Third World and the *Star Wars* technology of space combat.

Carl Nordin was the most familiar with the details of Lance's story, having heard them first from his father when he was twelve. But the other two cadets had learned the near-mythical dimensions of Sijan's heroism as Doolies and, as senior cadets, had, in turn, coached their squadrons' Doolies to memorize the pertinent facts of Lance's story.

Had this legend inspired them in any way during their four demanding years at the Academy? I asked.

They all nodded with spontaneous affirmation. There was a very tough survival course here, Carl explained, during which the cadets were subjected to an uncomfortably realistic simulation of what they would face if they ever found themselves prisoners of a communist enemy. They were harassed and deprived of sleep, pushed around and psychologically abused. The standard enemy torture techniques were vividly described. The purpose of the course was to force the cadets to consider the unpleasant possibility of their potential captivity and to assess the dimensions of their individual strengths and weaknesses. During this training the instructors repeatedly made reference to Sijan's long evasion, his escape from the mountain road camp, and his stoic defiance of his interrogators.

"Sir," Carl said frankly, "quite a few cadets think Sijan went too far . . . but in the SERE training, the fact that you can look at somebody like Lance Sijan, it gives you something to hang on to when you're sitting there in solitary."

Jim Post and Wynn Botts concurred.

We talked more about their future careers as professional Air Force officers. Why, I asked, did the cadets at the Academy opt for the dangers and hardships of such careers when the military profession no longer seemed so glorious or noble?

Again Carl Nordin took the lead in answering. "A lot of people here say they came to get a free education, to be able to buy a nice car their senior year, to be able to fly as a jet pilot, but not necessarily to serve their country." He looked across the table at his colleagues for the unspoken confirmation he knew was coming. "But on the inside, most of the cadets are here because they want to serve their country, to make a commitment." Again he looked to his friends. "And that commitment sometimes involves the risk of death. We understand that risk, and we accept it."

I posed a familiar hypothetical case. In two years, I pointed out, Carl and Jim would probably be flying high-performance combat jets like the F-15 or F-16. Suppose, I said, watching their faces, they were on final approach to a western air base and that approach took them over a school or suburb. Suppose they flew into a flock of migrating starlings and lost both engines. At that terrible moment, they would have the choice of ejecting and coming to earth safely while their crippled jet fell on the hapless people below, or they could wingover in a steep, powerless descent that would sacrifice altitude for distance so that the plane would impact in the empty desert scrub to the right or left of the glide slope. But in so doing, of course, they would have to stay with the jet until impact. This was the Great Santini dilemma, dramatically engrossing in a movie but a somberly real part of their lives' fabric as Air Force pilots.

Neither young man hesitated. Their duty, they said, was to prevent casualties, even if it meant their own death. They would stay with the planes until they were sure they were clear of inhabited areas. Then, *if they had time,* they'd eject. Not before.

Jim Post spoke now at length, with articulate feeling. In four years at the Academy, he said, he'd attended several memorial services for graduates who had died in almost exactly the manner we'd just discussed. So he'd had ample time to ponder his own reaction in those harsh circumstances. "One thing I learned at the Academy," he said with almost painful sincerity, "is that I have greater concern for other people than for myself."

After these rather standard hypothetical guessing games, I moved on to a more controversial area. What if America became involved in an armed conflict with Cuban troops in Central America, I suggested, and the young officers were flying fighter-bombers. What if the enemy infiltration route led through peasant villages where the Cubans—like their NVA counterparts years before—used the houses of the village as cover to hide their loaded trucks. Would Jim and Carl have the courage to attack those trucks, knowing full well that they would inflict civilian casualties in so doing?

Carl and Jim each spoke to different aspects of the problem, naturally assuming a team approach. If the mission order were *lawful,* they emphasized, that is, if they were ordered to hit the trucks alone and to minimize collateral damage and casualties, then they would have no qualms about flying the strike. They would, however, try to select their targets with great care, knowing full well that this meant increased exposure to antiaircraft fire.

We ended our discussion by ranging thirty or forty years into the future, toward the end of their careers. They spoke with unusual understanding of the world's political, social, and economic dynamics, easily discussing the history of totalitarian movements and the responses of the democracies to them; the role of the military in democratic countries; and the potential areas of conflict in a world beset by shrinking resources and exploding population.

I had taught graduate students at four American universities, but I had never before encountered three young graduates with such a breadth and depth of knowledge, that combined technical expertise and the humanities, as well as a mature, clear process of thought. Wynn Botts, for example, was twenty-three years old. Without further training, she could sit down at the navigator's console of a jumbo jet and guide it all the way from Denver to the Middle East. Once there, she could speak with reasonable fluency in Arabic to her local counterparts; in English, she could certainly discuss with them subjects ranging from the cultural and political history of the region to the thermal physics of a modern jet engine. Carl Nordin and Jim Post were equally impressive.

As we walked out of Arnold Hall into the sunshine, I understood what it was about this institution that formed such impressive young people as these three seniors and Lance Sijan. The Academy took good raw material—thirty-seven thousand potential applicants inquired about admission each year, and fourteen hundred were ultimately selected—then began the four-year education process that called for 180 credit hours and demanded consistently excellent performance. Maximum effort in academics, military training, and athletics was expected at all times.

During this four-year effort, as the commandant of cadets, Brigadier General Anthony Burshnick had pointed out to me, the unremitting demand for excellence was coupled with expanding leadership responsibilities within the cadet wing. The General, a 1959 Academy graduate, pointed out his office window at the Terrazzo where cadet formations were assembling. "That cadet wing is one of the greatest leadership laboratories in the world," he said. "The cadets run the organization. They train themselves. It's one thing for a general to order a colonel or a major, 'Do that. Get that done at once,' but for a cadet to earn the respect of his peers, he has to learn real leadership."

After I shook hands and said goodbye to Carl, Jim Post, and Wynn Botts, I again crossed the Terrazzo, moving this time toward the parade ground. High above, a Twin Otter aircraft hung in silent, level flight. As I squinted up, black dots detached themselves from the silhouetted plane . . . one, two . . . five . . . ten, twelve. Free-falling parachutists streaked down through the clear mountain sky, some trailing smoke plumes of red, white, and blue. Like a sequence of computer graphics, their rectangular blue sports parachutes popped open at exactly the same point above the parade ground and the jumpers spiraled down, one above the other, to land within twenty feet of the target on the grass. This was the Academy's Wings of Blue skydiving team, the national collegiate champions. By the time they graduated, some of the team members had over nine hundred jumps in their logbooks. The team, my escort explained, was entirely managed by cadets; they were responsible for their own safety, equipment, and training.

Watching them land with such amazing precision, I understood what General Burshnick had meant about the Academy building leadership.

Before I left the Terrazzo that afternoon, I paid the obligatory visit to the Academy's War Memorial. On the dark convex marble wall were carved the names of 125 graduates. The classes of the mid-1960s—'64, '65, '66—were disproportionately represented. These were the "two-tour" classes of F-4 pilots; the young lieutenants had flown their first tours as GIBs. If they survived, as had Joe Koz, they returned three or four years later to the same long war, as aircraft commanders, to again hear the rattlesnake buzz of the enemy's Firecan radar in their RHAW gear and again watch the glowing balls of flak rise up from the dark river crossings beneath the looming, bone-white karsts in "neutral" Laos.

I read Lance's name; I read a dozen more . . . thirty. Then, turning abruptly, I strode away to the visitors' parking lot. I preferred to envision the sinewy forms of the young people in the parachute team, caught above the parade ground in that clear helix of gravity, smiling into the bright wind at their own immortal skill.

This was a better picture to retain on leaving the impressive campus than images of a blackened corpse covered with the feeding tendrils of wait-a-minute vines in a smashed titanium machine on a ridge above Mu Gia or a starving, tormented skeleton in a dank cell of Hoa Lo Prison.

Chapter
Fifteen

★

Milwaukee,
Wisconsin

May 1983

My three days of interviews with Lance Sijan's family were painful, troubling, and, initially at least, disappointing. Later, when I wrote up my notes and began to block out this book, I realized that I had brought unrealistic expectations to my meetings with the Sijans. From them I had subconsciously hoped to gain sudden, piercing insights into Lance's character, to hear, perhaps, a half-remembered family anecdote that would unlock the lingering riddle of Lance's personality like a serendipitous key.

But there were no lightning bolts of insight, no quantum revelations of childhood trauma or victory that readily explained Sijan's adult courage.

Instead of easy insight, I found a mother and father, a brother and a sister still burdened with mournful loss fifteen years after Lance's death. Their grief, of course, was muted by a fierce pride in Lance's achievements and at the impressive recognition with which the Air Force has honored his memory. But the pain they felt talking about Lance and about the Vietnam War was palpable; it filled the sunny, tasteful living room of the brick home on South Shore Drive.

During the uncomfortable hours I interviewed Jane and Syl Sijan, Lance's brother, Marc, and his sister, Janine, I also came to see that they were not people of overtly heroic dimension as I had originally envisioned them. They were attractive people, well-respected leaders in their community, but overall, they seemed an eminently *normal* American family, responsible, patriotic citizens of Bay View, the Milwaukee neighborhood where Lance and I grew up in the relatively prosperous and untroubled years after World War II.

My initial disappointment at the Sijans' Midwestern normality, however, gave way to an understanding that it was exactly the family's decent, predictable stability, their spirit of community service and leadership, their uncomplicated and traditional values, and their unquestioning bonds of love that had molded Lance's adult character.

Jane and Syl Sijan had set about to raise an American family in the traditional pattern; that they succeeded in producing an exemplary American war hero should not have surprised me. Syl had spent his youth in the Depression, a time that taught him the value of self-reliance and determination to succeed. They also learned from those difficult times the self-confidence that comes from perseverence and eventually overcoming obstacles.

Syl Sijan had lost his father as a boy. He had witnessed his mother Mary's own resolve and determination when, widowed with four children at home, she had insisted that none of them quit school to work. She took over the family business, a tavern called the Log Cabin on Greenfield Avenue. Her children stayed in school. They worked odd jobs and helped out when they could. Mary Sijan was one of those first-generation American women who have become legendary in ethnic America. She overcame all the hardships; she persevered; she encouraged her children to succeed. Mary Sijan was Yugoslavian, but she could have been Jewish or Italian, Irish or German. She knew she was living in a country where hard work and opportunity could be combined to overcome adversity.

When Syl Sijan was about ten, he saw a girl play the violin on the stage of Allen Primary School and was enthralled by the beauty and precision, by the mastery of her skill. That night at the kitchen table he told his mother what he had felt in the school auditorium. Mary Sijan explained to him that if he worked hard, he, too, could master the violin. This was, after all, America. She was teaching Sylvester Sijan a lesson in practical optimism, a lesson he would teach his own children: Hard work and determination brought success. Two years later Syl Sijan stood on that stage with his own violin and played a schoolboy's recital piece, "Cavalleria rusticana."

When Lance was a teenager, he told his dad that it would be great to renovate the Model-T Ford sitting on blocks in the garage. You can do it, Lance, his father told him, if you really want to and if you work hard at the job. Two years later, Lance drove the restored car in a local parade.

Before Syl and Jane Sijan raised their family, they decided that Jane would not work outside the home while the kids were in school. Years later both of them still felt strongly that this was an important element in understanding not only their family but also the generation in which Lance was raised. Children, Jane told me, form their characters slowly, over hours, days, and years. They need advice and encouragement, as well as adult understanding, continually throughout the hours and days of their childhood. She always felt, Jane said, that it was important to her children that she was there at home when they left in the morning for Fernwood School; that she was there when they came home for lunch to tell her about their morning; and that she was there to advise them on their schoolwork when they returned each afternoon.

This was not a heroic or even fashionable portrait of the handsome woman to whom the President gave his arm following the Medal of Honor ceremony all those years later, after Lance had grown up and gone away to fight in Asia. As career options, housewife and mother had lost considerable luster among American women, Jane said, and that was regrettable. She herself, Jane added, had found great satisfaction and reward as a mother and housewife.

At this point Syl proudly announced that Jane had been the President of the Trowbridge Parent-Teacher Association for a number of years and in 1949 she had been elected Mrs. Milwaukee.

We talked into the middle of the first afternoon about Lance's childhood, and I made desultory notes. Again there was nothing sensational, only the outlines of a normal, Midwestern childhood:

Cub Scouts, Boy Scouts, YMCA, church choir, and model airplanes. True to traditional form, Lance had earned his own spending money from the age of ten shoveling snow and working a variety of after-school jobs. Later, at Bay View High School, the athletic awards and multiple honors began to accumulate.

But Jane and Syl had never pushed Lance toward those honors. It was important to remember, Jane added, that Lance's success had been achieved without compromise of his honest and faithful character. He never lost his loyalty to his childhood friends. It was a child's character that was important, Jane Sijan said; that stayed with him long beyond memories of a football letter or a committee chairmanship.

As she spoke, I remembered what Mike Smith had told me about Lance's honesty. During their third year, the Academy had been rocked by a cheating scandal of large enough proportions to crack the institution's seamless Camelot veneer. A number of cadets had been caught using a purloined physics exam, among them several of Lance's close friends. When the scandal broke, Lance was in the hospital recovering from a knee injury, and Mike was worried that Lance himself would be hauled before the Honor Code Board.

Mike questioned one of Lance's friends who was sullenly packing his footlocker in anticipation of the inevitable expulsion order. Had Lance been involved in the scandal in any way, had he broken the inflexible commandment: "We Will Not Lie, Steal or Cheat, Nor Tolerate Among Us Anyone Who Does"?

"Hell no," Lance's friend said. "We couldn't have brought *Sijan* in on it. That guy's too straight. If he'd heard we'd gotten ahold of that exam, he'd have had to turn us in."

"But he's your *buddy*," Smith exclaimed.

"Wouldn't have cut no ice with Sijan," the disheartened kid said. "That's the way they made him at the factory."

As Jane and Syl Sijan talked into the blue spring twilight, offering up the wholesome, perhaps predictable memories of Lance's childhood and adolescence, I slowly came to understand what I should have realized before I returned to Bay View to see them. There were no mysteries about Lance Sijan's indomitable character. He had been formed as a child, within the warm confines of this Midwestern American family, during a period of optimistic expansion that followed the long calamity of depression and global war.

Milwaukee, Wisconsin   245

The values that he and Marc and Janine learned centered around decency, responsibility, and loyalty to family, friends, and country. In the Sijan home, Jane said firmly, the words *nigger* and *kike* were forbidden; racial epithets were cruel, vulgar. She and Syl also taught the children that gossip was degrading, that it usually consisted of jealous lies. The respect a person showed to others reflected his or her own self-respect.

As I worked through the interview the next morning, I began to recognize the problem I would encounter trying to shape this background material into any kind of compelling narrative. One fundamental of storytelling I always emphasized with my fiction writing and journalism students was that they should find the *conflict line* of every story and follow it throughout the narrative. Yet there was little conflict here, almost no tension. Sijan had been a well-adjusted child in a happy family. He had matured in that ephemeral American Arcadia that had flourished between Hiroshima and the Battle of the Ia Drang Valley . . . Ozzie and Harriet land, when Father really did Know Best, the Tough Got Going When the Going Got Tough, and all the rest of it.

We transplanted Midwesterners living in Georgetown or the East Seventies might snicker now if we didn't laugh aloud. Yet we neosophisticates who trade names of undiscovered bays on the Turquoise Coast of Anatolia while sipping this year's proper Beaujolais *nouveau* often throw up our hands in sad frustration when we talk of our own children's failures. This girl disappeared into the Moonies; that boy short-circuited his frontal lobes with lysergic acid. They, to whom we gave everything . . .

A tough, honest Serbian tavern keeper who carved the word "Tradition" on the top of the ornamental cask behind his bar or the energetic president of the Trowbridge PTA who wore white gloves to her inauguration as Mrs. Milwaukee might not seem appropriate subjects of serious biography. They were, after all, relatively simple people, compared with the homicidal millionaires or voluptuous celebrities who dominate the publishers' nonfiction list each season.

On my last afternoon with the family, however, I did find the vein of dramatic tension I'd been prospecting for all week. Marc Sijan— who combined his brother's looks with the sensitivity of a mature artist—broke through his shell of mute grief and spoke with feeling about one of his last meetings with Lance. Marc is now an accomplished professional sculptor; then he was a college art student on Easter vacation, in California, visiting Lance during his final F-4 training before Vietnam.

They had always been close as kids, but at George Air Force Base, in the high desert evenings around the heated pools and barbecue pits, a distance separated them. Lance felt the chill loneliness of approaching combat. Marc brooded behind the invisible barrier that their conflicting feelings about the war had created between them, as silent but tangible as suspected cancer.

All of Lance's friends, it seemed to Marc, were professional officers, combat pilots either coming from or going to duty in Vietnam. He felt that their pride and professionalism might be an elaborate sham they had erected to hide the war's realities, its cruelties, and the terrible danger they were facing. Marc was troubled by Lance's seemingly stoic acceptance of his orders to a combat wing; Lance was harder now, so *serious*, even when they roared off to Las Vegas in his red Corvette in search of some easy money at the blackjack tables.

After a week of this tension, the conflict festered to a head on Marc's last night. They had a few beers at a pilots' bar near the base, but neither one was in the mood for a late night. Outside, in the parking lot, they stood beside Lance's car, looking up at the hard desert stars and the mustard-gas glow of vast Los Angeles to the south. It was time now to talk about the war.

"He told me that there was a good chance he wouldn't be coming back," Marc said in the Sijans' bright living room, fifteen years after that night in California. As he spoke, Marc's deep voice broke into a juvenile pitch, his angular face contorted with tears. Across from us Jane and Syl Sijan sat pale, unmoving. They had never heard this account of their two sons' final night in California. "Lance said that I should realize the risk he was facing. . . ."

Marc shook his head violently and tears spun away. "Because he was . . . my *blood*, I didn't want him to go. I . . . told Lance that he wasn't thinking clearly. The courage that he had, to face that risk . . . I couldn't believe it. I didn't know that side of my brother, that professional dedication."

Marc let the convulsive sobs run their course. He cleared his face of tears and looked up again. "Lance was so upset that I didn't understand what he was doing, that I didn't understand what he had experienced during all those years of training. He had been *trained* to accept . . . this . . . and I didn't understand it. I was too naive. Lance, he wished that . . . I would have understood. . . ."

Silent, painful minutes passed; then Syl Sijan went to the sofa to comfort his living son. But Marc had already begun to recover, to breathe more evenly after the unexpected catharsis, after the sudden expulsion of that guilt-bound memory of war and terminal separation. He and Lance had made up after this heated misunderstanding two months later, when Lance was home for his final leave. But Marc had never mentioned the encounter in California—so typical of the divisiveness engendered by the war—to his parents until this very afternoon.

The next morning, Memorial Day, the rain washed down in sheets, a summer storm off the lake, reminiscent, perhaps, of the northeast monsoon. I had planned to visit Lance's grave at Milwaukee's Arlington Cemetery off South 27th Street, and the grave of my brother, Bart, at Holy Trinity, a few blocks to the east. But the downpour gave me the pretext I needed to avoid possibly seeing the Sijans again under such wrenching circumstances.

Wednesday morning was cool and sunny. When I visited the two cemeteries, the grounds were empty beneath the fresh green trees under the rainwashed depth of the sky.

Lance's grave was in an oval section, near the stream and willow trees of a rock garden. The bronze marker that the Air Force had brought to Milwaukee along with his remains stood beside the headstones of his grandparents, Mary and Peter Sijan.

LANCE P. SIJAN

WISCONSIN

✝

CAPT US AIR FORCE

VIETNAM DFC—AM—PH

APR 13 1942   JAN 22 1968

On either side of this family plot there were dogwoods and flowering crabs. It was early summer in Wisconsin, a time of optimism, renewal. But I did not feel optimistically rejuvenated. I did not feel eager to begin the long process of writing this book. In the previous month on the road, I had encountered too many still-grieving and angry people for me to maintain my early optimism for the project.

Finally, however, I had answered to my own satisfaction the question of whether Lance Sijan's sacrificial struggle had been truly relevant to the defense of his country. It was now clear to me that he had done his duty well as an airman downed in enemy country and as a prisoner. The story of his struggle, of his astonishing resistance to interrogation, I had learned, had spread among American POWs faced with similar ordeals in the prison camps of North Vietnam.

Vice Admiral James B. Stockdale, one of the three living Vietnam veterans to receive the Medal of Honor that day in 1976 from President Ford, had assured me that Lance Sijan's sacrifice ". . . made him a hero to every American prisoner of war in North Vietnam. In spite of broken limbs, lacerations, concussion, lack of food and drink, he did it all: Evasion, Escape, Stoic Resistance under torture. What he did was truly above and beyond the call of duty. As the story of his heroic performance inspired us who were in prison with him, it will inspire future generations of our country's combat personnel."

And that inspiration, I had discovered, had helped foster resolve among the POWs during their lonely captivity. They had consistently resisted the protracted efforts of their captors to use them for propaganda spectaculars. The North Vietnamese interrogators like the Bug and Pig Eye had to physically break their victims all over again each time they wanted another war crimes confession or antiwar statement to be read to a visiting peace delegation. Rather than voluntarily sign a treasonous statement, men who had already undergone months of torture forced the enemy to again string them up in the knobby room until the interrogators once more, inevitably, broke them.

Ultimately this resistance convinced the North Vietnamese to abandon their propaganda campaign. And the former prisoners I had spoken to all assured me that the stories of men like Lance Sijan, Admiral Stockdale, and Colonel Bud Day, when passed along the clandestine prison communication network, had helped support the resolve that eventually defeated the enemy's efforts.

But several of these men felt emotions other than just pride when they talked about their captivity and the war. They revealed their sadness over the final defeat of America's allies in Indochina. They also urged me to write about the deep bitterness they still harbored toward former antiwar activists like Jane Fonda and her husband, Tom Hayden, who, they reminded me, had defied their country's laws by giving public aid and comfort to the enemy in his own capital yet now seemed to have become born-again capitalists, beneficiaries of America's short memory and overdeveloped popular-culture industry.

Other, perhaps more thoughtful, former prisoners suggested that I use this book as a vehicle to reexamine the geopolitical realities of the Second Indochina war, that I try to build Lance Sijan's story as the framework for a wider historical study. They reminded me that the seminal history of the Vietnam War still seemed to be Frances Fitzgerald's *Fire in the Lake.* This book, they suggested, was a ridiculously dated and simplistic paean to the National Liberation Front, the revolutionary organization that Fitzgerald had convinced so many was truly independent, not merely an organ of Hanoi's politburo. Now, they said, even the former members of the NLF publicly admitted that once the military victory was achieved in 1975, Hanoi simply annexed the South and abruptly disbanded the Front.

Several spoke with anger about the *Apocalypse Now* image of American servicemen in Vietnam. One pointed out that this distorted picture had become so ingrained in America's consciousness that a serious recent history of the war, Michael Maclear's *The Ten Thousand Day War,* had for a cover picture a lurid still photo from Francis Coppola's *Apocalypse Now.* In this surrealistic, carefully staged picture, an American tank turns its flamethrower on a thatched hamlet while craven G.I.s cower beneath a menacing chopper. The picture says it all: American technology perverted to genocide, and disillusioned troops obsessed with survival. It is a compelling image, but it is Hollywood artifice, not history.

These appeals, coming from men who had served their country with distinction, under arduous and isolated conditions, were hard for me to resist. But I was coming to realize that Lance's story and its underlying statement on America and North Vietnam's strategic motives would tell itself without blatant interlinear commentary.

Musing on these aspects of the book before me, I suddenly noticed that the list of abbreviations on Lance's government grave marker—Distinguished Flying Cross, Air Medal, and Purple Heart —did not include America's highest decoration, the Medal of Honor. Then I remembered that his body had been returned from North Vietnam in 1974, before he had been awarded his final medal. It seemed to me, however, that this omission of the Medal of Honor from his marker was symbolic of the way the country had treated all its veterans of that long, divisive conflict.

They had gone out there alone, as replacements, and they'd come back alone. Their honors were late in coming.

Bart's grave lay between two old elm trees that had somehow escaped the Dutch elm plague. I hadn't visited the cemetery for years and was glad to see that the Legion had placed a fresh flag in the bronze stanchion beside the flat government monument.

Unlike Lance's smooth bronze marker, Bart's gravestone was pitted by thirty-five years of acid rain and air pollution. But I was immediately struck by the identical form of the inscriptions the Air Force had provided when they returned the remains of the two young men from their foreign graves.

BARTLEY F. MCCONNELL

WISCONSIN

✝

SGT 852 AAF BM SQD

DEC 5 1925   JAN 5 1945

Bart was a ball-turret gunner on a B-24. He had been killed early in his tour during the Battle of the Bulge, on a bombing raid in support of the American troops that the Nazi counteroffensive had encircled in the Ardennes. After limping back across the Channel, the bomber crashed and burned on approach to its home runway in East Anglia. He was one month away from his twentieth birthday when he died.

When I was about ten, the government brought his body back from England and all my big Irish Catholic clan assembled for his reburial. I remember the smell of incense and the shocking noise of the Legion's honor volley above the open mud grave. I also remember sitting with my brothers when we got out some of Bart's last letters and the personal effects the Air Force returned from his base: strange little blue V-mail letters, a book of modern British poetry, a greasy repair manual for an archaic English bicycle.

Also among his effects were his Air Force ring and his Saint Christopher medal. The bronze was melted, twisted in strange pleats by the heat of the burning bomber. I will never forget handling that cool metal as a child, wondering what my brother had felt when the flames came for him, trapped, wounded in his glass-and-alloy turret.

Now, decades beyond those troubling events of childhood, I could understand the pain Marc Sijan still felt when he talked about his brother.

I knew that Lance and Bart had fought in different wars and that Lance had shown truly uncommon courage and incredible endurance, while Bart had been simply one of thousands of ordinary young men who went to war and died in heavy bombers. But, as I stooped to pull away some weeds from the edge of his pitted marble stone, I realized that Bart McConnell and Lance Sijan had much more in common than simply the identical forms of their grave markers and the somber fact that they had died as a result of aerial warfare.

They had both gone to Bay View High School, and they'd both been school leaders. Lance won an appointment to the Air Force academy, and Bart won a scholarship to study journalism at the University of Missouri.

But Bart had graduated from high school in 1943, a year of total war. College and scholarships were deferred until after the inevitable victory.

Like Lance, Bart volunteered for combat aircrew. Unlike Lance, Bart was slight, lithe, a gymnast not a football player. The Air Force needed small, dexterous men in the ball turrets that protected the bellies of the lumbering Fortresses and Liberators from the new jet fighters of the *Luftwaffe*. Like Lance, Bart went where he was needed, even though he knew full well that those Sperry turrets were too cramped for the gunner to wear his parachute and that they often jammed, trapping the man inside, when the plane's hydraulics were shot out.

Bart had originally been buried in the American military cemetery near Cambridge; the North Vietnamese buried Lance in a weedy plot across the Red River from Hanoi. A few years after their deaths, the Air Force escorted their bodies back to Milwaukee, to the South Side. Their coffins were expensive imposing bronze.

Two young men of warm, honest character and unusual promise, they went where their country's leaders ordered them. They did their duty, and that duty was dangerous. At very early ages, they both faced and accepted the terrible probability of their own deaths in combat.

We remember the war in which Bart was killed as a noble crusade against global fascism. Many Americans still consider the Vietnam War as a criminal folly, sullied by genocide.

Bart was never recognized a hero; his Air Medal and Purple Heart were posthumous bureaucratic afterthoughts. Yet his entire generation has been cast in a heroic light, their battles glorified by our best artists and poets.

Lance Sijan has received and continues to receive the recognition and honors that his incredible feat merits. But the majority of the men and women who served with him in that unpopular struggle remain in silent anonymity.

Perhaps, I thought, finally turning from Bart's grave, this book might help their country to remember.

Washington
December 1983

CPSIA information can be obtained
at www.ICGtesting.com
Printed in the USA
BVHW080313161221
624058BV00011B/113/J

9 780393 018998